MW01201400

NEWGRANGE

ABOUT THE AUTHOR

Anthony Murphy is a journalist, author, photographer and father of five children from Drogheda in County Louth. He has been writing since an early age, and has studied the astronomy, archaeology and mythology of the Boyne Valley monuments for the past 13 years, living just five miles from Newgrange. Author with Richard Moore of the acclaimed *Island of the Setting Sun: In Search of Ireland's Ancient Astronomers*, Anthony has written dozens of magazine and newspaper articles on the Boyne valley and astronomy. He has appeared in countless television and radio programmes, and has been featured in numerous films and documentaries, including a recent appearance on the History Channel as a Newgrange expert.

NEWGRANGE

Monument to Immortality

Anthony Murphy

The Liffey Press

Published by
The Liffey Press Ltd
Raheny Shopping Centre, Second Floor
Raheny, Dublin 5, Ireland
www.theliffeypress.com

© 2012 Anthony Murphy

A catalogue record of this book is
available from the British Library.

ISBN 978-1-908308-24-5

All rights reserved. No part of this publication may be reproduced or transmitted in any form or by any means, including photocopying and recording, without written permission of the publisher. Such written permission must also be obtained before any part of this publication is stored in a retrieval system of any nature. Requests for permission should be directed to The Liffey Press, Raheny Shopping Centre, Second Floor, Raheny, Dublin 5, Ireland.

The extract from 'Carnival' by Nuala Ní Dhomhnaill, translated by Paul Muldoon and originally published in *The Astrakhan Cloak* (1992), is reprinted by kind permission of the authors and The Gallery Press.

Printed in Spain by GraphyCems.

CONTENTS

To Ann, Amy, Luke, Josh, Tara and Finn, with all my love.

PREFACE

THERE IS A MAGICAL PLACE IN IRELAND where time and tide meet and the world melts away into a dreamy, tranquil otherworld inhabited by the most ancient gods of this country. That place is Newgrange, a 5,200-year-old megalithic monument fashioned by a commune of farmers and astronomers, distant ancestors of ours whom time has almost forgotten. There, heaven and earth become united in the most wonderful and spectacular fashion, and the dark interior of this palace of the gods was, and continues to be, illuminated by the rising sun on the shortest days of the year.

The mythology of Newgrange suggests that it is a magic portal to a heavenly realm, and that some of the most ancient deities of Ireland entered the mound to access a blissful eternity beyond sight and sense of the ordinary mortal human. The folklore of Newgrange suggests that these mythical gods, the Tuatha Dé Danann, are able to move between that world and this one, and that they are waiting for some appointed time in the future to return to Ireland once more.

Archaeologists, antiquarians, writers and researchers have been uncovering the secrets of Newgrange since its chamber was rediscovered in 1699. Much has been revealed about an enigmatic community, but much remains shrouded in mystery.

There are lots of books about Newgrange, and its archaeology and history. In particular, the works of Michael and Claire O'Kelly, and Geraldine and Matthew Stout, are foremost and will give the general reader a comprehensive overview of the monument and its landscape.

Newgrange: Monument to Immortality is an attempt to look beyond the archaeology and history of Newgrange to reveal a much more profound and sacred vision of the sophisticated people who felt compelled to create this wondrous testament to their time.

In this book, I attempt to show that not only is Newgrange a uniquely special place, marking the zenith in the achievements of a remarkable society of our distant forebears, but that it was an intensely cosmic, spiritual and eternal monument, designed to last the harsh ravages of time to speak to us out of the mists of prehistory.

It was not built by a grizzly mob of grunting barbarians, but rather by an advanced agrarian community who had developed competent skills in the sciences of astronomy, engineering and architecture.

What message does Newgrange hold for us today? With a society in turmoil, and its political, religious and economic institutions in crisis, is it any wonder that people are turning back to the most ancient and sacred aspects of our past to uncover some sense of comfort and belonging?

Newgrange belongs to a time when humans had taken the first steps towards modern society, when we emerged from the forests of the Mesolithic and began farming and keeping cattle and put in place the foundations of western civilisation as we know it today. For a relatively short period of time, known by archaeologists as the Neolithic – the New Stone Age – humanity expressed itself spiritually, creatively and cosmically in the most glorious way, requiring a superhuman effort to create remarkable monuments which were among the largest construction projects in prehistoric Europe.

There is a profound cosmology and spirituality underlying the design of Newgrange, and this book explores some of the more ethereal and mystical aspects of its creators, and the forces and motives that compelled them to create these vast stone shrines.

It is my contention that the Stone Age community of the Boyne Valley recognised the eternal nature of the human spirit, and that they were among the first to realise that the soul survived this life, to journey to another realm. Many people who have died and been brought back to life have described remarkable journeys down dark tunnels towards a brilliant light, and a meeting with a loving, luminous being in the next world. Is Newgrange designed to recreate, or perhaps to enhance this journey, from one life to the next?

There are many writers who have suggested Newgrange is more like a womb than a tomb, perhaps designed to celebrate the cyclical nature of life, and to recognise that death is just a natural process in the eternal movement of the soul from one world to another. The ancient Irish otherworld lay among the stars, but was accessed through the mounds. Its design was inspired by the stars, in particular the cruciform constellation of Cygnus, the swan, which might have been viewed as an ancient cosmic birth canal in the sky.

Newgrange is not just a tomb, it is not a dead thing. It is very much alive, marking the eternal cycles of the sun, moon and stars. It continues to function today, more than five millennia after it was built, and attracts many different types of pilgrim, the modern inquisitive men and women who come to marvel at its splendour.

Included among these many thousands of annual visitors are some wearisome and bewildered ones, lost in the modern technological and materialistic world, seeking answers about themselves, and their long forgotten roots.

A lot of people are seeking to connect with something ancient, something deeply rooted, something ancestral and something profound when they come to Newgrange. It has a message for us, speaking out across the millennia that have passed since its inception.

This is a very personal and in some ways philosophical exploration of Newgrange and its people. Were they so different from us? I invite you to join me on a fascinating and revealing journey into our most treasured ancient monument. It has a message for us, still resonating today, more than fifty centuries after it was built.

ACKNOWLEDGEMENTS

THERE ARE A GREAT MANY PEOPLE to whom I owe a debt of gratitude for their assistance and encouragement in helping *Newgrange: Monument to Immortality* become a reality. First and foremost among these is David Givens, Publisher, The Liffey Press, whose eyes lit up when he read the first draft of the first chapter of this proposed project in his office back in January 2012. As a writer it is important to have someone who supports your work, and having done such a terrific job on the production and editing of *Island of the Setting Sun*, it is a great pleasure, and a source of considerable comfort, to have the services of an excellent publisher to endorse my project.

To my wife Ann, and my children Amy, Luke, Josh, Tara and Finn, I extend my heartfelt thanks for their support and understanding during the past eight months. As the work intensified, so too did the time I spent writing and taking photographs. I am very thankful in particular to Amy for accompanying me on many of the recent trips into the Boyne Valley for the purpose of taking photographs. She kept me company on many an evening under the stars.

I am very grateful for the significant input into this project from archaeologist Conor Brady of Dundalk Institute of Technology. Although I tend to drift into ethereal realms, I believe in keeping my work firmly grounded, and Conor was there to make sure whatever I wrote from an archaeological viewpoint was based on reality.

To Clare Tuffy and Leontia Lenihan and indeed all the staff at Brú na Bóinne who have, over the years, allowed me to become part of the extended Newgrange family. Thanks to Kevin Kennedy and all the staff of the OPW Press Office for their courtesy and assistance, and for granting permission to allow me access Newgrange to take photos. The following images, taken by the author, are used with permission of the OPW: pps. 4, 5, 17, 23, 24, 25, 32, 35, 43, 45, 46, 55, 62, 111, 121, 122, 131, 135, 139, 143, 145, 147, 155, 157, 160, 162, 164, 170, 172, 180, 192, 194, 195, 196, 199, 201, 202 and 209.

I am grateful to all those who helped provide and locate sources for the text. These included Michael Fox, Ken Williams, Victor Reijs, Pat Burns, Martin Byrne, Colm Keane, and members of the Irish-Stones list among others.

A very special word of thanks to filmmaker Grant Wakefield who gave me my first opportunity, after many years of filling out lottery forms, to gain access to the chamber of Newgrange on the days of the solstice. I owe huge gratitude to Grant, who gave me permission to use several photographs from the shoots at Newgrange. The following photos were taken by the author on Grant's behalf and are used with permission: pps. 17, 65, 127, 131, 135, 139, 143, 145, 147, 157, 160, 162, 172, 180, 192, 194, 196, 199, 201 and 211.

Thanks to Ken Williams for his beautiful image on page 197, and to Michael Fox for the photo on page 191. Thanks also to Jane Brideson for permission to use her paintings of An Dagdha, Bóann and Aengus Óg from her collection 'The Ever-Living Ones'. For more information email morrigan@mac.com.

Thanks to those who provided an account of their experiences inside Newgrange, including Peter Kavanagh, Elizabeth Twohig, Dolores Whelan, Maggie McDonald, Jeremiah Keogh and Martin Dier. To Jim and Richard Smith for assistance with aerial photography, and to Liutauras Kepenis for his aerial photos of Newgrange.

Go raibh mile maith agaibh.

Anthony Murphy
September 2012
Drogheda, County Louth

If we were gods
here at Newgrange—
you Sualtam or the Daghda,
myself the famous river—

we could freeze the sun
and the moon
for a year and a day
to perpetuate the pleasure
we have together.

Alas, it's far from gods
we are, but bare, forked creatures.
The heavenly bodies stop
only for a single, transitory moment.

– Nuala Ní Dhomhnaill, from 'Carnival',
translated from the Irish by Paul Muldoon

1

CONNECTIONS

MY JOURNEYS TO NEWGRANGE are always about familiarity. I've held a deep wonderment for the huge Boyne Valley monuments for many years, and an arcane respect for their creators. I live just five miles away from Newgrange, in the town of Drogheda, where I was born and raised. Some of my fellow inhabitants have never been to see the wonderful sites that lie in the fields above the Boyne, about seven kilometres from the town, but I have always deemed them to be of major significance in understanding our history and our roots.

For we Irish are a deeply rooted people. We are rooted to land: to field, to river, to hill, to wood, to mountain, to lake, to shore, to valley. Our story is an ancient one. We came here, according to DNA studies, from Iberia, at the end of the last Ice Age, as the ice was retreating northwards. The Irish people, in the main, share the same DNA as those first inhabitants who came upon this place maybe 10,000 years ago. Newgrange and the Boyne Valley monuments are at least half as old as that, meaning that we had already been here a very long time before they were constructed. And what had Ireland been like before the Ice Age? What people, if any, had lived here, and what great monuments of their design had been gouged away by the ice sheets in the remote past? Who can know?

Visitors to Newgrange may find it difficult to relate to a time 5,200 years ago, when a community of people vastly different to us began their monumental construction projects in the Bend of the Boyne. There is a conundrum which presents itself to those who come here, especially to the Irish visitors. We share the same DNA, but our lives bear no resemblance to theirs. The builders of the great stone passage mounds set about their grand venture without the assistance of the sophisticated technology which we take almost completely for granted today. They had a much shorter life span, and a much tougher physical existence, and a fragile one at that. A broken leg during construction would have almost surely led to infection and death. Today, we can call for an ambulance and have surgery to repair bone breaks and, in most cases, return to health and fitness. But in the Neolithic, the period known as the 'New Stone Age', a bad fracture was a disaster, and one from which few would have escaped alive.

Language and communication among our distant relatives would have been very different too. And their appearance, their dress, might make them seem more like cave people than civilised and organised hu-

mans. I once imagined what it would be like if, by some universal magic, time could disappear and two people from different epochs might pass each other in a field in the Boyne Valley. I imagined one to be a Neolithic farmer and monument builder, the other myself, a modern day Irishman. This was an extraordinary vision; one spawned by some deep-rooted aspect of my spiritual self, a part of me which perhaps believed I might be descended from the great builders of Newgrange. But where I may have expected familiarity, I realised an acute sense of separation and unfamiliarity, bewilderment almost.

The Neolithic man in my vision was smaller in height than me but larger in stature. He was a strong man with hardened features. He had that caveman look which, through no fault of our own, we tend to transpose onto our prehistoric ancestors. We have seen this image in books and on television – a man with long, unkempt hair, with a rough beard, wearing some sort of animal fur and nearly always carrying either a wooden staff

A view of the Boyne Valley, where a community began building megalithic monuments over five millennia ago.

Our ancestors might have worn an animal fur such as this one, on display at the Brú na Bóinne Visitor Centre.

or a spear. And that's pretty much how it was in my vision. My 'ancestor' was abundantly familiar with the stereotypical history book image, but so vastly unfamiliar to anyone I know today. His most distinguishing features, apart from his tousled mane and his coat of animal hide, were his eyes. For it was in this man's eyes that an entire story could be told.

This vision occurred years ago, during one of my many daytime trances. I tend to drift off when I am bored, which happens surprisingly often because I find life to be sometimes excessively tedious and its small details vex me greatly. This sometimes happened in school, in fact quite frequently. I would often wander off into a waking dream, thinking lofty thoughts and imagining great things. These were qualities which were apparently frowned upon, but in retrospect I like to think that these are the qualities that make me what I am – a big thinker. And, in the time honoured fashion of big thinkers, every time I go looking for an answer to a question, instead I find at least three more questions, and sometimes many more!

It was in the midst of one of these dreamlike states that I imagined meeting a man from the Stone Age, in a field in the Boyne Valley, in a situation where our two times, the Neolithic and the twenty-first century, had become one. The field was full of very long grass, above waist height, which was blowing gently in a breeze. We passed each other, walking in opposite directions, about fifteen feet apart at our closest. He was walking towards the west, me to the east. As we passed, our gazes met. We fixed our stare upon each other as we walked, neither of us stopping or hesitating. But time did slow down, like a slow motion sequence in a movie, so that our passing seemed much longer, as if allowing us more time to peer into each other's inner thoughts. No word, no utterance, no spoken sound, was made between us. There was no conversation.

No words were necessary. A half a million thoughts travelled the void between us, as if a magical telepathic conversation was taking place across 5,000 years of history. His eyes told an entire story. They were deep set and blue, and his brow was stooped, so that he looked deeply suspicious of my presence. I was a complete stranger to him. He had never seen anyone like me, dressed in these bright colours in fine cloth,[1] not the animal furs and skins which he was familiar with. I had short hair and was clean shaven. I was an outsider in his world. And his eyes told that story. In those eyes I sensed wariness, fright, mistrust, confusion, animosity, contradiction, denial even. Denial that he was even seeing me, like I was some mysterious spectre appearing through a mist, or akin to some otherwordly deity about whom his fireside stories might have related wondrous attributes.

He had every right to be wary and frightened. At no time during the course of this man's existence would he ever have needed to give thought

A depiction of a Neolithic family around the hearth, from the Visitor Centre.

to what his distant offspring might look like. There were no Neolithic history books (not that we know of) relating to what people had looked like in the past, never mind how they might appear in the future. I recognised him as a prehistoric man, a familiar image from the history books, one I had seen over and over again in photo and moving image. But he had never, not once, imagined someone like me. I might have been a god, or a ghost, and I felt sure that if ever a meeting could take place between such a modern day Irishman and a Neolithic forebear, the image of the modern man would be forever ingrained in the ancient man's mind. For good or for bad, I would haunt this man all his life, if such a meeting were possible.

His eyes told many other things. He was a hard worker, and grafted a delicate existence in the valley using skills which had been passed down through many generations. He was a keen hunter and fisherman, but had also learned to sow crops and keep cattle. He could sail and swim and could navigate by the stars. He lived in a close-knit community who watched out for each other. He cared deeply for his family, and wondered often about what happens to people after they die.

In this last regard we find the most common ground. We are all part of a community, we are all part of a family, and there are very few of us who don't think about where we go after we die. We may be separated by five thousand years of history, but this ancestor and I share these universal attributes. We are descended from human families. We have seen our loved ones pass away, and we mourn their passing. We yearn for a better life, and a long and fulfilling one, with our own offspring. And, ultimately, we wonder about what will happen us when our own time comes to leave this life.

In my vision, I remained fixed on my ancestor's eyes after we had passed, such that we had to look over our shoulders to maintain our gaze. In a very short space of time, perhaps only seconds, we had learned a lot about each other. Alienation and mistrust turned to acknowledgement, acceptance and respect. We had no common language, very different manners and customs, bizarre clothing, alien appearances and we were

Standing beneath Newgrange, it can be difficult to glean a sense of what its builders were like.

separated by 5,000 years of time, but as we drifted out of each other's sight, each of us in his own mind accepted that we are part of the same human story. Without a single word or sound being uttered, we both realised that we are, in essence, eternal. His life had come and passed, and death had taken him to new realms. It is my turn now to live in this world, and it is thanks to my many thousands of ancestors that I am here at all. But my time will come, sooner or later, to go on to the next world, and long after I have departed, perhaps some distant future descendant of mine will imagine a meeting between himself and someone from the twenty-first century. Hopefully he will sense much fellowship and affinity amidst all the unfamiliarity.

When you visit Newgrange, and stand in front of its great edifice and survey the immense stones and the valley below, it can be difficult to glean any sense of what the monument-building community was like. There is much that is unfamiliar. These are a people who have lived and died, and whose language and customs and beliefs have, to a large extent, passed on with them. There is no book, no story teller, that can relate the fine details of what motivated them to such great achievements and how and why they undertook these momentous exploits. You can stand at the front of the monument and take a sweeping view of the Boyne Valley beneath, and you can sense that you share the same space which these people once lived in, that, somehow, you walk the same ground as they did. But beyond that you can become overwhelmed with the feeling of disconnection. This might be because you are surrounded by tourists, that tour buses from the nearby visitor centre are constantly coming and going, that you can see the chimney stack of a cement factory across the

The valley beneath Newgrange looking towards Red Mountain.

hills, or maybe that you can hear the whine of aircraft engines as they approach Dublin airport. This is the same landscape that your ancestors lived in, but it is utterly different, and they are not here to share their story. They are utterly gone. Their way of life is a very distant memory, lost on the remote paths of time. You are alone here with your thoughts, trying to reconnect with deep-rooted things which time has almost completely forgotten. So many generations separate you from your ancestors that it hurts the heart even to think about them. The very thought of connecting across the ages moves some visitors to tears. I have spoken with lots of people who have come to the Boyne Valley, many from distant shores, and a common thread in many of their stories is that they feel a connection with lost ancestors, and that somehow they feel at home here. This is how I have always felt in the Boyne Valley.

You can stand beneath the monument, on the road, and watch after the evening's last tour has departed and the staff have gone home, as the dusk draws in around the valley, with nothing but the sounds of the birds and the livestock as company, and feel little sense of connection with whatever forces conspired here in the vague yesteryear to bring a community of your ancestors together to build this gigantic edifice.

There are reasons for this. As the day's light fades, artificial lighting comes on. There will be an occasional car or van to break the silence along the road, and the sound of distant traffic near Rossnaree on the opposite side of the valley is always to be heard. There are hedgerows and fences to prevent access to Newgrange, and there is always the sense of something forbidden, something beyond the reach of the ordinary wanderer who has been drawn to this place to connect with something distant.

To envision any sense of connection with the megalithic community which assembled these great monuments of Newgrange, Knowth and Dowth, you must first sweep away your own trappings and impressions and preconceptions. You are vastly different to those people. Not necessarily better, as we will see, but very different.

You have to imagine a world without artificial light, beyond what can be provided by flame, whether it be a roaring hearth, a wild mountain gorse fire, or the glow of a smouldering tinder. This world has no electricity, no 'power supply', no appliances, no cookers or fridges or microwave ovens, no televisions or computers, no electrical or mechanical devices. There are no hospitals or schools or police stations. There are no shopping malls or hardware stores. There is no transport system, beyond what your own legs can provide, and your own sailing skills.

You have to imagine a world where the only technology is made of stone, bone and wood, as we shall see in Chapter 2. The tools of the Neolithic are stone axes, flint scrapers and arrowheads, and there is no metal. Personal belongings, apart from clothes, amount to decorated beads and stones and bones. It is this world into which you have to step in order to glean some sense of the immensity and the difficulty of the task of building Newgrange.

The barriers, the fences, hedgerows and the grass verges at Newgrange today seem to convey the sense of something untouchable, something that has climbed to a plane of awe and splendour, beyond the grasp of us mere mortals, the 'modern' men and women that wish to probe it and disturb it and to ask questions of it. We would wish that we could scale the fence, walk right up to its gleaming facade, and ask the very monument to speak to us of matters cosmic, of creation and the journey of life and, ultimately, why we are here and where we are going.

But it might not answer back. Perhaps there are too many barriers. There's the barrier of time.

Over 5,200 years of precious time. There's the barrier of dimension. New-grange was created in a different world, a place which heaved to vastly different natural rhythms. There is the barrier of our own language and appearance, our customs, our new beliefs, our strange dress code. If the monument were ever to speak, surely it would not speak to someone as unfamiliar as us? There's even the barrier of cosmetic transformation, for Newgrange is not now as it once was. Its gleaming quartz is supported by a gigantic concrete wall, built by archaeologists. I stand under it some-times, right there near the kerb, and look up, and wonder whether it's 12 feet tall, or maybe 15, or perhaps even 20. Its fastidious 'reconstruction'

The fences and hedgerows around Newgrange convey a
sense of something untouchable.

The quartz wall, built by archaeologists, could be 20 feet tall.

does not take into account that its creators did not have concrete, nor might they have used it even if they did.

This sleeping giant was awoken in the seventeenth century after millennia of sleep, and it was woken with a violent shudder, like a child being poked by a cruel stepmother, squealing in a harsh tone, 'wake up child, wake up, and speak to me of the dreams you've been having'. But the dreams of Aonghus Óg are not lightly imparted, and if we truly want Newgrange to yield her secrets, we have to become like the innocent miracle child of the divine parents, whose union in the womb of the earth gave rise to the enlightened star child. We must retreat into the darkness of the cave and be born again.

In creating all the barriers around the monument, we have acutely acknowledged that Newgrange is not ours, that it belongs to another time and another people, and all we can do, for now, it to keep it under control, lock it up at night, and bring people in during the day and tell them all about its stones and where they come from. But we cannot relate to them the real story of *Sidhe an Brugh*, for to do that we must first learn the story. And us modern Irish folk are not as good at telling stories as we used to be. We are distracted now by other things.

But can we go back?

Can we yet recover something of the past? Is all of the glorious yesterday gone, forsaken, lost to the ether of time? Can we retreat back inside Newgrange, like the Tuatha Dé Danann, and commune with our ancestors? Is it possible for us to peel back the layers, like archaeologists, except in a metaphorical sense, and uncover the secrets of Newgrange? Can we yet hope, earnestly and honestly, that we can learn something about why it was built there, what its importance was, why it survived until this time, and what message, if any, it might have for us?

Should we go back?

Why would we want to? Maybe we need to. Isn't there an overwhelming sense that we are lost? Isn't it true that our feet no longer tread firm

Newgrange belongs to another time.

paths? Are we not detached from what it is that makes us firmly rooted on the earth? Have we not forsaken our own ways and customs, our language and music and crafts, and largely abandoned what it is that makes us the true descendants of the builders of Newgrange? Does the charge that we have ceded our power and authority to foreign gods not ring true? Are we not empty, lacking a true grounding, a real sense of place in the world? Do we not feel like abandoned children, walking empty streets, in hope of an absolution? Did we not trade riches of the soul for riches of matter? Are we not now broke, desolate?

The monument and its giant stones in the glow of moonlight.

We have lost our power. We are floating, adrift, on a lonely ice sheet in a remote ocean, with no sense of direction, and no impression of our destination. And worst of all, we don't know where we have come from. In order to complete a journey, we must first understand where we have started from, where we are going to, why we are going there, and what route we must take in order for the journey to be successfully and safely completed.

How do we go back?

This is essentially a spiritual journey, not an actual trek across the landscape. The spirit is capable of very powerful things. Materially, we

are made of the same basic components as the people who built Newgrange. We are all children of the cosmos. We share a common origin, we live on the earth and breathe its air, we behold its beauty and its awful tragedy, we grow old, we die. At a certain fundamental level we are one and the same people. Those who carry the same DNA as the builders of Newgrange – and there are many – can lay the best claim to being deeply rooted, at least in the sense of having ancestors who have lived in Ireland for many thousands of years. But there are so many people whose distant family trees can never be known, that it would be nigh on impossible to ascertain whether any particular individual has ancestry in Neolithic Ireland. On a spiritual level, however, it is possible to believe that we are all descended from those early ancestors. We all yearn for the same things – for a happy, fulfilling and peaceful life, for the flourishing of our offspring, for the safety of the world, and for a happy and peaceful passing into the next life. Are these not also the things for which the people of Newgrange yearned?

Spiritually, we must return. We must go back. We must retreat into the womb of Newgrange and be reborn. There, in the dim winter light, we might recover some sense of our journey. In the warm bosom of the earth mound, we might find succour. The supernatural star children, Aonghus and Sétanta, were each conceived by the miraculous union of the father sun and mother moon, the sky king and the earth queen, Daghda and Bóann, Lugh and Deichtine, in the deep belly of Newgrange. The Tuatha Dé Danann have long since retreated into the chambers and vaults and mounds and raths of Ireland, waiting there to be roused for a great battle to restore Ireland's glory. Surely the time has come to rouse the sleeping gods of our hearts and consciousness, to stir the spirits of the Tuatha Dé, to bring forth light from the darkness, and to restore the glory of forgotten kings, so that once more we might find our path in this world. Not all of the glorious yesterday is forsaken. We can, once again, become children of the stars, walking enlightened through the worldly life.

We must mend the broken path that brought us on our journey out of the amnesia of prehistory. We must reconnect with that which is old and arcane and sacred. 'The old that is strong does not wither, deep roots are not reached by the frost.'[2] Something of who we really are, a part of that ancestral foundation we hold to be so special, remains. It has never been truly lost. We might have forgotten who our Neolithic ancestors really were, or what they looked like, and what their names were. But we are, and we remain, one and the same people, living in vastly different times and circumstances.

So now we should look upon our visit to Newgrange with a fresh pair of eyes. Let us not consider the barriers, the fences and hedgerows, the modern roads and buildings, the artificial lighting, the tour buses and the locked gates. Let us instead behold the miracle that is Newgrange. Here is a vast edifice, constructed with immense toil and zeal and enthusiasm by a unified community who endeavoured to create something truly monumental as a gift to the world and as a sacred space within which the rhythm of cosmic movements could perform their eternal dance. Here is a giant earth mound, dedicated to the gods and spirits and fairies and

Neolithic carvings on a Newgrange passage stone –
Dagda, Bóann and Aonghus?

all of the cosmic forces which influence life and everything that happens during it. Here is the sacred womb, where birth and death and rebirth are understood as part of the pattern of life, the great circle of existence. Here, we shall celebrate who we are, and not who we once were.

Here, we shall feel at home.

We feel at home in the ancient Boyne Valley.

2.

STONE AND BONE

OWN ALL THE DAYS SINCE ITS massive stones were hauled into place, beneath the thousands of full moons which have crossed the sky since then and now, Newgrange has endured, above the everlasting flow of the river Boyne, a permanent memorial to a people whose fleeting lives were devoted to a grand cause, the memory of which might otherwise have vanished in the dim mists of time.

On a lowly ridge peering down upon the silvery waters of the Boyne below, its giant belly sits, the great mansion of the ancient gods, long forlorn but never forgotten, an ancient experiment in scientific study and spiritual endeavour, enduring the battle with time to speak to us of our long gone family of yesteryear.

This 5,200-year-old monument, and its sister sites of Knowth and Dowth, represent cocoons of sorts, the empty caterpillar skins of butterflies that have long since flown away. By examining these giant stone remains, we hope to learn something of the magnificence of the ancestors who endowed us with such remarkable memorials.

By the time of their construction, the people who built these giant mounds had already become talented at many things. They were farmers, who had learned to sow crops and to keep domestic animals. The forests which once enveloped the bend of the Boyne in a canopy of green had long before been cleared away for the purposes of agriculture and monument building. They were also keen astronomers, but in those far-off times when humans lived much closer to nature, a detailed understanding of the heavenly movements was not only essential to everyday life, but was probably ingrained in the minds of children from an early age.

We do not know exactly how long the megalith builders had been in the valley before they commenced their construction work. What we do know is that the landscape they inherited was already very ancient when the first stones were being carefully manoeuvred into place.

> The geological foundations of the Boyne Valley landscape were formed over a period of 500 million years. The broad shape of the countryside emerged during the latter part of the Tertiary Period (2–60 million years ago) but the final touches were put to the emerging physical landscape during the ice ages of the past 1.65 million years, in particular the last great ice age which ended 10,000 years ago.[1]

The forests of the Boyne were cleared away for monument construction and agriculture.

It is a remarkable and spectacular landscape, and yet there are no features that rise to any great height. The waters of the Boyne loop dramatically around a giant peninsula of land upon which the great mounds sit. Foremost in prominence is Newgrange, which appears to stand out in front of its sisters, and from various vantage points in the valley it dominates all the rest, giving rise to the notion that it is the focal point of the whole monument assembly.

The gushing glacial melt waters which flowed through the great channel now occupied by the Boyne as the Ice Age ended were immensely powerful, depositing millions of tonnes of sediments consisting of 'glaciofluvial sands and gravels'.[2] It is partly to this large-scale deposition of material that the valley owes thanks for the richness of its soils. It is a widely known fact among the Irish farming community today that the most fertile soils can be found in the east, and this has been the case as long as people have been farming on this island. This, coupled with the proximity of the Bend of the Boyne to the sea, along the east coast, must have made it an ideal haven for the people whose farming practices were imported from overseas.

That's not to say there were not a pre-existing people living in the Boyne Valley before the farmers came. DNA studies have shown that an ancient genetic marker which dates from about 10,000 years ago can be found in a majority of Irish men today.[3] The marker is known as 'haplogroup 1' and geneticists believe that most of the population of Western Europe carried this gene over 10,000 years ago. Through time, though, the gene became diluted through the movement and intermingling of peoples, leading to a situation today where it is found in many fewer people in Europe.

> The greatest movement and migration of peoples in Europe has been the movement of farmers from the southeast of the continent after the invention of agriculture about 10,000 years ago. The farmers moved with their new technologies northwest into Europe, probably displacing the local hunter-gatherer populations that were living there at the time. In this way the haplogroup 1 genes in Europe were diluted, the farmers introducing new and different genes.[4]

Interestingly, the lowest concentration of these genes is in Turkey, and the greatest distribution is found in Ireland, where 78.1% of all men have the haplogroup 1 gene.

Some experts believe there may have been some interbreeding between the old population and the new. One school of thought suggests that those who built the great monuments of the Boyne and elsewhere were immigrants, who brought new methods and systems of living from mainland Europe across the sea. But it was not an invasion as such. It is suggested that this westward-moving people, whose civilisation had originated in Mesopotamia, introduced their farming and cattle breeding techniques to the:

> . . . earlier Mesolithic populations scattered around the forests and scrubland, with whom they would, in time, have interbred, so that by the end of the Stone Age the Irish population was a successful blend of old and new, strong enough to supply the basic and important gene-pool for the people of Ireland today.[5]

It would appear that some archaeologists and anthropologists have come to believe Newgrange and the monuments of the Boyne were built by a single community which consisted of a benevolent mix of a precursory race of Mesolithic foragers, fishers and hunters and their newfound Neolithic friends who had migrated gradually westwards across Europe, bringing with them a new economy based on agrarian practices, the breeding and keeping of cattle and the construction of monumental stone structures.

Precisely when, and how, this benign intercultural change took place is a matter of considerable debate, and some conjecture. Asked to put a date for the 'beginning' of the Neolithic in Ireland, archaeologists will generally answer 'circa 4000 BC', with Neolithic settlers beginning to build dwellings in the Boyne Valley around 3800 BC.[6] However, the earliest cereal production in Ireland, which is strongly associated with the beginning of agriculture, can be seen at least as early as 4500 BC, with some evidence from radiocarbon dating of domesticated cattle being kept around that time too.[7]

Whatever the time frame for the transformation, it is clear that archaeology believes the change, while bringing about substantial adjustment of social and subsistent habits, was largely altruistic and non-confrontational. There is still room, though, for discussion about the possibility that localised crop use and cattle domestication found in the late Mesolithic meant that the pre-existing aboriginal hunter gatherer population had already begun the developments which we largely associate with the Neolithic.

Archaeologist Gabriel Cooney, an expert on the Neolithic, argues that the distinctive characteristics of their stone tools along with a focus on fishing and gathering in the late Mesolithic:

> . . . do not suggest much contact with either Britain or adjacent continental Europe. In this context it may be difficult to argue for a propensity to take on the importation and management of unfamiliar domesticated animals and crops from off-island sources.[8]

The breeding and keeping of cattle in the Boyne Valley, represented in a model at the Brú na Bóinne Visitor Centre.

A model showing the new farming community of Newgrange.

In other words, the indigenous population had their own way of doing things, and might not have been open to the substantive social transformation brought by the foreign farmers, who no doubt would have been viewed with some scepticism and mistrust. After all, the Mesolithic way of life had existed in the Boyne Valley and elsewhere across the island of Ireland at least since the last Ice Age, a period of several thousand years. Why would such a long-established population with its own social patterns and abilities and beliefs allow itself to be circumvented by the supposed ingenuity of a group of foreign invaders who doubtlessly spoke an unknown tongue, and possibly had a very different dress code and maybe even dissimilar spiritual beliefs and customs?

What we do know is that around 4000 BC there were remarkable changes in the social and economic fabric of life and that there was something of a scientific revolution at the time. New stone tools were being used, and pottery was being produced. Domesticated cattle, pigs, goats and sheep had been introduced, as had cultivated cereals which included wheat and barley. The animals, and the cereal grains, were not native to Ireland and thus had to be brought here from elsewhere.[9]

Cooney suggests the possibility that a 'small-scale colonisation' of Ireland by the New Stone Age people might help explain the spread of the Neolithic in northwest Europe, particularly in an island context.[10] Professor Michael O'Kelly, the archaeologist who excavated Newgrange, pointed out that the belief of many archaeologists was that only immigration could account for the very drastic change from hunter-gatherer to farmer.[11] But O'Kelly also alluded to the 'other view', that 'the Neolithic way of life was introduced by a slow and complicated process resulting from overseas contacts – there was no invasion and no arrival of a great colony of foreigners'.[12] He went further by saying that the Neolithic way of life:

> ... could have been introduced by Irish natives returning from travels abroad and by small family groups enticed here by what they had heard of Ireland from Irish travellers. At first, and indeed for a long time to come, the way of life must have been a mixed one. Hunting, fishing and food collection must have gone on while the practice of agriculture and pastoralism was slowly developing, so that no hard-and-fast line can be drawn between the end of the Mesolithic Period and the beginning of the Neolithic proper.[13]

Stone Age axe replicas, on display at the Visitor Centre.

In other words, the indigenous fisher foragers brought the new farming practices and stone technology into Ireland themselves, resulting from their own journeying abroad and contact with the Neolithic communities in Britain and further afield. Certainly this explanation would fit much more neatly with the lack of dilution of the haplogroup 1 gene in Irish males today. If there had been a widespread influx of Neolithic immigrants and a large-scale intermingling of the old and new populations, one might expect a lower incidence of haplogroup 1 in today's Irish population. Interestingly, the highest concentration of the haplogroup 1 'Mesolithic' gene can be found today in Connaught, the westernmost part of Ireland, and indeed the most extreme westerly point of Europe. There, almost all men, 98.3%, carry the Mesolithic gene.[14] It is an incredible statistic. One could attempt to argue that in western Ireland, the furthest extremity of Europe, the Mesolithic people might have been least influenced and transformed by the influx of the Neolithic culture from the continent, but one would have grave difficulty with this hypothesis,

The transformation brought by farming continues to resonate
in the Boyne Valley today.

principally because there are megalithic monuments in the west, chiefly in Sligo, which are widely held to be more ancient than the Boyne monuments, perhaps by as much as 1,000 years.[15]

If the Neolithic culture was brought into Ireland by immigrants coming across the Irish Sea landing on the east coast, one might have trouble explaining why the monuments further west are older than those in the east. Archaeologists acknowledge the quandary of explaining how the New Stone Age culture was introduced here. There is no single accepted theory as to how it happened.

What is known with absolute certainty was that the new farming practices were introduced, that new stone tools were being manufactured, that pottery was in widespread use, and that huge monuments were being built. This was a clear departure from the foraging lifestyle which had been prevalent since the Ice Age. In a relatively short period of time, perhaps 500 years or less, the everyday routine of the people had changed considerably. Previously there was a very high dependency on hunting, fishing and scavenging. If a man and his family were hungry, their food had to be caught or found, often a very time intensive and labour demanding affair. From about 4000 BC onwards, food was being grown and cattle were being grazed in fields of tillage and pasture that were separated by some sort of hedging material.[16]

> The introduction of arable and livestock farming during the so-called 'Neolithic Revolution' did more to transform mankind's way of life than anything before or since. It created permanent, settled communities, which may be seen as the kernel of civilisation as we now understand it.[17]

Large-scale forest clearance had been undertaken, mainly to provide areas for these new agricultural practices. It is highly probable that the Boyne Valley was heavily forested in the Mesolithic, and obviously for the new agrarian practices to thrive, in turn allowing for the construction of the monuments, significant deforestation at the hands of the mound builders was required. This deforestation of the Bend of the Boyne is apparently mentioned in mythology. Sláine, a Fir Bolg king who is said to

The manmade deforestation of the valley is mentioned in mythology.

have been buried under a mound on the nearby Hill of Slane, was identified as the one responsible, in the *Dindshenchas*, a collection of stories
about ancient place names:

> Sláine, king of the Fir Bolg, and their judge, by him was its wood
> cleared from the Brugh.[18]

The cutting down of forested areas across Ireland to create space for
farming is seen as one of the key indicators of the dawn of the Neolithic.
In many cases, archaeological evidence showed the decline of certain
species of tree and a striking increase in the presence of grasses. However, this activity is not confined to the accepted time of the beginning of
the Neolithic, circa 4000 BC. In fact, there are several sites where clearance had taken place earlier. In Cashelkeelty, County Kerry, on the Beara
Peninsula, for example, Dr Ann Lynch found evidence of cereal cultivation during the period of 4700 to 3800 BC,[19] from which we might deduce

that farming practices were being introduced by the existing Mesolithic population.

Those days, when land clearance was beginning, marked a dramatic change in the landscape, when mankind first started to have profound effects on the earth. The days were ending where the scrublands and forests could grow on the hillsides and in the valleys with free will, and the days of open fields and pasture lands and hedgerows and permanent human habitations had begun to dawn. In reality, the ending of the Mesolithic period represented the last time that the earth was a truly natural place in which humankind wandered at ease. Beforehand, people lived in commune with the natural surroundings, and their presence on the earth might, in places, hardly have been noticeable. Thenceforth, the mark of human hands was on everything, and the coming of the Neolithic was just the first stepping stone towards today's world, when man's influence on everything is much more drastic.

The question of who the real builders of Newgrange actually were is clearly still a major one for archaeologists and anthropologists. Were they a 'new people' as such, a wave of immigrants from overseas, or were they the indigenous gatherers, who had developed the new farming customs and pottery making skills with the help of an outside influence? Or a cordial mix of the old population mixed with the new?

Whatever happened during the millennium in the run-up to the beginning of the construction of the monuments, there was a prehistoric industrial revolution of sorts. The new technology outlined earlier, consisting of innovative stone tools and pottery, along with the land clearance and budding farming industry, are indicators of a substantial evolution of human life patterns in the Bend of the Boyne and elsewhere. There was a greater availability of food as a result, which enabled a radical transformation in the habits and lifestyle of those who had chopped down the trees and begun sowing crops. Less time was needed for foraging and hunting in the wild, and more time could be given to other pursuits. Without doubt the greatest of these pursuits was the construction of the huge monuments of the Boyne.

The impressive scale of the main monuments, and the immense amount of labour and material required for their construction, in addition to the building of the many smaller mounds, suggests that a substantial population existed in the Bend of the Boyne from around 4000 BC on-wards. Archaeologist Conor Brady undertook a fieldwork study involving a systematic survey of the so-called 'ploughzone' of the Boyne Valley, an area measuring six kilometres by four kilometres.[20] Almost 8,000 stone artefacts made from a range of materials including flint, chert, quartz, shale and porcellanite were recovered during this survey. Brady says the results demonstrate 'clear evidence that there was substantial settlement and related activity not only in the immediate area of the monuments but also on the south side of the river where no monuments remain'.[21] Activity obviously extended beyond mere habitation and construction. There would have been various areas in the valley dedicated to activity and work, the procurement of raw materials, processing and disposal areas, as well as the ritual and ceremonial sites.[22]

The impressive scale of Newgrange indicates the immense labour and material required.

It is difficult to imagine this busy scene today. Standing atop Dowth, or on Red Mountain, or walking along the Boyne on its southern shore at Staleen, one is afforded sweeping views of this ancient landscape. Today, it is mostly farmland, part tillage, part pasture, and here and there are dotted houses and farm buildings, erected in modern times. There are hedgerows and fencing, and some trees, and telegraph poles, and even modern roads with tarmacadam surfaces. At certain times of year one can see large flocks of sheep, and herds of cattle, not to mention the large quantities of bird life that flourish here, particularly along the river's edge. It is a landscape that has changed dramatically since the far-off days of the Mesolithic, and yet those changes are largely on the surface only. Archaeologists Geraldine and Matthew Stout paint a beautifully descriptive picture of the scene beneath Newgrange in ancient times:

> Here, five and a half thousand years ago, the sea tides ebbed and flowed beneath its feet, and streams and rivers flowed down from Redmountain into the Boyne creating a swirling cauldron rich in the fruits of sea and river, field and forest. Red deer, boar, wild cats and foxes emerged from a canopy of hazel, birch and alder to drink here. A yearly cycle of migrant birds halted here in the Boyne Valley: the whooper swan, water rail, woodcock and pied wagtail. This is a special place, a fitting home for such an extraordinary monument.[23]

To truly appreciate what life might have been like in the Neolithic age, one has to grapple with certain key concepts and take stock of the harsh realities of prehistoric life. Nothing was as convenient as it is today, and life was fraught with a mixture of onerous day-to-day duties and ever-present dangers, including the threat of disease or serious injury.

While one might have expected the advancements in agriculture and stone technology to have led to an improvement in the quality, and indeed the length, of life in the Neolithic, the opposite was the case. There was, in fact, a decline in life expectancy during the so-called 'Neolithic Revolution', brought about by an increased exposure to environmental hazards like infectious diseases which resulted from an enlarged population density and an increase in manual labour.[24] It is likely that the people who built Newgrange had a lower average life expectancy than their Mesolithic forerunners.

> Most comparisons between hunter-gatherers and farmers . . . suggest that, in the same locale, farmers suffered higher rates of infection due to the increase in human settlements in size and permanence, poorer nutrition due to reduced meat intake and greater interference with mineral absorption by the cereal-based diet. Consequently, Neolithic farmers were shorter and had a lower life expectancy relative to Mesolithic hunter-gatherers.[25]

Let us go back to those far-off times, and look into the mirror at our ancestors who lived on the sloping terraces above the Boyne in the New Stone Age. To do this, we need to imagine a radically different world. Imagine a world without artificial light, beyond what a raging fire or a single flame could provide. We are surrounded in our lives today by arti-

The fireside played an important role in the Neolithic community.

ficial light sources, from street lamps to indoor lights to advertising displays to illuminated shop windows. In the Neolithic, there was only the light provided by fire, beyond that provided by the sun and moon and celestial bodies. In the absence of artificial light, we would find it difficult to survive today. We are simply not used to the dark. During the course of the past century, with the introduction of electrification and the constant illumination of nighttime street lighting, we have grown afraid of the dark.

In the Neolithic, nighttime darkness was simply the natural way of things. There was no need for the mound builders to become accustomed to this situation, for they and their ancestors had been acclimatised to the dark since time immemorial. The fireside played an important role in community, especially in the long winter nights. Many hearths have been found during the course of archaeological digging at Neolithic sites, and indeed at older places of settlement and activity. Indeed, in the Neolithic the hearth was always found centrally in houses, whether circular or rectangular. One can imagine that the great tradition of storytelling around a raging fire was well established in the Neolithic, if in fact it had not been a way of life since the time men and women could first speak a language. Today, we flick a switch and a light comes on. Five thousand years ago if you wanted to create light at nighttime, you had to make a fire, or a flame of some description. That's not easy when you don't have simple devices for creating flame, such as the matches or cigarette lighters that we have today.

It goes without saying that there was no electricity in the Stone Age, and obviously all of the comforts and conveniences that power brings into the modern home were not available in prehistory. There were no televisions or radios, no computers or games consoles, no domestic appliances to do the washing and the drying of clothes, no microwave ovens to heat food, no toasters, no fridges to preserve food. There were no food blenders, no coffee makers, no vacuum cleaners, no blow heaters or cooling fans, no battery chargers, and indeed no electronic devices of any kind.

There was no central heating, no readily available system to heat the home, apart from the fire mentioned before, which would have needed constant fuel, which in turn required sourcing and collection. And of course while we cannot put an exact number on the population of the Bend of the Boyne during the monument building years, we can only speculate that it must have been at least several hundreds of people, if not more. With a much reduced presence of wood and forest in the immediate vicinity of the Bend of the Boyne, such a large population of monument builders would have needed to look further afield for their fuel supplies, perhaps beyond the southern bank of the Boyne, up on the hills. In the long cold nights of winter, the availability of dry tinder and wood to keep these fires ablaze would have been critical. No doubt a serious effort to keep these supplies topped up was required, and indeed one might wonder how such a fuel supply was kept dry, especially if the climate at that time was anything like the climate today.

While there is no doubt that natural springs and wells have been held sacred in Ireland since the earliest days, water was not available at the turn of a tap in every home, as it is today. Water for drinking and cooking had to be sourced, probably from springs in the immediate area, and brought to the homestead in some sort of containers, presumably using ceramic pots or bowls, or maybe wooden vessels or even goat skins. We could speculate that water for certain purposes might have been drawn from the sacred Boyne, but the river was tidal up to Newgrange at the time of the New Stone Age, so perhaps only those sources guaranteed to produce clean freshwater might have been used. Furthermore, any population engaged in farming practices would have required a secure supply of water. Water storage in the home for the purposes of food preparation and cooking would have become possible in the Neolithic with the introduction of pottery vessels capable of storing liquid. This would have meant that a vessel, or vessels, could be filled at the spring and enough water brought to the homestead to ensure a supply for the day's needs. This might have seemed more than adequate at the time, but it is a far cry from today's convenience of an ever-available water supply from the tap.

Water might also have been used in ritual and ceremonial practices at Newgrange.[26] Indeed a natural spring under one of the orthostats, or supporting stones, in the passage of Newgrange produced a small stream of water in the passageway in wintertime.[27] A drainage pipe was laid during restoration of the site so that this no longer happens.

The Neolithic world was one without the trappings and conveniences of modern life. Transport, for instance, was confined to walking on land or sailing on water. There were no roads as such, no chariots, and only trackways and pathways through the wilds. Travel by water was by far the most convenient way of getting around. The boat was the chief mode of transport, and was the key to the maintenance of links between the Neolithic communities of Ireland and Britain and near Europe. There were no motorcars in the Stone Age, no bicycles, no buses, trains, or airplanes. A journey which we today might consider short and convenient, maybe a distance of about seven or eight miles, would have represented a day's journey in the Neolithic, unless of course that journey could be made completely by water.

Health care as we might understand it today was all but absent. We could reasonably suggest that there was no treatment for disease or serious illness beyond herbal and homeopathic methods, and that medication not immediately obtainable from local plant life was otherwise unavailable. There were no hospitals of course, no treatment clinics, no intensive care units, no x-ray machines, no diagnostic instruments, no hypodermic needles. A serious injury, such as a broken limb, would spell doom for most. Mortality rates would have been much greater than today without

Stone and bone.

the intervention of competent medicine and properly equipped practitioners.

There were no convenience stores, no specialist shops to buy foodstuffs or clothing or tools. The Neolithic equivalent of the hardware store was the place, or places, where the manufacture of flint tools was taking place. In the New Stone Age, there were no screwdrivers, no chainsaws, no electric drills, no spanners, no nail guns, no spirit levels, no wood glue, no screws or nails or anything metallic. The only tools available were those made of stone and bone. And perhaps wood. Stone was the chief material for tools, with flint foremost as the stone from which many practical implements were made. Axe heads in Neolithic Ireland were largely made from porcellanite and shale, although examples made from many other types of rock have been found.[28] Several bone implements found at Newgrange might have been tools, including one which excavator Michael O'Kelly describes as a 'chisel', a polished bone which had been rubbed smooth, found in the east recess of the chamber.[29] Other

Newgrange was assembled without any of the tools we have today.

Agriculture continues to flourish around Newgrange to this day.

tools at Newgrange included flint knives, trimming flakes, flint axes, hollow scrapers and various other blades and scraping stones.

It is against this backdrop that one has to paint a picture of the people who built Newgrange. They assembled its 200,000 tonnes of material without the aid of modern heavy plant machinery, and with none of the surveying and construction tools that we have today. In addition, they built the two other massive mounds, Dowth and Knowth, and a sizeable amount of smaller mounds and monuments, all apparently without any of the aids and techniques which make such large-scale projects so much easier today. They did it all without the assistance of anything made of metal. All their work was done with their simple tools of wood and stone and bone.

This happened during a period when there had been a considerable evolution, a Stone Age revolution, a renaissance of sorts, when humans first began to farm and to keep herd animals and to make pottery, and when mankind finally turned his back on the simple but fraught hunter-gatherer existence, a lifestyle he had known since the earliest times.

The results of this humongous collective effort have stood the test of time, over 5,000 years of time, and these great edifices of the Neolithic remain standing today, stark reminders of a time in distant human history when we took the first steps out of our wild, animal-like existence, towards what we might call civilisation.

An examination of those stone remains, and an investigation of the people who built them, will reveal much about who we really are today.

3.

COMMUNITY EFFORT

THERE ARE SO MANY QUESTIONS about Newgrange. And the chances are that if you ask a question about this remarkable monument, you will reveal more questions, and probably not find the answer that you were looking for. There are many reasons for this. The primary reason is the fact that Newgrange was built so long ago, and its people have long vanished, their existence representing a mere speck on the long pathway of the human story which meandered out of the Palaeolithic and down the long ages, all the way to today.

The persistence of curiosity about our past, and the very recent upsurge in fascination with our ancestors, has resulted in many developments in our knowledge of Newgrange. These factors were some of the driving forces behind the excavations at the monument, as indeed they are driving forces behind this book. This absorption with the past, this charm with the ancestor's tale, represents one of the primary reasons that a visitor centre for the Boyne Valley mounds was constructed along the Boyne in the early 1990s. Up to a quarter of a million people come to Brú na Bóinne every year. A great deal of them are intrigued by Newgrange, and share a widespread fascination with anything that is really ancient. Of course, Newgrange is not unique in that regard. Ancient sites all around the world are being opened up to the flow of tourists, archaeologists, researchers, writers, photographers, and a vast range of people with different interests, all eager to see a piece of prehistory, and to ponder on some of the big questions.

Foremost among the questions about Newgrange are, 'how did they build it?' and, 'why did they build it?', but there are a plethora of mysteries and puzzles about a great many things, matters that are beyond the scope of archaeology alone to answer. In the space of a few moments, it is possible to think of a dozen questions and, over time, many, many more. How many people built Newgrange? How long did the construction take? Was it a tomb, or something greater? Why are there 97 kerbstones? Why are only some of its kerbstones decorated? Why did the builders use a mixture of turves and stones in the mound? Why are some of the large stones decorated on the rear, where the artwork cannot be seen? What is the meaning of the triple spiral on the entrance stone? Where did they source the stones from? What was the special significance, if any, of the milky white quartz at the front of the monument? Where did the people who built Newgrange actually live? Why did people stop building passage-mounds after Newgrange was completed?

How many people built Newgrange, and how long did construction take?

Sadly, there is nobody that we can talk to who has the answers. The people who crafted these great earthen mounds passed on many moons ago, and little of their spirit lingers in the valley beyond what one thinks one can sense in the quiet evening air. All that remains physically is mostly stone and bone. And it is very difficult to piece together a coherent narrative of a people based solely on some of their buildings and artifacts. We need to speak with them, to commune with them, to listen to them tell their story. When you've spent enough time in the valley, over a period of years, it is possible to imagine that you have discerned various aspects of their story, almost as if you've heard them speak. It is not in the digging or probing or photographing or drawing that you get all the answers. Sometimes it is in the still moments of contemplation that a thought or revelation will come, like a distant whisper on the winds of time, resonating in the ether.

There are many for whom the exploration of Newgrange, Knowth and Dowth is a largely esoteric experience. Archaeologists are, somewhat understandably, sceptical about such folk, whose number includes spiritualists and druids, pagans and shamans, mystics and diviners, meditators and astrologers. Some interpretations, say the archaeologists, are 'untethered from the actual' and 'soar into speculative realms, which belong to a mystical dimension of the human spirit'.[1] We might not argue with that, except to say that Newgrange itself represents a grand expression of the mystical dimension of the human spirit, and that its secrets will not be revealed by archaeology alone. But we have no great quarrel with the archaeologists, whose work is the foremost aid in reconstructing the past, and to whom we are greatly indebted for their skill and diligence in piecing together the Neolithic puzzle.

Wouldn't it be fabulous if we had some ancient volume, a manual written by the builders of Newgrange, explaining in great detail how and why it was constructed? Such a guide, which might be titled *Brug na Bóinne: An A-Z Guide*, or *Newgrange for Dummies*, would give us all we needed to know about Newgrange and its people, where they came from, what they looked like, how they built the mound, and why they did it, among many other things. How many of us would be greatly surprised and shocked by some of its contents? Probably all of us, to some extent.

Within the pages of such a manual, we might glimpse something even more precious than the answers to our lingering questions. We might, perchance, get a glance at something profound and arcane, yet familiar and heart-warming. We might just see what the people of the Neolithic were like, and what the forces were that drove them to such brilliant endeavours in the days of stone and bone. We might get an insight into the very spirit of these people. Perhaps, if we did, we would see something very familiar. Might we not be looking at ourselves at some very fundamental level?

Such a manual does not, obviously, exist. If it did, there would be little or no interest in Newgrange. It would cease to be mysterious, and we would have all the answers. Humanity has a habit of casting profound knowledge and experiences aside, of growing tired and bored easily, and of constantly searching for something new and undiscovered. We sent men to the moon in the 1960s. Today, we're not that interested in going back. If we were we'd have done so already. We're more interested now in going somewhere further, more hostile, more mysterious. Like Mars.

As long as we have questions about Newgrange, we will continue to explore it, and we will carry on trying to quench our thirst for knowledge. There is great mystery yet attached to it, despite all our scientific and technological advances. This one of the fascinating qualities of Newgrange and its sister sites – they hold much intrigue for us. We still cannot figure out much of what they were about, the hows and whys. It is this that keeps us on our perpetual quest to learn more.

Not much is known about the size of the community that lived along the shores of the Boyne during the time of the forest clearance and subsequent construction phase. We know that the land had been cleared during the 500 years previous to the building of the mounds.[2] The limited evidence we have of habitation around the time of construction shows that the builders lived in fragile homes built mostly from wood with straw or rush roofs. The remains of between ten and 14 houses were found during

*The builders of Newgrange lived in fragile homes built
mostly from wood with straw roofs.*

excavations at Knowth, some large enough to accommodate perhaps a family of between five and ten people. There is a lack of evidence of habitation sites from the limited excavations at Newgrange. While evidence of some timber structures was found during excavations carried out by George Eogan at a small passage mound at Townleyhall,[3] a few kilometres to the north of Newgrange, it is safe to say that the size of the extant community in the Boyne Valley at the time the great monuments were being assembled can really only be guessed at until the remains of further habitation sites are found.

But the sheer volume of material involved in the construction of Newgrange alone suggests a substantial community was involved in putting it together. There were an estimated 200,000 tonnes of material used at Newgrange, and similar if not greater amounts used at Dowth and Knowth. When we consider that there are 31 known 'passage-tomb' monuments plus a possible nine additional sites in the Bend of the Boyne,[4] we begin to see the mammoth scale of this vast construction project. And we begin to encounter some of the questions that are apparently beyond the grasp of any of us to answer definitively at this time.

It seems unlikely that the community of the Boyne was less than a hundred people, and it would be more appropriate to suggest a population of several hundreds. A thousand inhabitants might not have been sustainable, even with the substantial agricultural activity in the valley at the time. But we are playing a guessing game here.

The archaeological evidence suggests a settled population existed in the area before the main mounds were built. Archaeologist Conor Brady of Dundalk Institute of Technology points to the pre-passage tomb activity in the valley, and indeed beyond, including a number of sites that were uncovered during construction of the nearby M1 motorway at the turn of the last millennium. 'There was an established population in the area, probably relatively small, before the passage tombs.'[5]

One difficulty with ascertaining probable population size and growth lies in the lack of radiocarbon dates for the beginning of the passage mound phase.

> We don't actually have a huge number of dates from the World Heritage Site[6] from passage tombs. There is a good collection from Knowth but many of these relate to samples that probably pre-date the tomb construction in each case. Indications are that the earliest dates are c.3300 BC although there are dates for human bone from tomb 3 Knowth of 3600-3400 BC.[7]

Brady ascertains that the tombs were probably built in stages over a drawn-out period of time, and suggests it is likely that the population was increasing during that time.

> Not all of the builders were necessarily resident in the Bend of the Boyne. There is extensive settlement evidence in the form of lithic scatters from outside this area and along the corridor of the river. There may have been an element of pilgrimage involved with movement on a temporary basis from other areas, especially as the scale of the tombs increases. The scale of the complex suggests a regional hinterland.'[8]

Was Newgrange built during quiet times in the agricultural calendar?
(Image from the Brú na Bóinne centre.)

Trying to guess the exact population of the Bend of the Boyne when Newgrange was being built is akin to asking 'how long is a piece of string?' There are some indications that the construction of the large monuments was not a continuous process, according to Brady. 'Construction might have been carried out at quiet times in the agricultural year rather than having a dedicated 'supported' workforce'.[9] This is intriguing. In other words, despite the free time which the introduction of agriculture provided for the community of the Boyne, the fact remains that someone had to carry out the actual activities of farming, especially at those times of the year where considerable labour might have been required to do so. Did this agricultural activity and the associated effort mean that the building of Newgrange had to be abandoned for parts of the year?

If this is the case, it might perhaps indicate a sense of organisation and purpose about the Neolithic community. It couldn't have been easy to run the farming operations of the valley and keep everyone fed, while at the same time hauling massive stones through the valley for the colossal construction projects taking place at Dowth, Knowth and Newgrange.

The organised community showed significant logistical expertise.

If current theory holds true – that there was a sequence to the construction of the monuments with no great overlap between each – then this would further underline the logistical expertise of this incredibly organised community, because they could concentrate their efforts on one project at a time instead of sharing resources between three. However, the opposite is also true, that if a commune of people using only stone and wood as technology could build three great monuments in the same time frame, there were considerable skills of coordination and planning.

One way or the other, it is clear that the people who fashioned these colossal monuments were highly organised, dedicated and motivated. Balancing the requirements of agriculture and domestic activity, and the provision of food, with the manufacture of tools and materials required for the work of building, in addition to the actual time and effort necessary for the construction, could not have been an easy task for a people who didn't have any metal, nor the plant machinery that would make such exploits so much easier today.

One of the difficulties with estimating the scale of the task facing the farmers and star gazers of the New Stone Age is that it is not pos-

sible to ascertain the population size just from looking at the archaeological finds. Because the rate of use of raw material is variable, there is
no simple equation stating that X number of tools = 1 resident. Thus, the
discovery of hundreds of lithic items in a particular corner of the Boyne
Valley might not necessarily indicate a higher population at a particular
time in that location. Rather, it might illustrate activity over a prolonged
period of time, by a smaller number of inhabitants.

However, what the distribution maps of the finds do indicate is that
'very large areas of the landscape were occupied and that the population
of the wider landscape could have been greater than has been assumed'.[10]
Excavations on the M1 showed that were was a 'major focus on the river
corridor'. Activity stretched from Brú na Bóinne out to the coast, some 15
kilometres or so downstream from Newgrange. There was considerable
activity along coastal areas at that time also.

The picture that we are seeing is one of regional, not just local, activity. In fact, the size of the district from which materials were sourced for
Newgrange was so expansive that we really have to view its construction
almost in terms of a national project. In addition, the logistical chal-

*The entrance kerbstone at Newgrange, which, like the other kerbs, is of
greywacke, brought here from Clogherhead.*

The white quartz and granite cobbles fronting Newgrange were brought from Wicklow and Rathcor, respectively.

lenges posed in bringing that material over many miles to Newgrange, which was carried out without any transport infrastructure to speak of other than the rivers and the sea, gives us a much greater appreciation for the colossal task that our ancestors faced in turning the vision of Newgrange into reality.

Earlier interpretations of Newgrange suggested that its giant kerbstones were glacial erratics, deposited by glaciers at the end of the last Ice Age, around 10,000 years ago. However, this view has changed dramatically in recent years as the study of the Boyne complex by archaeologists, geologists, anthropologists and all manner of other scientists has broadened our knowledge of the area.

While all the kerbstones at nearby Dowth, thought to have been built before Newgrange, are irregular, suggesting that they were glacial erratics,[11] the kerbs at Newgrange are all made of greywacke.[12] Most of the kerbstones and the orthostats in the Boyne tombs are of a stone called Lower Palaeozoic greywacke.[13] Recent studies have suggested the greywacke kerbs at Newgrange were sourced at a place called Clogherhead,[14] located along the east coast, a distance of some 19 kilometres northeast as the crow flies, and perhaps 25-30 kilometres by boat down the Boyne river and up along the coastline. There is considerable evidence for this deduction from the work of the late Professor Adrian Phillips and the late Mary Corcoran, which has yet to be fully published.[15]

The dramatic façade of Newgrange consists of a mixture of large quantities of white quartz which were interspersed with dozens of large cobbles of granite, each perhaps the size of a rugby ball or slightly smaller.

In the words of the late archaeologist and geologist Frank Mitchell, these granite cobbles 'could not be obtained in quantity less than 30 kilometres from the site'.[16] In fact, the source of these cobbles has been identified as Rathcor beach,[17] on the Cooley peninsula, almost 37 kilometres away as the crow flies, overlooking Dundalk Bay, in the shadow of the Cooley Mountains. There were 103 of these granite boulders used in the façade of Newgrange. Despite the fact that these stones were sourced by the builders of Newgrange at Rathcor beach over 5,000 years ago, their origin can be traced even further north. These cobbles consist mainly of Newry granodiorites and Mourne granites, that is, they come from the Mourne Mountains, even further away from Newgrange, and some 20 to 30 kilometres northeast of Rathcor.

A journey by some sort of barge or boat[18] with a cargo of these stones might, we can speculate, have made a beeline from Rathcor across Dundalk Bay in a straight course towards Dunany Point. This would have made sense because hugging the coastline might not have been practical due to the shallow nature of the bay along the coast at Dundalk and

An inlet at Clogherhead where there are significant amounts of large greywackle slabs lying about the place even today. Was this one of the locations from which Newgrange's kerbstones were brought?

*The greywacke kerbs had to be brought from the Boyne to Newgrange,
a distance of one kilometre, up an incline of 60 metres.*

Blackrock. From Dunany, the boat or boats might have rounded Clogherhead and sailed on down the coast, maybe half a mile from the shore or
less, until reaching the Boyne estuary.

We are back in the realm of speculation here. It is not known how the
stones were transported from their various locations to the Newgrange
site. What is known with a great deal of certainty is the source of the
Newgrange stones. There were diverse locations for these sources, which
have been identified thanks mainly to the diligence of modern geologists.
And when we examine the great distances from which large quantities of
this material was brought to Newgrange – and indeed scrutinise the possible nature of the transportation involved – we begin to appreciate not
just the regional scale of the project but also the baffling quandary of how
such an apparently primitive community managed such a humongous
logistical operation.

For instance, the white quartz which features so brilliantly on the
modern reconstruction of the Newgrange façade was originally brought

here in the Stone Age from the Wicklow Mountains, the source of these stones lying some 70-80 kilometres south of the Boyne Valley. A total of 607 water-rolled quartz pebbles interspersed with 612 pieces of quarried angular quartz and 103 of the Rathcor granite boulders were found during O'Kelly's excavations at the front of the monument.[19] More questions spring to mind. What was the average stone-carrying capacity of whatever boats were used to bring these stones from Wicklow, and indeed from Rathcor? How many journeys might have been necessary before all the material was actually available on site for construction? Were the granite selection and quartz quarrying operations at Rathcor and the Wicklow Mountains coordinated in such a way as to allow the stones arrive at Newgrange at the same time?

Perhaps the biggest questions though are reserved for the larger boulders at Newgrange, the kerbstones and some of the orthostats and roof stones. There are 97 kerbstones in total, weighing between one and five tonnes apiece, the average weight being around three tonnes. How they were brought here, from the coast at Clogherhead, is a mystery.

Current convention holds that the stones were somehow strapped to the underside of a boat at low tide at Clogherhead, and when the tide came in the boat, with boulder attached, became buoyant.[20] From there, the boat sailed down along the coastline and up the Boyne, the total distance from Clogherhead to Newgrange being approximately 30 kilometres. Due to an interesting quirk of physics, a stone weighs less in water than it does in air, making large slabs such as those used in the kerb of Newgrange easier to transport while immersed in water. Exactly what material was used to lash these enormous slabs to the underside of the boats is not known. In fact, the whole theory about how these great stones were transported to Newgrange is just a hypothesis. However, with no roads to speak of, and no indication of how these giant greywacke slabs might have been dragged across land – and all the streams and waterways encountered along the way – transport by sea and river seems more likely.[21]

Some experiments have taken place in England to reproduce the transportation of similarly large stones, the so-called 'Blue Stones' of

Stonehenge, which weigh between two and four tonnes apiece. The Blue Stones were found to have been brought from a site in Wales, some 160 miles (257 kilometres) from Stonehenge, an astonishing distance.[22] Forty-three of these stones remain at Stonehenge, but it is thought there were originally more. How they were brought from Wales to Stonehenge is the subject of much debate, and the notion that the stones were carried from the Preseli Hills at least some of the way towards the Stonehenge site by a glacier in much earlier times has not been ruled out.[23]

Transporting these large stones by land or sea, or a mixture of both, would have been a precarious venture in the Stone Age. Indeed one experiment to bring a slightly lighter blue stone from the Preseli Mountains to Stonehenge ended in failure when the stone in question 'slipped from its lashings, fell into the water and sank 60 feet to the bottom of Freshwater Bay, Pembrokeshire, with its sharp currents.'[24] The failure of the experiment did, however, illustrate the difficulty and danger involved in the transportation of large stones over long distances.

A journey by water alone, however, would prove equally fraught with danger.

> The endeavours of crews attempting to manoeuvre a heavily-laden, clumsy raft along the seas of the Welsh coast would have been perilous in the extreme.[25]

Without the assistance of modern navigation and propulsion systems, such a venture would have constituted a maritime suicide mission:

> On a floating platform without sails, with propulsion dependent on paddles and poles, with little control over steering, and affected by every capricious current of the Bristol Channel, the crews would have faced the vicissitudes of weather and a recurring series of threats: strong tides, undertows, lethal sandbanks.[26]

Could the same not be said for the transportation of greywacke slabs 30 kilometres down the Irish Sea coast from Clogherhead to the Boyne, and then up the river towards Newgrange? Are we missing part of the picture here, a piece of the puzzle about how this great monument was built?

In addition to the fact that there are 97 large greywacke kerbstones at Newgrange, each weighing an average of three tonnes, there are many more heavy slabs which were used in its construction. Claire O'Kelly, who accompanied her husband on the excavations of Newgrange, gives us an approximation of the number of boulders involved: 'On a rough estimate, at least 200 slabs were required for structurally prominent positions. This does not include the stones of the Great Circle but takes in the orthostats of passage and chamber, the passage roofslabs, the roofslabs and corbels of the three recesses and the ninety-seven kerbstones.'[27]

If Clogherhead was the site of the greywacke quarry for Newgrange, we have to imagine a total of 200 precarious journeys up and down the coast and then along the river channel, which itself is peppered with danger spots. Because the Boyne would probably have been tidal as far as Brú na Bóinne in prehistory, each journey from the estuary up to a land-

At low tide, several islands appear in the Boyne west of Drogheda,
a popular spot for anglers today.

Several granite cobbles gathered by the author at Rathcor beach.

ing site below Newgrange would have been necessary during full tide. There are places where the Boyne is shallow, and dangerously so at low tide. For instance, at a place not far from Yellow Island, just west of the modern town of Drogheda, and some eight or nine kilometres downstream from Newgrange, the river is so shallow that fishermen can easily wade out onto some of the natural islands that appear when the tide is out.

Further to the dangers of being lashed about mercilessly by the waves of the Irish Sea followed by the very precocious navigation of the Boyne which would have been necessary to bring each stone towards Brú na Bóinne, there was the challenge of somehow hauling the stones from the river bank up to the site of Newgrange, a distance of one kilometre, up an incline of about 60 metres.[28] A reconstruction of this effort at the nearby Brú na Bóinne Visitor Centre appears to show a large boulder being hauled up a steep incline on some sort of wooden sled. The cargo is pulled by perhaps as many as fifty men using ropes, and moves along on wooden rollers, which are constantly taken away from the rear of the sled and brought back to the front as the stone progresses towards its destination.

It is possible also that the sled might have been rolled across round stones, ancient 'ball bearings' so to speak, such as was done in Malta,[29] and might also have been carried out at Stonehenge.[30]

We cannot say whether there was a fleet of vessels used to bring material to Newgrange, but it seems likely. In addition to the 200 very large greywacke slabs, a further 200 boulders of greywacke make up the corbels of the passage and chamber roof.[31] These were probably also sourced from Clogherhead. That's a total of 400 large boulders, some weighing

A model at the Brú na Bóinne Visitor Centre depicting how the large kerbstones might have been moved up the hill towards Newgrange.

as much as five tonnes,[32] which had to be brought from quarry to construction site. Were there five boats making the trip each time, meaning that each boat would have to make 40 round trips of 60 kilometres? Or were there perhaps 20 ships, each required to make ten such 60 kilometre journeys? It's simply impossible to tell at this point.

Further to the greywacke transportation, the large amounts of quartz and also the granite cobbles had to be brought from Wicklow and Rathcor respectively. Coordinating the logistical operation involved in bringing all this material to Newgrange in a timely fashion – without the modern communications technology that we take for granted – would have been an immense task.

But it wasn't an impossible task, and the fact that all those stones are there today, making up the great monument that we stand in awe of, is testament to the fact that it was indeed possible, whatever the methods of transportation might have been. Archaeologist Conor Brady does not believe we are missing part of the picture:

The same kind of work has been achieved elsewhere with similar technology. An organised workforce with a workable plan can achieve a lot. Experimental work has been done elsewhere showing it is entirely possible.'[33]

Brady believes the wide geographic spread of the material used at Newgrange demonstrates the degree of mobility that existed among the population and highlights the regional scale of the construction project. Indeed, the distribution of certain types of pottery and axes in the New Stone Age suggests that there were 'widespread contacts during Neolithic times'[34] and that 'Neolithic people were not as parochial as we may at first think'.[35] Porcellanite is a special stone which can only be found in the extreme northeast of Ireland, and yet over half of the known Irish axes were made of it, and such axes also appear in Britain. It is now an established certainty that there was trade and exchange between the islands of Ireland and Britain in the Neolithic. Why should we be surprised about the ability of these people to transport stones to Newgrange from remote locations?

It would be nice if we had all the answers, but then the mystery of Newgrange would be diminished, and we would be less interested in its exploration. Future examination of the river bed might yet reveal great greywacke slabs which were dropped or otherwise lost on the journey from Clogherhead.[36] This would certainly help to prove the theory. In the meantime, all we can do is stand in awe of the great monument and pay homage to its builders, who risked life and limb to ensure its completion.

4.

SUN, MOON & STARS

O N THE SHORTEST DAYS OF the year, in the middle of winter, when light is most scarce, there is a deep sense of longing that rouses itself in the innermost recesses of the human heart. This acute desire is for light and warmth, those things that bring comfort to the spirit of mankind, and this desire is sensed with much greater intensity at more northerly latitudes, where the winter days are shorter and the nights longer. In Ireland, the seasons of winter and summer are in dramatic contrast, not just because of the difference in temperature, but more especially because of the enormous difference in the length of day.

The varying duration of day occupies a special place in conversation in modern Ireland, where you will hear with diffident regularity phrases such as, 'the days are really closing in', especially around September and October, and conversely, 'there's a great stretch in the evenings' in February and March. Even modern folk, with all their indoor comforts and conveniences, notice this stark disparity in the length of the day from season to season. In midsummer, the sun rises just before 5.00 am and sets just before 10.00 pm, and there is no real dark night, because twilight lingers in the northern portion of the sky where the sun hasn't sunk far enough below the horizon to allow complete darkness. In midwinter, conversely, the sun rises at around 9.00 am and sets after 3.30 in the afternoon. The winter nights can seem very, very long, and the days fleeting.

So it should be no great wonder, then, that a people who lived without artificial light, except for whatever brightness a fire could afford them in the deepest nights of winter, should consider the winter solstice to be a very special and sacred occasion. For the solstice is not just the lowest ebb of the sun's cycle, nor is it the absolute end of long and cold nights, but rather it is the day after which the sun can sink no lower, the day when the sun becomes renewed, and begins the slow turn towards the lengthening days and shortening shadows.

We should not think that there is anything special about the ability of people in the Neolithic to recognise this cyclical behaviour of the sun. It was common knowledge to them just as it is common knowledge to us today, except it must have been much more acutely obvious to them because they spent a lot more time out in the open air and among nature. Like us, they needed to have a means to track time. Unlike us, they did not have wristwatches and other electronic devices to allow them conveniently announce the exact moment in the year, so they used different methods, which we shall examine.

The megalithic civilisation, if we can call it that, which existed on the periphery of Europe in prehistory, stretched from Iberia and the Mediter-

The sun begins to peer over Red Mountain on Winter Solstice.

ranean through France, Britain and Ireland, and up into parts of southern Scandinavia. If the influx of farming practices and giant monument building was indeed fed by some great migration of ideas and people across Europe, it must have been acutely apparent to these people that the length of the winter days in, for instance, Spain, was much different to the length of day in northern Scotland.

The slow movement of the sun's rising position along the eastern aspect, like a giant pendulum, swinging from solstice to solstice, would doubtless have been apparent to the very earliest of peoples. No matter how far we go back in the human story, right back through the Mesolithic and the Palaeolithic into the unknown realms of the origin of the first men and women, we can say with a degree of confidence that this innate recognition of the sun's cycle – one of them simplest and most recognisable of nature's patterns – was inherent in the human psyche since people first walked upright on this earth.

If there is something remarkable about the winter solstice at Newgrange, it is the grandeur of the celebration and the monumental labour that was imbued into the effort surrounding its commemoration. At 8.54 am on the shortest day, the sun begins to peer over the hill of Red Mountain, across the valley from Newgrange. As it creeps over the crest of the hill, the landscape around the monument becomes bathed in golden light, and the chill morning is momentarily banished as the great glow warms even the spirits of those who have gathered to watch. All the time,

the front of the monument is aglow, and its stones have turned from shades of pale grey to radiant hues of yellow and orange.

Four minutes after the sun first makes its appearance, a shaft of its light has penetrated deep into the mound's interior, reaching the chamber floor more than 20 metres inside. At its widest, the beam is 17 centimetres on the floor of the chamber. It reaches towards the end recess, and when the sky is clear enough the light is sufficient to see details in the recesses of the chamber. At 9.09, just 11 minutes after it first illuminates the deep interior, the light beam begins to narrow, and by 9.15 am it has become 'cut off from the tomb'.[1]

The winter solstice alignment of Newgrange is trumpeted worldwide as a remarkable achievement of ancient engineering. And rightly so. For here is a structure which is made of largely unhewn stones – many of the stones are 'surface dressed', which means they were smoothened by a percussive hammering action – but none is 'worked' into a block with straight edges. Unlike the corridors in the pyramids in Egypt, which have exceptionally straight walls, formed by blocks with extremely even surfaces, the passage of Newgrange is created with humongous rocks which have barely been altered in shape at all.

With these enormous stones, the creators of Newgrange cleverly created an aperture which was able to admit just a very thin beam of sunlight onto the chamber floor. The passage meanders to an extent, and there are passage uprights which lean inwards, an intentional effort on behalf of the builders to help narrow the beam to their exact specifications. In essence what they achieved was extraordinary. Not only did the roofbox and passage and chamber have to be very carefully designed and constructed, to focus a 17 centimetre beam of sunlight into the back of the chamber, but they had to be built in such a way as to sustain the weight of the cairn material above. And, it is suspected, they built Newgrange as an everlasting memorial, designed to withstand the harsh ravages of time, long into the future.[2]

It is clear that the winter solstice held a great significance to the people of the Boyne Valley. Once the autumn equinox has passed, the posi-

Winter Solstice sun bathes the Boyne Valley in light.
In the foreground is Mound A, down the fields from Newgrange.

tion of sunrise moves steadily southwards along the horizon. It may have seemed to the people at that time, and probably since much earlier ages, that perhaps some year the sun would just continue sinking southwards, and maybe the time would come when it would never rise again.

Solstice is a word which comes from the Latin *sol* (sun) and *sistere* (to stand still). In Irish, solstice is *grianstad*, meaning 'stopped sun'. There is no doubt that the standing still of the sun's rising position marked the turning of the year, and that this was recognised, as stated previously, from the very earliest times by humans. In *Island of the Setting Sun*, Richard Moore and I made a substantial case that the builders of the monu-

*The builders of Newgrange were adept astronomers,
long before modern telescopes were invented.*

ments of the Boyne were adept astronomers and cunning surveyors and engineers. They needed to be. Such wondrous constructions would not have been possible without a good working knowledge of the sky and the movements of the celestial bodies. Just how advanced this knowledge actually became is still the subject of considerable debate.

While the solstice held a great importance to the Neolithic inhabitants of Ireland, and it might have helped the builders of Newgrange to enumerate the days in the year, a calendar based solely on the movements of the sun is pretty much useless. It is useless because even if you move half a mile away, to another part of the valley, all your reference points on the horizon for sunrises and sunsets at solstices and equinoxes have changed. Simply put, you have to stay in the same spot for a year and mark the various positions of the sun before you can then know more precisely what time of year it is. And even then, you are limited to a basic calendar, divided into four by the two equinoxes and two solstices, or into eight if you have marked out the half-way points between the solstices and equinoxes, known as the cross quarter days.

While we might heap praise on the builders of Newgrange for meticulously constructing this marvellous time-keeping device, we must also take cognisance of what other heavenly objects might have been its target, and how much more advanced their calendar needed to be as an agrarian society. The rising and setting positions of the sun alone would not constitute a functional and practical calendar. In addition to the problem of having to mark out the positions of sunrise and sunset, whether with standing stones or wooden posts or chambered cairns, there would have been the problem of weather. What happens when you miss a solstice because it's been cloudy for a week? You are into guessing game territory.

If you wish to more accurately mark out the time of year, you need to make reference to the moon and the stars. Only then can you properly tell what day of the year it is.

The builders of Newgrange and its sister monuments knew this very well. They and their ancestors spent a great deal of their time out in the open air, living lives free of the distractions that make us, their modern descendants, all but ignorant of the movements of the sun, moon and stars except what we read in books and learn on television and the in-

One needs to make reference to the stars to form an accurate calendar.

ternet. How many people today know, for instance, that the sun rises in the northeast on the longest days of the year, and the southeast on the shortest? How many know that the moon goes through a monthly cycle, growing from a thin crescent to a half moon to a full moon and then waning back to a half moon and down to a slender crescent before disappearing for a few days? How many know that the moon completes a loop through the sky, doing what it takes the sun a year to do, in just 27 days? How many know that the twelve constellations of stars, which we refer to as the Zodiac, form the backdrop against which the sun, moon and planets pass as they wander through the sky?

The answer, of course, is 'not many'. And that is unfortunate. We have allowed ourselves to become parted from nature and its innate rhythms. We still perceive the cycles of nature, mainly the seasons, although it's hard not to in Ireland because of the often inclement nature of our weather. We do still understand that the days are long in summer and the days are short in winter, but beyond that people today have little grasp of the cosmic cycles. Part of the reason for this is down to our own time-keeping devices, the wrist watches and clocks which are an everyday part of our general attire these days. Every mobile phone has a clock and a calendar on it, and a great majority of people own mobile phones. So with such powerful aids at our disposal, why would we need to take notice of what's going on in the sky?

Such a flippant dismissal of the importance of the sky cycles would have been lethal in the Neolithic. In fact, scant regard of cyclical cosmic activity would be a difficult indulgence at most periods of our history, except perhaps for the last century or so.

One of the reasons winter solstice was important to the builders of Newgrange was because it was one very obvious way to mark out the beginning and end of a period of time, a year. When a Stone Age observer watched the standstills of the rising and setting sun in the northeast and northwest in summer and then the southeast and southwest in winter, they could literally see the turning of the year, those times when the brightest days would begin to wane, or the darkest days would soon lengthen. Why was this important? For several reasons. The change in direction of the sunrise position following a solstice enabled people to readily perceive that the sun's course through the year was cyclical, that it followed a pattern, that it went through predictable motions that regularly brought it back to the same places on the horizon at time of sunrise and sunset. More importantly, the changes brought about by the waxing and waning strength of the sun could be directly seen in the landscape and in nature, something that was of fundamental importance to a society that practiced agriculture. A community rooted to the earth in one particular location, such as the Bend of the Boyne, lived or died by the cycle of the sun. Much as perhaps their Mesolithic ancestors had done, except the Neolithic population were growing crops and keeping cattle, practices which were ultimately governed by the motions of the sun. Who, after all, would plant crops in November or December or January, with the threat of harsh frosts always looming?

Sunlight enters the passage of Newgrange at Winter Solstice,
the end and the beginning of the year.

Winter solstice was important to the builders of Newgrange because it marked the death of the old sun, and the birth of the new. These were the shortest days, and the longest nights, but the return of the light beam to the inner chamber of Newgrange brought great hope, a light in the darkness, the promise of the return of the stronger days and the renewal of the year. The death and decay of winter, and the cold and darkness, would be shaken off by the reinvigoration of spring. In the days following the maximum penetration of the sun beam into the rear of the chamber, each dawn would bring a retreat of the light back down the passageway until, within days, the light would no longer reach the chamber. This was the one certainty from which the creators of Newgrange could draw the greatest comfort. The shortening of the light beam in the passage meant that the year had indeed turned again, and the sun was once more on its inexorable dance along the horizon, this time heading north and strengthening, meaning the longer, brighter, warmer days were coming.

The moon, Venus and Jupiter hang in the evening sky over Newgrange.

As a permanent timepiece, set with great effort into the landscape so indelibly, Newgrange would have worked very well in this regard. It was a precision chronograph, able to pinpoint the days of the standing still sun with great accuracy. However, with the sun shining into the chamber for just a number of days at one end of the year, Newgrange can hardly be described as a practical calendar. With only the solstices as reference points, any dates in the year would have to be referred to as, for example, 'fifty days after *grianstad*' or something similar. And that highlights the shortcomings of a 'solar calendar', one based on the movements of the sun alone.

A Neolithic astronomer or farmer might not enjoy the prospect of pinpointing the shortest days without some monument like Newgrange, or a set of standing stones, or some other structure to aid them. A good working knowledge of the movements of the moon, and also a reference to the positions of the stars, would have been absolutely necessary in order to keep a precise reckoning of time.

While it travels along its path through the Zodiac – those twelve constellations which we know today as Aries, Taurus, Gemini, Cancer, Leo, Virgo, Libra, Scorpius, Sagittarius, Capricorn, Aquarius and Pisces – the moon also changes shape, as discussed earlier. It starts in invisibility and then grows from crescent to half to full back to half back to crescent before disappearing again. One of the simplest astronomy lessons, which one can imagine a Boyne Valley farmer teaching his or her children, is this changing shape of the moon. The next lesson would involve telling the kids that the moon makes one complete circuit of the sky in 27 days. This is something the sun takes over 365 days to complete. Interestingly, the Zodiac was known in Irish as the *uair-chrios*, the 'turning circle',[3] a concept which might have originated in the far-off days of the Stone Age.

Following on from their rudimentary astronomical explorations, the farmer might tell his children how the 'half' moons, those phases which we ironically call 'quarter' moons today,[4] can help show what constellation the sun is currently located in, and where it will be situated in three months' time. In the Neolithic, at the time Newgrange was being built,

The changing shape of the moon is one of the rudimentary lessons of astronomy.

the sun was located in the constellation we know today as Aquarius at winter solstice. At that time of year, a 'first half' moon (what we call 'first quarter' today) would be located in the constellation we call Taurus, which most likely also seen as a bull constellation in the New Stone Age.[5] Thus, not only would the farmer tell his children that in three months' time it will be spring equinox, because the half moon is three months ahead of the sun, but also that by extension it must now be winter solstice and the sun is located in the constellation Aquarius. Curiously this constellation is referred to in an old Irish manuscript as the 'lunar leper'[6] and this may be connected with the story of how the Boyne river was formed after the goddess Bóann was washed out to sea by the rising waters from Nechtain's well, which she had been forbidden to approach.[7]

The full moon, which comes 14 days after the invisible moon, is always located in the opposite part of the sky to the sun. Often one can watch the sun setting in the west and within a short time the full moon rising in the east. This is another elementary lesson in lunar astronomy, and something that would have been very obvious to anyone who watched the moon's movements over a period of time. At winter solstice in the Neolithic, the full moon rose in the constellation we know today as Leo, but which was likely known as *Cú*, the Hound, in ancient times.[8] The full moon indicates where the sun will be located in six months' time. During those gloriously long days of summer, with the sun rising early in the northeast, the full moon would be located in Aquarius. It follows from all this that the 'last half' moon, the one we call 'last quarter' today, would mark out the place in the sky where the sun would be located nine months from now. Thus, our Neolithic farmer would tell his kids at winter solstice to expect the following autumn equinox's sun to be positioned in the Milky Way, the river of the sky, where it runs down between Sagittarius and Scorpius.

There are some natural astronomy lessons which follow on from an introduction to the lunar movements. If the full moon is always opposite the sun, it follows that the full moon at the time of winter solstice will occupy that part of the sky where the summer solstice sun will be located in six months' time, and therefore while the winter solstice sun remains low in the sky throughout the day, the full moon would climb very high in the sky during the night, rising in the far northeast and setting in the northwest. It is not beyond the realm of possibility that a Stone Age farmer in the Boyne Valley could have taught his kids these simple lessons in one single evening. Of course, they would have to watch the moon's movements among the stars for several months in order to see his predictions in action.

It would not take the farmer, or his offspring, too long to notice that the moon's course through the sky is not entirely straightforward. There are two immediately obvious reasons for this. The first is that the time it takes the moon to return to the same place among the stars, what we know today as the siderial or tropical month, is about 27 days, which is around two days shorter than it takes the moon to return to the same phase, something we call the synodic month. For example, if you see a full moon tonight, you will see another full moon in roughly 29 days' time. So the moon completes a circuit from, say, the horns of Taurus, the bull, in 27 days, returning to approximately the same place in that length of time. But if you had seen a full moon between the bull's horns the previous month, the second return to the bull's horns will be an incom-

The moon's path through the sky (yellow line) is tilted against the sun's path (red line). Image from Stellarium with some modifications.

plete full moon – it would have a chunk missing off it ! It would be a full two nights before you would see a full moon, and of course it would have moved on, across the upraised hand of Orion towards the feet of Gemini, the twins.

To help them understand the path of the moon through the stars, the early astronomers had their own Zodiac, their *uair-chrios*, the 'turning circle'. The word *uair* can mean time, thus *uair-chrios* might have meant the 'time circle'.[9] Many of their constellations might have been similar to those we know today. Some were different. Their *uair-chrios* helped them to 'mark out' time, so to speak, by watching the moon's position against the background of the stars from night to night, from week to week, and from month to month.

The second reason the moon's movements are not straightforward relates to the fact that its path through the stars is inclined slightly to the path that the sun takes, which we call today the 'Ecliptic'. The result is that during its meanderings, the moon will wander some distance north and south of this imaginary line through the stars. It makes sense that if the moon's path were not tilted against the sun's path, there would be a total eclipse of the sun every month when the moon is invisible and a total eclipse of the moon every 29 days when the full moon is exactly opposite the sun. The inclination of one path against the other means that eclipses can only take place when the moon is on the Ecliptic.

The apparent complexity of all this represents the main reason some modern day academics refuse to explore the notion that the ancients could have developed a complex calendar based not only on the sun, but the moon and stars also. If the moon's movements are complex, and perhaps too complex for us to understand, then how possibly could people living 5,000 years in the past possibly have done so, they argue. But our single biggest problem in approaching this matter is the fact that we no longer take notice of what's happening in the sky. We rely on computer software to show us the movements of the heavens, and we can see the sky as it was at any time in the past by a few clicks of a mouse button and a few keystrokes on a computer keyboard. This is, of course, a massively powerful tool at our disposal, but without the direct observation and perhaps the enjoyment of spending time under the night sky, how can we ever expect to appreciate the very movements which we deem complex?

> The moon is an important test of the abilities of ancient astronomers because its movements are more complex and demand more skilful observation than those of the sun. In urban surroundings we may notice the different phases of the moon from time to time, but the place in which it appears in the night sky can seem quite haphazard from one week to the next. Actually, the movements of the moon are perfectly regular, as most people not hemmed in by tall buildings or dazzled by city lights are well aware.[10]

The fact of the matter is that, over time, people in prehistory would have discerned that, despite the seeming convolution of the motions of the moon, its movements still follow patterns. Almost everything that happens in the sky, with a few exceptions such as meteors (falling stars), or the appearance or comets or Aurora Borealis (Northern Lights),[11] fol-

The moon's movements follow discernable patterns.

lows a cycle. And this is the key to understanding ancient astronomical knowledge – the idea that the heavenly bodies obey sequences. It might also represent one of the reasons the great monuments of Newgrange, Knowth and Dowth were built in quasi-circular shapes, and had giant rings of kerbstones around them – were these huge sequences of stones designed to represent some sort of counting aid, a useful assistance in discerning the patterns of the sky? The idea that the number of kerbstones at Newgrange, Knowth and Dowth relates to patterns of the moon has already been explored in *Island of the Setting Sun*. If they were indeed counting sequences, one might expect that certain noteworthy stones might represent significant moments in those cycles, and this has been suggested to have been the case. Furthermore, some of the carvings on certain kerbstones have been shown to represent lunar counting sequences, most notably the 'Calendar Stone' at Knowth.[12]

One difficulty with convincing modern onlookers – and especially non-astronomers – of the intricate level of knowledge of the ancient sky watchers lies in the fact that some of the cycles are extremely long. The Metonic cycle, named after a fifth century BC Greek named Meton, sees the same phase of the moon return to exactly the same background stars after a period of 19 years. Because of the difference in the length of the tropical month (27 days) versus the synodic month (29 days), combined with the moon's inclination to the Ecliptic, the same phase of the moon never seems to come back to the exact same background stars – even after a full year. It might be located in the same approximate area of the sky, but not exactly. And the number of lunar months never seems to quite fit into a full solar year of 365 days, sometimes falling short by a number of days, and sometimes being longer by a few days. It is only on completion of a full Metonic Cycle of 19 years that the moon seems to harmonise with the sun again. This represents 235 synodic lunar months – in other words, 235 full moons – and 254 tropical months – that is, 254 returns of the moon to the same constellation, perhaps the upraised hand of Orion, which was seen as a very significant point on the ecliptic, where the path of the sun, moon and planets appeared to cross over the Milky Way, the bright river of the sky from which the Boyne takes its name.[13]

One of the things that helps to simplify the enumeration of the Metonic Cycle is the fact that the monument builders did not need to count the actual number of days involved, but rather the number of full moons. This makes it much easier to count. As it happens the lunar tropical month and the synodic month do not fit an exact number of days. The tropical month is about 27.32 days long, and the synodic month is 29.53 days long. There is no evidence to suggest the astronomers of the Neolithic understood or cared for fractions or decimals. It is more likely that they developed a counting system based on full moons, which are easy to observe, and days and years. All of these things were within their capability to observe and enumerate. The day is marked out by the passage of the sun from sunrise to sunset, while the year could be seen at the time of solstice at Newgrange. Full moons might not always be observable due to weather, but as the synodic month progresses the moon passes through various phases and it would not have been difficult for the astronomers to work out on which day the full moon actually fell.

In addition to all this, the Stone Age astronomers are likely to have watched tropical lunar movements as well, using certain key locations in the sky to watch as the moon made complete circuits of the *uair-chrios*. By counting both tropical circuits and synodic returns, they would have developed a useful calendar enabling them to mark out time much more minutely and efficiently than if they just watched the movements of the sun alone.

At some stage in the distant past, probably long before the first stone monuments were assembled in Ireland, people living a Mesolithic existence might have perceived the discrepancy between the lunar year and the solar year. It would have been quickly obvious to anyone with a basic counting ability that the number of full moon synodic returns does not fit into a whole year. In fact, 12 synodic months falls short of a full year by 11 days. At the time Newgrange was in use, this would have been starkly obvious. For instance, if there was a full moon on the day of *grianstad* one year, it could be easily observed that the twelfth full moon after that solstice occurred a whole 11 days short of the next solstice. And that's why the period of time we know today as the Metonic Cycle might have been important to the people who built Newgrange. The solar and lunar year were out of synch – they did not 'fit' together. Knowledge of this discrepancy, and in particular of how the moon eventually did fall back into synch with the sun once every 19 years, would have been very beneficial to the community at Newgrange, who viewed the cosmos as sacred. As an agrarian society, they would have appreciated how the earth was governed by the sky, the seasons for sowing and harvesting being dictated by the strength of the sun.

A number of years ago an American medical doctor named Charles Scribner tried to teach me about the Metonic Cycle based on his own direct observations of the heavens over a long time. Dr. Scribner developed a notation which helped me more easily understand how a more primi-

*The astronomers of Newgrange watched lunar and
stellar movements as well as the sun.*

tive, less numerate, society in the past might have been able to mark out
the progression of the Metonic Cycle without any recourse to fractions or
decimals, or indeed to huge numbers. The number of days in 19 years is
6,939 and a half, a fairly substantial number for a community who did not
have pen and paper or such luxuries as calculators. Did they ever need to
know how many days there were in a whole Metonic Cycle? It's doubtful.

Watching full moons and counting twelves and thirteens was a much
simpler method. Thus it could be seen that 12 synodic months is 11 days
short of one solar year, and by extension 24 synodic months is a whole 22
days short of two years. To bring the solar and lunar years closer together, the addition of an extra month (that is, thirteen full moons instead
of twelve) in the second year gives us 25 synodic months ending eight
days after two years. Another 12 full moons later and we have 37 synodic
months ending three days before three years. Thus the counting continues, with the number of full moons never seeming to exactly fit into a
solar year. Another dozen moons brings us to 49 synodic months ending
14 days before four years. Then we add a thirteen, with 62 synodic months

Full moon rises over Red Mountain across the valley from Newgrange.

ends five days after five solar years – this is perhaps the Metonic interval recorded on the Calendar Stone at Knowth.

The counting continues each year, with the addition of either a dozen full moons or sometimes 13 required to bring closer harmony with the solar year, so 99 synodic months ends two days after eight solar tropical years, and this is the cycle which ties in with the planet Venus which might have particular significance to Newgrange. One of the Metonic intervals which brings the sun and moon counts very close is the 11-year interval, so that 136 synodic months ends about a day before 11 solar years. Just one day out – but still not perfect. We have to go all the way to 19 years to achieve exact harmony, when 235 synodic months is exactly equal to 19 solar tropical years. This is the equivalent of 254 tropical lunar months. This is a complete Metonic cycle, one of the natural rhythms of the sky, and it can be stated with some degree of certainty that this cycle was studied and perceived and 'figured out' by the people who built New-grange, Knowth and Dowth over 5,000 years ago, almost three millennia before the Greek Meton, after whom the cycle is named, ever existed. And the Irish astronomer builders probably had their own names for this cycle, as we will see in the next chapter.

There are other cycles which were probably observed and figured out by the builders of Newgrange. The bright planet Venus, which is the third brightest object in the sky after the sun and moon, follows a distinct pattern over the course of eight years, after which its movements seem to repeat themselves exactly. Joseph Campbell recorded a story in the Boyne Valley which suggested that Venus cast a beam of light into the chamber of Newgrange once every eight years.[14] *Uriel's Machine* authors Christopher Knight and Robert Lomas suggest that a series of eight markings on the lintel stone above the roofbox of Newgrange represent the eight years of the Venus cycle.[15] In her guise as the morning star, Venus was known in Ireland as *caillichín na mochóirighe*, which means the 'early-rising little hag'.[16]

Another cycle which was perceived and recorded in the Boyne Valley in prehistory was the so-called Saros Cycle, the cycle of eclipses. Significant discussion of this was presented in *Island of the Setting Sun*. At Newgrange, a number of significant kerb counts could relate to eclipse intervals, as suggested by Dr John Gordon.[17] Eclipses were held to be extremely significant events, particularly the much rarer solar eclipses, and indeed it has been suggested that the legend of Dowth was inspired by a total eclipse of the sun. Lunar eclipses, during which the moon appears to turn red, may have given rise to stories and place names involving a red cow. The proliferation of bovine mythology and place names in Ireland could well relate to the moon, especially because the gestation period of a cow is strongly connected with lunar time. Bóinn, also Bóann, the goddess who gives her name to the Boyne river, may well have been a lunar and stellar goddess, the river having the same name derivation as the Milky Way, which was known as *Bealach na Bó Finne*, the way of the white cow.

If all of the above is true, it could be suggested that the Neolithic mound builders of the Boyne Valley had developed an accurate and complex calendar, based not just on the sun's movements, but on those of the moon and perhaps some of the planets. A lot of these movements were observed against the backdrop of the stars, particularly the *uair-chrios*, the time circle. Such a calendar did not rely exclusively on precise observations of the sun at its standstills, but rather involved watching the sun, moon, planets and stars and therefore gave the people of Newgrange a much more reliable time-keeping method, something which could keep time even if certain observations were missed due to inclement weather.

Even if the builders had only been interested in observing the sun, then Newgrange would have been able to show them what we call the 'leap year' today. The length of a year is 365.24 days, something that would have been observable at Newgrange because every four years the solstice would seem to 'fall back' by a day. Presuming they did not deal with decimals or averages, the builders would have seen that the pattern of days between each solstice was 365, 365, 365 and 366.[18]

In addition to all this, it is highly probable that the builders of Newgrange perceived another cycle, something called precession of the equinoxes, which is very slow wobble of the earth's axis, causing the positions of the equinoxes to gradually regress through the Zodiac over a period of 25,920 years. The most immediately observable evidence of this precessional drift at the time the great monument was built involved the

Winter Solstice sunrise viewed from the entrance of Newgrange.

brightest star in the sky, the one we know today as Sirius, but which has long been known in many traditions as the 'dog star'. Sirius is the main star in a constellation we know today as Canis Major, the Greater Dog, which was known from the earliest times as the 'Dog of Orion'.[19] It may be purely a coincidence that at the time Newgrange was built, Sirius shared the same declination as the winter solstice sun, and therefore would have been visible from inside the chamber from night to night during certain parts of the year.

Precession of the equinoxes is the process by which the sun's vernal point, or its position on the spring equinox, drifts slowly westwards at a rate of one degree every 72 years.[20] This process is caused by a slow wobble of the earth's axis, which appears to draw out a giant circle in the northern part of the sky over 25,920 years. Currently, the axis of the earth points roughly at Polaris, which we know as the 'North Star', but at the time of the Neolithic the north pole of the sky was located in the constellation Draco, the Dragon. The gradual drifting of the stars would have been observable over a period of years as the position of Sirius in the roofbox of Newgrange, as viewed from its central chamber, would have been seen to be moving. In fact, Sirius would have been gradually climbing in the sky. Just 200 years after Newgrange was built, Sirius would no longer have been visible from the chamber. Some markings on the rear kerbstone at Newgrange, K52, could be interpreted as representing the belt stars of Orion pointing at the Dog Star.[21]

Of further interest to our discussion of precession is the constellation Cygnus, the swan, whose giant cross-shape may have inspired the design of the passage and chamber of Newgrange. At the time Newgrange was built, the brightest star of Cygnus, known today as Deneb, from Arabic, meaning the 'Hen's Tail',[22] was scraping the horizon during certain times of the year. It was in the epoch during which Newgrange was built that Cygnus was at its lowest declination. It is a fascinating astronomical coincidence that, at the latitude of New-grange, the bright star of the swan, Deneb, appears to remain circumpolar throughout much of the cycle of precession. In other words, it is a star that never seems to set. Except, that is, during the Boyne Valley monument epoch, when it appeared to set, or at least 'touch' the horizon, for a brief period in the Neolithic.[23] At lower latitudes, Deneb would appear to set completely for a time, while at more northerly latitudes this bright star of the swan never sets, at any time in history. The axis of the passage of Newgrange, when extended into the distance, points to another passage-mound some 15 kilometres to the southeast called Fourknocks. The passage and chamber of Fourknocks are aligned towards the place in the far northeast where Deneb would have been rising off the horizon in the Neolithic.

This is made even more fascinating by the fact that the owner of New-grange, the god Aonghus, was said to have taken the form of a swan when he fell in love with the swan maiden, *Caer Iobharmhéith*. The story relates how, after finding Caer at a lake in Tipperary, Aonghus was transformed into a swan and they flew together to Brugh na Bóinne where they remained. Newgrange is an important wintering ground for the whooper swan, which comes to the Boyne valley in large numbers from Iceland every winter.[24]

From the smallest cycle – the day – to the larger cycles of lunar months, solar years, Saros and Metonic cycles, to the biggest cycle of them all, precession of the equinoxes, it seems that the people who built Newgrange, a quasi-circular earthen mound surrounded by giant stones, were aware of the cosmic patterns that marked out time. Fascinatingly, we might now be able to present some of the names that they had for some of these cycles.

5.

VALLANCEY AND
THE ARMED KING

L
ONG BEFORE THE MODERN archaeological investigations were begun at Newgrange and its sister monuments, people had come to
the Boyne Valley to investigate these mysterious sites. Newgrange
had lain forlorn and abandoned for four millennia, without much notice
from anyone. In 1699 the lands containing Newgrange passed into the
hands of Charles Campbell, one of the many protestant settlers who were
establishing themselves in the region following the victory of William of
Orange at the Battle of the Boyne at nearby Oldbridge in 1690.[1]

Campbell is the one credited with 'discovering', or rather 'rediscov-
ering', the passage and chamber of Newgrange around this time. This
was not through any particular care for the monument or an interest
in antiquarianism. In fact, Campbell had been making good use of the
stone from Newgrange with some construction projects connected with
his new mansion and its outbuildings.[2] Professor Michael O'Kelly, the
archaeologists who excavated Newgrange in the 1960s and 70s, wrote:
'The discovery of the 'cave' at Newgrange came about through the need
for stones on the part of the then landowner.'[3] It was while his labourers

were carrying away stones from the mound that the passage entrance was discovered.

Since that moment, antiquarians and explorers and visitors of all description have been coming to Newgrange to study its many mysteries. One of the first was Edward Lhwyd, an antiquarian and scholar from Wales, who happened to be on a tour of Ireland at the time of Campbell's discovery. Lhwyd made the first known drawing of the passage and chamber and wrote letters to his friends describing some of the features of the interior.[4]

Lhwyd was followed some time after by Sir Thomas Molyneux, a Professor of Physics in the University of Dublin, who had amusingly described the height of Newgrange as being 150 feet.[5] It was, in fact, closer to 40 feet! A later visitor was the antiquarian Sir Thomas Pownall, who came to Newgrange in 1769. It was a good three-quarters of a century after the rediscovery of the Newgrange chamber, in the 1770s, that the military surveyor, Charles Vallancey, came to the Boyne Valley. It is difficult to find any book or work about Newgrange that does not mention Vallancey.

Charles Vallancey

He was the first to make accurate drawings of the passage and chamber.[6] Not all mentions of Vallancey paint him in a positive light. His reputation suffers somewhat as a result of his suggestion that Newgrange had Chaldean origins.[7]

Vallancey was one of a growing band of antiquarians and writers who were trying to put their own interpretation on Newgrange. Some of these ascribed its origins to the Vikings, which was a popular supposition of the times. Vallancey contributed much to the debate about ancient Ireland and the origins of its language and monuments, but unfortunately he became embroiled in what one expert on his life describes as 'fantastic theorising.'[8]

Charles Vallancey, who was born around 1725, was descended from a French family who settled in England. He attended Eton and entered military service and quickly established himself as an adept engineer. By 1761 he became Major of Engineers and around the same time was transferred to Dublin.[9] During his time in Ireland, he undertook a military survey of a great chunk of the southern half of Ireland, a task that was to take twenty years. It was described at the time as 'the most elaborate cartographic project attempted in Ireland since the time of Sir William Petty'.[10] In 1777 he began an inspection of Charles Fort in Kinsale, County Cork, and it is thought that it was his time in Cork that 'sparked his interest in Irish culture and language'.[11]

Vallancey would marry a total of four times during his lifetime. He had ten children to his first wife. It was clear that he was a busy man, with family, career and antiquarian interests keeping him well occupied. He was a prolific writer, and would leave a large corpus of works, including the *Collectanea de Rebus Hibernicus*, in six volumes, the first of which was written in 1770 and the last in 1804. He describes the *Collectanea* as a collection of papers about Ireland which are the 'first fruits of many years of research'.[12]

Unfortunately, his writings are often described in terms of being the fruits of a fertile and fantastic imagination. Antiquarian George Petrie later said of Vallancey: 'It is a difficult and rather unpleasant task to follow a writer so rambling in his reasonings and so obscure in his style; his hypotheses are of a visionary nature.'[13] *The Quarterly Review* declared: 'General Vallancey, though a man of learning, wrote more nonsense than any man of his time . . .'[14]

However, his reputation is not altogether tarnished. He did, as stated previously, provide the first reasonably accurate survey of Newgrange in 1776. He designed the Queen's Bridge in Dublin, which took four years to build and was completed in 1768, a work which was 'frequently praised'.[5] He was a founder member of the Royal Irish Academy.

He gives one of the earliest accounts of some of the carvings at Newgrange, although his interpretations are wild and fanciful. However, his claim about the antiquity of these engravings is not without merit: 'The most ancient inscriptions now remaining in Ireland, if not in these parts of Europe, are undoubtedly found in the tumulus or mount of NewGrange near Drogheda in the county of Meath.'[16]

But it is not Vallancey's writings on Newgrange that provide the most fascination to our exploration of this fascinating ancient site, but rather something he wrote about ancient Irish astronomy. Although many archaeologists refer to Vallancey's work, few seem to have delved into his work beyond what he writes about Newgrange.

In Part II of Volume VI, the final volume of his *Collectanea*, published in 1804, he presents a chapter entitled 'Astronomy of the Ancient Irish'. While he makes an ill founded attempt to show that the ancient Irish gained their knowledge from the Chaldeans, this essay does, however, provide some interesting nuggets of information, specifically relating to Irish words for astronomical concepts and cosmic cycles. These words are repeated in another work by Vallancey, with some additions and changes, called *Oriental Collections*, published in 1798.

In these two works, although it is difficult sometimes to extract the Irish words and their meanings from a body of text in which Hebrew and Phoenician and Greek and Chaldean words are interspersed, there are a fascinating collection of Irish terms and words and phrases relating to astronomy, some of which are very familiar, others completely obscure. Indeed some of the words Vallancey writes about do not seem to exist in other dictionaries and sources and one wonders if he didn't misspell them completely. In his preface to *Collectanea*, Vallancey claimed to be a 'master of the ancient language of Ireland', but 'modesty was not in Vallancey's nature'![17]

Despite his significant drawbacks, Vallancey nonetheless gives us some valuable information about the 'Astronomy of the Ancient Irish'.

Vallancey's writings about Newgrange and astronomy are fascinating.

He indicates that, during his time in the south of the country, he gleaned some interesting information about the apparently advanced astronomical knowledge among local peasants.

While in County Kerry, Vallancey related that, 'I saw a poor man, near Black-stones, who had a tolerable notion of calculating the Epacts, Golden Number, Dominical Letter, the Moon's Phases, and even Eclipses, *although he had never been taught to read English*.'[18] The Golden Number, not to be confused with the Golden Ratio, is a counting system which determines which year of the 19-year Metonic Cycle we are currently in. The epact is the number of days difference between the lunar year and the solar year, the epact of one year being 11, because, as stated in Chapter 4, 12 synodic months is 354 days, 11 days short of a solar tropical year. Vallancey refers to the fact that the Black-stones peasant had never learned to read English, and goes on to suggest, 'Consequently this man must have received his knowledge from Irish manuscripts.'[19] However, it is more likely that the man could not read at all, and that his knowledge had been passed down to him orally, as was and has been an Irish tradition for many centuries.

Vallancey refers to another incident which occurred in a mountainous area of West Cork not long after he had come to Ireland from Gibraltar. Here, an 'aged cottager' offered to be their guide on a 'fine starry night'. The peasant pointed out the constellation Orion and 'he said, that was *Caomai*, or the armed king; and he described the three upright stars to be his spear or sceptre, and the three horizontal stars he said was his sword-belt.'[20] He infers that *Caomai* is 'an armed man' in Shaw's dictionary, but in fact Shaw spells it *Caomhaigh* and explains it as 'a man expert at arms'.[21]

This might seem like a peculiar reference to the constellation Orion, but in *Island of the Setting Sun* we explored the idea that some of the principal characters of ancient Irish myth might have been inspired by this brilliant anthropomorphic constellation. Included among these was Nuadu of the Silver Arm, who lost his arm in the first battle of Moytura but had a silver one fashioned for him by the healer, Diancecht, and was able to return as king of the Tuatha Dé Danann for the second battle of Moytura, in which the king and his army were victorious in routing the Fomorians. The upraised arm of Orion is immersed in bright band of the Milky Way, the heavenly Boyne, and it is at this point that the sun, moon and planets cross the cosmic river on their journey around the *uair-chrios*.

One of the less familiar, or rather one of the totally unfamiliar, words thrown up by Vallancey in 'Astronomy of the Ancient Irish' is the word *Nag*, which he says is 'a star', *Maidden Nag* being the morning star, Venus. He furthermore suggests that this word 'is in every dictionary and in every peasant's mouth'.[22] However, it is not in Shaw's dictionary, where we only find the familiar words *reul*, *reult* and *realt* for star. In a later dictionary by R.A. Armstrong we find the word *maidneag*, meaning 'aurora, or the morning star'.[23] But the word *nag* is missing from most dictionaries, and it seems Vallancey was trying to make something of the word nag so he could compare it with the Chaldean word *nag*, meaning 'star'.

Occasionally in the text of his chapter on astronomy, Charles Vallanc-ey tries to connect his researches on the astronomical words with his own explorations of the Irish landscape. He refers to *Ti mor*, 'one of the old Irish epithets of the Supreme Deity', which also meant 'the great circle'.[24] 'The sphere shows the divine nature to be without beginning or end,' he says, adding, 'the ancients represented the Deity not only by a circle, but by volutes of circles.' Such symbols, he adds, 'we find on the stones in the *mithratic* cave of New Grange, described in my Vindication of the ancient History of Ireland.'[25]

He suggests the Irish referred to the Pole Star as ''N'iatha*, from the negative *ne*, and the verb *iatham*, to turn, signifying that which turns not.'[26]

He further tells us that in Irish the word *Sodhac* signified an eclipse of the sun, from *sodh*, dark, obscure, and that the *Sodhac* 'was so named, because they observed that the sun is always eclipsed in that line'. They

A time exposure of the stars shows how they appear to move around the pole star, which was known as N'iatha, that which does not turn.

might well have observed that the sun was eclipsed while on the zodiac, but I am unable to find the words *sodh* or *sodhac* in any dictionary![27] He relates another Irish name for the Zodiac which sounds much more familiar. *Crios-griain*, Vallancey states, is 'from *crios*, an eclipse, obscure, and *grian*, the sun'. Here he mistranslates the word *crios*, which means belt, girdle, circle, cincture, sash, garter, etc. Thus we could more accurately translate *crios-griain* as the 'sun's belt' or 'sun circle', that is, the imaginary loop that the sun forms on its yearly journey through the Zodiac.

The signs of the Zodiac are known in Irish as *comh-ardha*, 'that is, the *mansions* of the *zodiac*, or of the signs'. Indeed we find in other dictionaries the word *comhartha* or *comhthara*, meaning 'sign'. Another name for the zodiac signs is *talla-griain*, 'the halls, palaces, or mansions of the sun . . . synonymous to *comh-ardha*'.[30] Interestingly, Newgrange is sometimes described as a palace of the gods, or a mansion of the sun.

Vallancey introduces a section on cycles, and speaks of an Irish word *Losca*, meaning a period of five years, which he says is one of the Egyptian cycles. He enumerates it as 1,825 days, which is basically 365 multiplied by five, but one wonders if this is not supposed to refer to the Metonic interval of 62 synodic months falling five days after five years.

The smallest cycle of the 'Hibernian astronomers' was, of course, the day, which was reckoned from sunrise to sunset. 'This they named *lilai*, from *liladh*, to turn round, to turn any way; as, *go ros lil*, from the beginning of that *turn* or day.'[31] The setting sun is *Noin*, and *noin realt* is the evening star, Venus. They had another beautiful expression for a day:

> But the Irish astronomers and poets use a remarkable expression
> for a day, viz. *faigh*, or *faic-iula*, a turn of the horizon . . . poeti-
> cally, a day, at the end of which man laid himself down.[32]

There follows a lengthy section dedicated to the 'Cycles of the Irish Philosophers', which contains some very interesting astronomical words and concepts which are relevant to our study, and indeed to a lot of the evidence unearthed in *Island of the Setting Sun*. Whether these words or ideas are very ancient or not, we cannot know, but the notion of cosmic cycles and patterns and revolutions being observed and recorded by astronomer farmers in the Bend of the Boyne in distant prehistory is not at all far fetched. Newgrange itself is an expression of cosmic union, of the belief that life on earth is intrinsically linked with the heavenly cycles. Indeed, the monument may represent something which encompassed both a concern with death, the degradation of the corpse and the corruption of physical death, and the rebirth of the soul into the next world. The cyclical nature of life is enshrined into its very design, which follows a rough circle of stones in a continuous journey around the mound, reflecting the cyclical nature of the cosmic movements, which in some way can be said to have no beginning and no end, just a never-ending repeating pattern.

Vallancey starts his long list with the word *Bar*, meaning 'a cycle, revolution, a month', and there are many words that follow which mean cycle, although he doesn't always state exactly what cycle might be referred to. For instance, he mentions *Barbhis* or *Beirbhis* as 'a cycle, an anniversary' and goes into considerable discussion about a similar word in Egypt. Such is the nature of Vallancey's work. There are some gems of information in there, but you have to look for them! It is interesting to note that Shaw's 1780 dictionary lists *Beirbhis* as meaning 'anniversary feast, vigil'.[33]

Bis, *Beis*, *Baisc* and *Baischarm* are given next, again meaning 'a cycle'. However, of particular interest to our exploration of Newgrange and its ancient astronomer architects is the fact that 'from *Baisc* comes *Baisc-bhuidin*, the golden cycle or number.'[34] *Baisc-Bhuidhin* (pronounced *bais-cvooin*), is the golden number, also known as *Naoidheachda*, the nineteenth, that is, 'A space of nineteen years, at the end of which the new moon comes in the same month, and on the same day of the month.'[35] This is the so-called Metonic cycle, the 19-year lunar sequence which represents 235 synodic months, the cycle whose discovery is credited to a fifth century BC Greek, but which there is compelling evidence to show was known about at Newgrange, Knowth and Dowth almost three millennia previously. Is it possible also that these words, *Baisc-Bhuidhin* and *Naoidheachda*, have a very ancient origin, and that one or both were used in remote prehistory to describe this cycle which we refer to today as the Metonic Cycle?

In his writings in *Oriental Collections*, Vallancey adds:

> This famous lunar cycle was well known to the Hibernian Druids; many of their circular astronomical temples consisted, and do yet consist, of 19 stones: others of 48, the number of the old constellations.[36]

The Moon with Venus and Jupiter near Taurus and Orion.

Another nineteenth century author reaffirms this, saying that the 'cycle of 19' is 'a common number of the Irish stone circles'.[37]

In *Collectanea*, Vallancey refers to a stone circle in Cornwall, England, called Biscawoon. He describes the temple as consisting of nineteen pillars in a circle, with a 'kebla' in the centre. He says of Biscawoon that 'the name corresponds so exactly with the *Baiscbhuidhin*, or golden cycle, I think there can be no doubt of the derivation'.[38] There is indeed a stone circle in Cornwall, near Land's End, called Boscawen-Un, containing nineteen stones, one of quartz and the others granite.[39] The eighteenth century antiquarian William Stukeley claimed that Biscawoon was the 'first circle to be built in Britain, erected by the proto-Christian, Tyrian Hercules'.[40]

Another cycle mentioned by Vallancey is *Beacht*, or *Grian beacht*, which is described as, 'The cycle of the sun; the space of twenty-eight years that the sun takes to go through the twelve signs.'[41] This is confusing, because it takes the sun just one year to make a circuit of the Zodiac, and the only other cycle that takes the sun through the *uair-chrios* is the 25,920-year cycle of precession. Shaw's dictionary gives *grianbeachd* or *greinbheachd* as 'zodiac'. Another dictionary gives *beacht* as 'a circle, a ring', and *go beacht* as 'perfectly, entirely, for ever'.[42]

A cycle of 60 is called a *Seasga*, which is a multiple of the five-year *Losca*, and the 12-year cycle of Jupiter, according to Vallancey.[43] This *Seasga*, he says, is a tenth of a greater 600-year cycle called *Phennicshe*, 'the Phoenix, a celestial cycle', although it is difficult to find out where this latter word comes from. In *Oriental Collections*, he renders it *Phenicshe*, 'i.e. *ain naomhag*; the phoenix or celestial cycle' and suggests that the phoenix, when restored to life, lives 600 years, or '600 turns of the *Beal*, the sun'.[44]

Yet another phrase for the Zodiac is introduced by Vallancey in *Collectanea*. He claims to have uncovered the real meaning of the name of another English stone circle, called Rolldrigh (now known as the Rollright Stones) in Oxfordshire. Of course, Vallancey throws out his modesty and claims 'all these works to have been performed by *Coti*, or ancient Irish, the *Cuthi* of the learned and venerable Bryant, who lays the same claim to them, I beg leave to look for the etymon of the name in the Irish language.'[45]

He claims Rollright gets its name from *Dra* and *draoch*, meaning a wheel, a circle, a cycle, and *Reall*, a star or planet. Indeed, both Shaw and Armstrong give *droch* as 'coach wheel', while Dinneen gives it as 'the wheel of a chariot'. Vallancey says of Rollright:

> This temple has been so destroyed, that the number of stones it originally contained cannot be ascertained. It is supposed the number was sixty, of which twenty-two only remain. I should think, if the great circle contained sixty, there was a smaller that contained twelve, the number of signs in the zodiac, which in Irish is expressed by Real-draoch, the circle or wheel of the stars. The wheel was certainly an ancient emblem of the zodiac.[46]

He then makes a fascinating and extraordinary claim. He says that the sun in Irish is known as *Daghdae-rath*, the Sol of the wheel. What he appears to miss completely, despite all his claimed expertise, is that *Dagda* (also *Dagda Mór*, *Dagdae*) was the chief of the Tuatha Dé Danann and owner of Newgrange! *Dagda* was also known as *Deirgderc*, 'red eye, i.e. the sun'.[47] It has been said that *Dagda* was also 'a sky-god . . . or the sun itself'.[48] We will explore *Dagda's* relationship with the sun in more detail in Chapter 9.

Vallancey appears also to have unearthed another name for the solstice. He says that the word *Aonac*, also given as *Aineac* and *Eang*, means 'a period, cycle, year', and that *eang-la* meant 'an anniversary day'. *Tach-fhang*, pronounced 'tacvang', means a cycle, a revolution, a year, and furthermore, *Teachbhaidh, teacfhaidh, teacphai*, mean the solstice.

> The Irish *teacphai* is thus explained; *an tan Grian nac eidir dol uirde, ni as isle sa la as foide*; i.e. when the sun can go neither higher nor lower; when the longest and the shortest day comes.[49]

This *teacphai* is likely the same word as *tiocfad*, meaning 'to come',[50] also rendered *tiocfaid*, 'they shall come' in Shaw's dictionary, and hence the phrase '*Tiocfaidh ár lá*', 'Our day will come', which became the slogan of the Irish republican movement during the troubles in Northern Ireland.

Many other words and phases are given by Vallancey in his sweeping study, of which we will give quick mention here: *Ais, Eis, Ois, Easc*, a cycle, whence *Eas*, and *Easc*, the moon. *Fonn*, a cycle; *fonnsa*, a hoop; *faine*, a ring. If there was a ring around the moon, one might say, '*Tá fáinne ar an ghealaigh*'.[51] Vallancey says *Aim-sire* means a revolution of time. The word *aimsear* also means a season, or even the weather.[52] *Mascaor* means 'a cycle' and *Mithis, Mithich, Mithr*, 'a period, season, cycle'.[53]

The word *Gall* means a wheel, circle, or cycle, with *Sior-gal* meaning 'a complete revolution', hence *Feigal, fagal*, a revolution, anniversary, holyday, fair-day. *Sao-ghal* is a 'revolution, orb, life, age, the world; that is, the revolutionary planets'. *Saoghal-gan-saoghal* is 'world without end'.[54]

Chuig, Chuiggeal, Oig is a 'period, a cycle'. *Cuig-bhreith* is an annual sacrifice. *Cuig-maddin* and *Oig-maddin* means 'Aurora, i.e. the return of the sun in the east'. *Rath* is a cycle, circle or wheel. *Nidhe* is a time period.

An interesting one is '*An, Ana, Aine, Uine, Onn*, plural *Anith*. *Bliaain*, the cycle of *Bel*, the sun, a year.'[55] There is an ancient goddess called Áine, who draws many attributes from another goddess called Ana, from whom it is said the Tuatha Dé Danann were named.[56] Vallancey says that *Ain naomhag* was 'the heavenly revolutioner', and that an Irish astrologer or astronomer was known as *Anius*. He furthermore states that *Ana-mor* was 'the zodiac, the great circle'.

The word *Saobha* is a cycle, and *Seona Saobha*, a cycle of Saturn. *Saobhal* or *Siobal* is a cycle, with *Siobal na greine* meaning 'the sun's path, the zodiac'. *Cuaran, Curuinne, Cruine* is a cycle, sphere, globe and even an onion! *Casar* is a period, cycle, return. *Crios* is a cycle, the sun; *Grian-crios*, the zodiac; *Crios-bacht* is the circle of the sun, the zodiac. *Ear, earrach, eiris, iris, uiris* is a cycle or an epoch, whence *Leabhair iris*, an ephemeris. *Duir, dra, drach, draoch*, means a wheel, circle, cycle, period. *Easc* is a cycle, the moon, the cyclic moon. *Ainbhih*, pronounced 'ainwy', 'literally signifies a knowledge of the stars'.[57]

In ancient Ireland, long before words and language were written down on paper, intelligent astronomers and farmers were studying and marking out cycles of the sun, moon and planets. Whether they had names for these cycles similar to those listed by Vallancey, we cannot know. Language changes much during the course of history, and indeed many of the older words found above are now redundant, and in some cases the very ideas they represent are now forgotten.

Vallancey's writings were carried out in the late eighteenth and early nineteenth centuries. He does not state how ancient these words and phrases are, how far back into the past they reach. He is unable to. He draws comparisons, many of them flimsy and even downright incongruous, with the Chaldeans and other ancient cultures. His linguistic reputation suffers a great deal as a result. There is, however, a grain of truth and an element of sense in much of what he writes about the Irish words. Many of the words listed in his *Collectanea* still exist in some form, with similar meanings to those which he attempted to give. He deserves much credit, if not for his comparative linguistic work, then certainly for the fact that he has preserved much older knowledge. His work on the 'Astronomy of the Ancient Irish' has helped in some way to provide a link between the present and the distant past. He provides us with a gripping insight into much more ancient knowledge, information gleaned in far-off times by people who were much more in tune with

The stars over Newgrange.

nature and the cosmos. How far back did this knowledge enter into human consciousness?

Martin Brennan, the pioneering author who discovered the winter solstice alignment at Dowth and the equinox alignment at Loughcrew with Jack Roberts, is fulsome in his praise of Vallancey, although accepting that he did have flaws.

> Regardless of how these interpretations were arrived at, Vallancey anticipated the modern realization that Newgrange is oriented with reference to the rays of the sun. This is one of the reasons why I consider Vallancey to be the most important of the Irish antiquarians. Many of his insights are now being substantiated by current research.[58]

Brennan adds that Vallancey came close to uncovering the astronomical functions of Newgrange and his sources largely appeared to be the local population or, as he called them, 'the common people'.[59] Brennan tips his hat to Vallancey, who could not have known that the mounds had been built long before the emergence of the Druids:

> Matching his interpretation of the mounds, Vallancey was the very first to advance an astronomical explanation of the rock engravings. Where other antiquarians could see only 'rude scribblings' and 'barbarous carvings', Vallancey saw the stars in the stones. These he aptly described as 'the most ancient inscriptions now remaining in Ireland, if not in these parts of Europe'. To him they were 'Hibernian Druidic Symbols', representing the cycles of the sun, moon and stars, 'the chief if not the only deities of the heathen Irish'.[60]

Newgrange and its sister sites represent an interest in cyclical cosmic activity. The return of the *teacphai*, the solstice, was certainly celebrated at Newgrange. Was this the word that the Neolithic astronomers used to describe the return of the shortest day, the lowest sun? Did they, in those far-removed times, have spoken words, similar to some primitive form of Irish, which represented many of the cyclical cosmic concepts described by Vallancey? Unfortunately, my own linguistic skills are not much better than those of the military engineer Charles Vallancey, whose work is largely derided in so many quarters today.

What we can say with certainty is that the great passage-mounds of the Boyne reflect a significant fascination with the cosmos on behalf of their builders. They not only knew about and marked out solstices and equinoxes, but also lunar standstills, solar cross-quarter days, the risings and settings of significant stars and they even knew about the periods of at least some of the planets, especially Venus, the *maidneag*, the morning star which would have been visible in the chamber of Newgrange once in eight years.

There are so many words and phrases representing cycles of the sky that it's difficult not to think that our distant ancestors were not utterly devoted to the study of the heavens. The idea of a supreme being, or chief god, being represented by a great circle, or the sun, is not lost in our study of Newgrange, which had at one time as its owner the great Dagda. The concept of a sphere or circle showing the 'divine nature to be without be-ginning or end' resonates deeply at Newgrange, where the solstice marks neither beginning nor end, but a yearly return in an ever-ending cycle.

> So why do we struggle so hard to understand our ancestors? Why do we continue to wonder how, without telescopes, their eyes could penetrate the intricacies of the visible universe? Without computers how could they precisely predict the positions of celestial bodies? Without writing how was it possible to keep records of observations on which to base accurate predictions? Without mathematics how could they calculate all those cycles? I think part of the answer is that we simply don't know enough about them; the more we dig into the record of the past the more we come to realize that our low-tech predecessors, with perspica-cious eye and attentive mind, accomplished extraordinary feats.[61]

Vallancey was the first to advance an astronomical explanation for the rock engravings of Newgrange.

One of those extraordinary feats was to construct huge stone monuments with primitive technology and to compose them in such a way that they would endure the harsh ravages of time, surviving as they have done for over 5,000 years.

How did the builders of Newgrange calculate the cosmic cycles?

6.

THE TEST OF TIME

THE ETERNAL RHYTHM OF THE cosmic cycles and the enduring continuance of the sky's patterns, repeating themselves over and over again across vast aeons of time, imbue the human watchers of the earth with a salient sense of the fleeting nature of corporeal life. We are here only for a short time.

This gripping sense of the brevity of human life entangles us all at some stage. It is difficult to grow into adulthood without inevitably wondering what is going to happen to us. When will we die, and how? These are the questions that puzzle us all, and an understanding and recognition, and even acceptance of, physical death, is something that bonds together all of humanity, through all of the ages. It is likely that no generation has lived on this earth since the remote beginnings of humankind that hasn't wondered about the whole purpose of this life, which can be cruel, and harsh, and short.

Many generations of people throughout Irish history and prehistory have lived and died and left no mark on the earth, no reminder of singular achievement, no memorial to their labours and beliefs. When our time comes, what reminder will we leave behind? What great gift will we bequest to the earth, as a reminder of the fact that we ever existed?

The word 'memorial' means something that is designed to preserve the memory of a person, or a people, or an event or happening. Many people have lived long lives and contributed much to their community and the only memorial to their existence is a headstone. Many more, buried in countless *reilig* (graveyards) across Ireland, are not even afforded such a luxury. Their dry bones lie in the ground, and the earth has forgotten who they were. They might not have existed at all.

The same could easily have been said for the New Stone Age farmers of the Boyne Valley, except for the fact that they constructed some of the largest and the most enduring monuments of this island's history. Their vast shrines of stone and earth are grand memorials to lives spent toiling in honour of greater ideals. The people who built the passage-mounds are gone from the earth, their time long over, their memory almost erased

Newgrange is an enduring monument, similar to a small hill.

from the human story. But something of their spirit remains, and something of their story can be pieced together. Their legacy, gifted to us modern folk across countless generations, comes in the form of stones and stories. By looking at these stones, and by reading these stories, we can catch glimpses of distant lives lived in the hoary yesteryear, in a time when men and women had begun to leave their nomadic hunting lifestyles behind, and had begun to declare their presence on the earth.

Whatever the forces were that drove them to such memorable feats, they were likely many. The sheer scale of the effort involved, especially for a technologically primitive society, is impressive. The hundreds of thousands of tonnes of stone and earth required for Newgrange, and for the other large mounds, were wrought into giant mounds that were so large that they could almost be described as hills.

Indeed, one of the old Irish words which is sometimes used to describe a man-made mound or a tumulus, is *cnoc*, which also happens to be a word used to describe a hill.[1] In the Metrical Dindshenchas, a collection of very old place name stories contained in the twelfth century *Book of Leinster* and some of the later manuscripts, both Knowth and Dowth are described as hills. Dowth is described as 'the solid hill' while Knowth is equally described: *Cnocc ic Búa i medón Breg*, which translates as 'A hill had Bua in the midst of Bregia'.[2]

If it was the desire of the Neolithic community of the Boyne to build enduring monuments, constructions that would stand the test of time, then certainly they chose wisely in their design plans. The erection of enormous mounds and cairns of stone on ridges and hilltops across Ireland in prehistory in large numbers is testament to the persistence and ingenuity of the builders. Archaeologists refer to Newgrange as a passage-tomb, and it is estimated that there are over 300 passage-tombs in Ireland.[3] However, there are many more mounds, cairns and mottes which have been unexcavated which might in the future be found to contain passage-tombs.[4] The total number of surviving megalithic tombs, if one also includes court tombs, portal tombs and wedge tombs, is 1,500, although wedge tombs date to the end of the Neolithic, after 2500 BC.[5]

This is an astonishing number, especially when one considers the amount of vandalism and destruction of monuments that has taken place in Ireland during the past three centuries. Even large stone monuments were utterly destroyed. One such example is the so-called 'Ireland's Stonehenge' at Carnbeg outside Dundalk, County Louth, a series of concentric rings of stones and a large circular embankment of which no visible trace remains, except what has been revealed by specialist ground-probing archaeological techniques.[6]

The quarrying of material from Newgrange, carried out by Charles Campbell at the end of the seventeenth century, was thankfully not extensive, and not nearly as destructive as that which occurred at nearby Dowth. Sir Thomas Pownall, who visited Newgrange in 1769, seemed to believe that Newgrange was 'but a ruin of what it was' and that a large amount of material had been removed from in front of the entrance 'as from a stone quarry'.[7] However, Professor O'Kelly gives us some comfort in the matter:

> This statement of Pownall's gave rise to the belief frequently expressed even in modern times, that vast quantities of material had been removed. Undoubtedly some amount of stone had been taken but . . . during the recent excavations no evidence was found that wholesale removal of cairn material had taken place, such as happened at Dowth, for example.[8]

One wonders what moved Charles Campbell and his labourers to stop carrying off stones from Newgrange for the construction of his new mansion. At Dowth, much larger quantities of stone were removed. Sir William Wilde, writing in 1847, says:

> . . . a considerable gap occurs in the western face of the mound, caused by large quantities of the stones of which it is composed having been removed at different times to erect buildings or to break up into macadamising material for the road which passes at its foot. It has been said, we hope without truth, that the grand jury of the county have, in form, presented for the stones of Dowth, to improve the condition of the roads . . .[9]

It is a firm testament to the labours of the builders of Dowth that such a large quantity of material could be removed from the cairn and yet such a great deal of it still exists. There is today a very large crater in the top of the mound, sadly the result of an invasive and destructive excavation carried out by R.H. Firth at the behest of the Committee of Antiquities of the Royal Irish Academy in 1847-8.[10] It is interesting to note that, in the middle of the Great Famine, during which a million Irish people died and another million emigrated, the esteemed gentlemen of the privileged class had nothing better to occupy their thoughts than an ill-conceived and unsuccessful 'treasure hunt' at Dowth, for which a special subscription fund had to be raised, while the population was suffering one of the worst calamities in Irish history.

The efforts of the 'archaeologists' were eventually abandoned when they failed to find a central chamber which they believed might have been found under the cairn. The absence of this chamber 'probably convinced the committee that Dowth was a monument of little importance after all'.[11] For this, we must be grateful, for a continuance of this butchery, even for another season, might have flattened the cairn completely. And no effort was made to restore the monument to its previous condition. Reverend James Graves of the Archaeological Association of Ireland, writing in 1879, says:

> We must lament that this grand national monument has been left to destruction. It would also be well to remark that the 'archaeological society' which 'devastated' the tumulus was not our association. It was explored about thirty years ago by private individuals. No account of the exploration has ever been published and when I saw it, the materials of the tumulus were lying about in sad confusion, and evidently had never been placed back. Being so, Mr Elcock, the tenant of the land, naturally thought they would form good building materials and acted accordingly. Thousands of tons of stones for 'road metal' were also taken from it, for Mr Elcock was a road contractor as well as a house builder.[12]

Thankfully, Newgrange was spared the gross vandalism suffered at Dowth. After the discovery of the passage entrance by Campbell's labourers in 1699, the Welsh antiquarian Edward Lhwyd visited and 'took careful note of all that was to be seen and heard'.[13] Perhaps it was the arrival of such a luminary as Lhwyd that convinced Campbell of the importance of the site and thus prevented further destruction? This did not prevent Lhwyd from describing Campbell as a 'gentleman of the village who had employed his servants to rob stone from the tomb at Newgrange'.[14]

Newgrange did not suffer from human intervention and alteration to the extent that its sister sites did. At Knowth, for instance, there are several phases of activity during which considerable alterations to various parts of the structure were undertaken. These included the creation of an enormous ditch behind the kerbstones during the Iron Age, the building of souterrains, underground passageways dating from the Early Christian period, and the fortification of the mound in Medieval times. One result of these destructive later phases of human activity at Knowth was the

An aerial image of Dowth, showing the crater left by the 1840s excavation.

foreshortening of the passageways which had suffered Early Christian remodelling.[15]

If anything, most of the serious damage that took place at Newgrange occurred naturally, and long before the days of Charles Campbell, as Frank Prendergast of Dublin Institute of Technology explains:

> For reasons unknown, the cairn underwent a catastrophic collapse sometime during the Bronze Age, causing an outward slip of stones and boulders. This slip reached as far as the great circle in front of the passage entrance and completely covered the great circle to the East and West where it runs nearest the cairn. The slip completely concealed the kerb and sealed the entrance.[16]

The great circle referred to by Prendergast is the ring of standing stones around Newgrange, of which 12 survive. With the exception of one of these great stones, there was no significant displacement caused by the collapse of material from the main cairn.[17]

The remodelling that took place at both Knowth and Dowth in later times did not occur at Newgrange. Professor O'Kelly wrote that although it was not possible to specify the time frame in which the sides of the Newgrange cairn slipped outwards over the kerb, 'it is at least possible to say that no secondary interments or any modifications of the structure, such as occurred at many chambered tombs, were discovered here'.[18] O'Kelly points out that it is not known whether the collapse of the cairn and the concealing of the entrance led to the abandonment of Newgrange at that time, or whether it had already been abandoned when the collapse occurred. The quartz and granite stones which were found in a layer at the bottom of the cairn slip at the front of the mound had 'come down in a fairly rapid and clean collapse', according to O'Kelly.[19] This was followed some time later by a 'sudden great slide of stones, the cause of which is unknown'.[20] He speculates that it could have been brought about by a sudden thaw after a severe frost, or perhaps even an earth tremor.

The collapse of the cairn material covered over the kerbstones and blocked up the entrance, and the general profile of the cairn remained the same from that time until Charles Campbell's disturbances in 1699

when the entrance was rediscovered. In other words, Newgrange lay concealed, its secrets hidden, for the best part of 4,000 years. The conceal-
ment of the kerbstones beneath the mound slip material resulted in the
inadvertent protection of those stones that had carvings on them. The
blocking up of the tomb entrance meant that whatever bones and other
material were contained in the interior were not disturbed or removed by
visitors or intruders, at least until Campbell's time.

A steady stream of visitors and explorers after 1699 probably caused
severe disturbance of bone remains and any burial goods and artefacts
that might have been inside. By the time of O'Kelly's excavations, there
were only bone remains from five individuals found in the interior. The
discovery of the chamber allowed people 'to trample the ground of both
passage and chamber ever since, probably removing or destroying any
small artefacts which might have survived from the Stone Age . . .'[21] Contemporary accounts from the time of the tomb's rediscovery suggest
that there were 'a great quantity of bones', including animal skulls and
horns.[22] The quantity and type of finds which might have been present in
1699 will never be known.

Despite the collapse of material over the edge of the cairn, the actual
height of Newgrange is not thought to have changed much since it was
constructed.[23] This can be taken as a vindication of the design, which not
only kept the structure of the interior chamber intact for five millennia,
but which also kept it largely dry for most of that time.

Faced with the design and engineering of monuments which were to
be used for many purposes, including the placement of the bones of the
dead, for astronomical observations and perhaps even to aid the journey
of the spirits of the deceased into the next world, the question begs as to
why the designers of Newgrange, Knowth and Dowth went to such great
lengths to ensure the durability of these huge structures.

If you wanted to build something that would tolerate the ravages of
time and weather and nature, what better structure could you choose
than a miniature hill? Apart from any gradual settling of material, and
perhaps some subsidence as happened at Newgrange, it would take forc-

es of mighty proportions, or certainly a great human effort, to undo such a grand work.

Newgrange, Knowth and Dowth mark the zenith of the Irish megalithic culture. They are the largest and most lavishly designed of all the passage-tombs. One question which arises time and again is whether or not durability was a key aspect of their design. In other words, were they created with the intention that they would survive long into the future? Certainly some archaeologists think so.

Matthew and Geraldine Stout, who have carried out excavations in the Boyne Valley and have been studying Newgrange for the past two decades, suggest so:

> One of the marvels of the construction of the passage tomb within the cairn is that it remained basically intact and almost completely waterproof to this day. It was, in other words, built not for a generation but for all time.[24]

Archaeologist Dr Carleton Jones of the National University of Ireland Galway says:

> Megalithic tombs endure. They are still here today for us to marvel at long after just about everything else Neolithic people made has either disappeared or lies buried and unseen.[25]

The mounds represent a permanent presence in an ever-changing landscape, a lasting memorial to the zeal and toil of an extraordinary community.

> The stones, and the tombs which they form, endure unchanged against the changing seasons and the passing generations and this permanence was probably one aspect that appealed to the Neolithic builders. The stones, and therefore the tombs, were good symbols of ancient origins, ancestral lineages and 'timeless' traditions.[26]

There is no doubt this symbolism is part of the appeal of Newgrange today. Irish people, and descendants of the Irish from abroad, mostly

The mounds represent a permanent presence in an ever-changing landscape.

from the United States, come here in search of some arcane connection with forgotten ancestors, cherished forebears, and a journey to Newgrange represents a pilgrimage of sorts, a bonding of human spirits across thousands of years. This great shrine, this temple of stone and earth, ingeniously fashioned by bright men and women of the distant yesteryear, stands today as a sanctuary for the human spirit, for the lost ancestors of the hoary past and for the modern day pilgrim who comes here to commune with them. Newgrange endures, more than 5,000 years after it was built, and with its survival, the memory of the ancestors also endures, for this great monument was a product of their spiritual and scientific endeavours, grafted in stone and earth as an everlasting memorial to their brief time on this planet.

There is an old poem about Newgrange which was uttered to Fionn Mac Cumhaill by a poet who put him under a spell so that he could understand it:

I saw a house in the country
Out of which no hostages are given to a king.
Fire burns it not, harrying spoils it not.
Good the prosperity with which it was conceived the kingly house.[27]

Finn indicates that he understands the meaning of the verse, saying that Newgrange 'cannot be burned or harried so long as Aenghus still lives'. Newgrange survives today, and its perpetual endurance might signify, in some people's minds, that the spirit of Aonghus, and perhaps also of the people who built it, lives on.

Fascinatingly, there might be some cosmology underlying the need for Newgrange to survive into the modern age, which we will explore in Chapter 14.

The passage-mounds are in stark contrast with whatever homes the builders lived in. Of these, little trace has yet been found in the Boyne Valley. Evidence from excavations at Knowth shows that rectangular houses were being built around 3800 BC, but apart from these examples the homes of the builders 'have largely managed to elude us'.[28] The Knowth houses, like other rectangular Neolithic dwellings, were constructed using upright wooden posts. One of the dwellings found at Knowth had been partially built over when the main mound was constructed, and it is possible that the Knowth dwellings do not belong to the same people who were responsible for building the passage-tombs.

But what is clear is that the homes of the Neolithic are fleeting, almost temporary structures in comparison with the great mounds and cairns which survived for millennia:

> No greater contrast could be imagined than that between these meagre rectangular houses and the curving kerb and circumference of the massive stone-built mounds that constitute the three great Passage Tomb cemeteries of Dowth, Knowth and Newgrange.[29]

We may be able to tell a lot more about how the builders lived if and when we find their dwellings. There are lots of unanswered questions

*A reconstructed Lough Gur Neolithic house from the
National Heritage Park in Wexford.*

about the builders of Newgrange and this is one aspect of the mystery surrounding who they really were. Will archaeologists some day find evidence of a massive cluster of homes in one particular field in the Boyne Valley, indications of village living, or will they find homes scattered here and there throughout the valley? To sustain the level of construction that took place in the valley during a concentrated period lasting perhaps a couple of centuries, a substantial settlement such as that indicated by Conor Brady's ploughzone finds (see Chapter 2) would have been necessary. Where was this substantial settlement? We don't yet know.

Another mystery surrounds the burial practices of the mound-building community. Even with all the disturbance inside Newgrange after the time of Campbell's discovery of the chamber, it is unlikely that bone remains from the entire community had been placed within and that these had been carted off over the past few centuries. Even in that scenario Professor O'Kelly should have found the bones of several dozen individuals.

A reconstructed Neolithic home on display at the Brú na Bóinne Visitor Centre.

Were the ordinary labourers and farmers of the Bend of the Boyne buried in the smaller tombs in the valley, or were they buried somewhere else? We will explore the matter of the extent of the role of burial at Newgrange in the next chapter.

A further aspect of the survival of Newgrange relates to the common folk belief that damaging or vandalising an ancient site would result in revenge by the 'fairy folk'. The fairies were known as the '*daoine sídhe*', the 'people of the mound',[30] and they preferred to 'live underground, especially under a hill, in a cave or burrow, or in a heap of stones, such as the raths of Ireland'.[31] Although fairy lore only appears within the last millennium, the enduring tradition of such folklore suggests that the *sídhe* (fairy mounds) were considered the places 'where the semi-divine Tuatha Dé Danann fled underground after their defeat by the mortal Milesians'.[32] Essentially, the fairy folk are 'composed of the discarded gods and diminished heroes of the old native religion', as one theory of the origin of fairy faith suggests.[33]

As a renowned palace of the gods, Newgrange – *Síd in Broga* – would have held particular reverence. Its association with some of the supreme deities of the Tuatha Dé Danann probably resulted in a fastidious observation of a 'no trespassing' rule of sorts which resulted in many prehistoric monuments around Ireland being protected from damage over the centuries. Rural dwellers in particular held fast to deep superstitions about the possible outcomes of damaging raths and mounds and stone circles. A common tale to be heard at various ancient sites around Ireland, akin to a modern urban myth, tells of how a particular farmer starts breaking up stones from a cairn or mound only to be informed, within a short time of his vandalism, that a member of his family has died in a tragedy, such as a drowning. This persistent and widespread folklore held that any damage to a fairy mound might result in a catastrophe for the vandal, and as a result of this many farmers even today won't go anywhere near sacred mounds of ancient sites on their land.

It was not unknown in the nineteenth century for roads to be rerouted around fairy mounds,[34] and 'the sídh was not to be disturbed by grazing cattle, and most farmers would avoid both the sídh and perceived paths to and from it'.[35]

The special reverence surrounding Newgrange likely shielded it from the sort of reuse that had occurred at Knowth and Dowth, but it did not altogether escape damage. A number of the Great Circle stones had been removed before the coming of the Romans, although it is not known when this vandalism took place.[36]

In the twelfth century Newgrange and the lands around it fell into the ownership of the Cistercians, who had founded the nearby Mellifont Abbey in 1142. The sprawling estate of the Cistercians constituted 20,000 hectares, which was divided into smaller farms known as 'granges', and 'it was at this time that the ancient name of *Brú* passed out of general use in favour of Newgrange'.[37] Intense ridge and furrow cultivation at this time is thought to have played a part in the destruction of at least one smaller passage-tomb near Newgrange, and it is possible other sites were damaged during this period. The Cistercians might not have concerned

An aerial photo of Mellifont Abbey. In the twelfth century Newgrange fell into the ownership of the Cistercians.

themselves too much with the supposed reverence associated with New-grange: 'One cannot imagine the hard-nosed Cistercian farmers paying much heed to pagan legends.'[38]

One of the most ironic results of the passing of Newgrange into the hands of the Cistercians was that, while it lost its old name, it gained the name by which we all know it today.

> By 1378 the mound had been completely stripped of its former identity and was called merely 'the new grange'.[39]

One folk epithet of Newgrange is *Uaimh na Gréine*, the 'cave of the sun'.

The endurance of descriptions which may refer to the gleaming white quartz of Newgrange is also fascinating, especially in light of the cairn collapse which appears to have resulted in much of this milky white stone being buried and hidden from view. Archaeologist Claire O'Kelly, wife of Professor Michael O'Kelly, said, 'It is tempting to see in such phrases as 'Mac an Og's *brugh* brilliant to approach', 'yonder *brugh* chequered with the many lights', and 'the white-topped *brugh* of the Boyne', references to the glistening white quartz of the Newgrange mound.'[40] Interestingly,

The white quartz of Newgrange lay hidden from view for millennia.

Yonder brugh *chequered with the many lights.*

the word chequered is translated from *brecsholus*,[41] from *brec* and *so-lus*, meaning 'speckled' and 'light'. In *Island of the Setting Sun*, it was suggested that the milky quartz which adorned the monument might have been considered 'a sanctified reflection of the Milky Way'.[42] At the time Newgrange was built, the Milky Way galaxy would have been seen to settle along the horizon in a complete loop, something which does not happen today. Of significance is the fact that the Boyne (river of the white cow), which is the earthly Milky Way (Way of the White Cow) also loops around Newgrange on three sites, to the east, south and west, that is, on the pretty much the same sides of the monument as the quartz.

If these epithets of Newgrange do refer to the quartz, it is possible that they are memories of Newgrange as it appeared before the Bronze Age cairn collapse? Professor O'Kelly found the quartz layer at the very bottom of the cairn slip material, which means a great deal of this quartz, if not all of it, was hidden from view for four millennia. Perhaps there was originally an entire covering of quartz over the mound and this was gradually taken away over time, perhaps piece by piece, as keepsakes by visitors to the site? This seems unlikely though, especially in light of the aforementioned fairy folklore which would have forbidden any interference with the mound.

Newgrange has largely stood the test of time, however unlikely that may seem. By fortunate happenstance its cairn material suffered a partial collapse not long after it was built which helped to seal off the kerbstones, and the chamber, for 4,000 years. As a revered palace of the gods it was bestowed with a greater superstitious and spiritual aura than many other sites, and was, fortunately, left alone throughout the long years of prehistory and historic times, almost untouched by human hands. Its remarkable state of preservation into the modern age is due to a combination of its ingenious construction, and a mix of fortune and fairy tales.

For that, we are extremely grateful. We have inherited a temple, a shrine, a tomb, a monument of remote ancestors, which stands today as an everlasting memorial to their accomplishments.

7.

TOMB OR WOMB?

THERE IS A LONG-RUNNING DEBATE between archaeologists and other researchers and experts about the true nature and purpose of Newgrange and its sister monuments. Archaeologists say they are primarily tombs, used to inter the remains of the dead, with possible secondary functions. Others say they are temples, shrines, observatories, portals to the otherworld, sound amplification chambers and there are even some who say ancient sites such as Newgrange were inspired by visitors from space at some time in the distant past. There are dozens of published theories, and probably hundreds more unpublished. Tour guides at Newgrange hear a range of speculative ideas on a daily basis from visitors eager to share their own theories about the function of the site.

There has been much disagreement between the various parties to this debate. Archaeologists love labels, and 'passage-tomb' or 'passage-grave' is a label that seems to suit Newgrange quite well, in their opinion. Others deride what they consider an over-simplification of the function of such a truly remarkable site. One argument holds that there was simply too much effort expended in the construction of Newgrange, Knowth and Dowth just so that they could be used to inter the remains of a select few people. They must, therefore, have been constructed for some greater purpose.

Since the popularisation of Newgrange following Professor O'Kelly's excavations, a succession of writers has attempted to remould the story of Newgrange, reinterpret the meaning of its design and layout and to redefine its purpose. Some of these have, with perhaps some degree of hostility and even a touch of naiveté, dismissed the 'tomb' idea completely, preferring instead to thrust their own lavish interpretations on the masses.

A great deal of hostility was generated in the 1980s, when Irish American artist Martin Brennan and his coterie of friends and researchers came to the Boyne Valley. Brennan discovered that one of the chambers of Dowth was illuminated by the light of the setting sun on the winter solstice. That was 1980, the same year he and Jack Roberts had discovered that Cairn T at Loughcrew, County Meath, some 50 kilometres or so northwest of Brú na Bóinne, was aligned on the equinox sunrises. These discoveries were very significant, making major media headlines, and thrust the whole area of ancient astronomical knowledge and scientific endeavour into the limelight. However, both sides became entrenched, with archaeologists sticking to their guns in calling Newgrange and the other Boyne sites 'tombs', while the Brennan camp said that the apparent

The author pictured with Martin Brennan at Newgrange in December 2009.

refusal of archaeologists to investigate the astronomical purpose of the mounds was, in many ways, 'one of the greatest blunders of modern Irish archaeology'.[1]

Things got ugly. Brennan claimed archaeologists were not objective enough and that their reconstructions of the mounds had been 'disastrous'.[2] The archaeologists, meanwhile, were naturally upset at being insulted, and contemporary anecdotal accounts would suggest that a war of attrition broke out, with both sides equally engaged.

Newgrange archaeologist Claire O'Kelly was less than gracious in her 'review' of Brennan's book *The Stars and the Stones* in 1983:

> As an archaeologist I find myself at a loss as to how to attempt a review of this book or to say anything favourable about it beyond the fact that it is well produced . . . it contains errors, misrepresentations, innuendos, and even sneers at the expense of what the author calls 'modern archaeologists' – of the Irish breed, of course.[3]

It might have been difficult for an objective casual observer to discern the motives behind the disagreement and understand the finer intricacies of what should have been a much more friendly discourse. The main problem was that there was a perception that Brennan and his team were stepping on the toes of the archaeologists, and claiming new discoveries from under their noses, while archaeologists were apparently not ready to accept cosmology as a key function of the 'tombs', especially when these ideas were, metaphorically, being rammed down their throats. The divisions between the two sides were too deep, and they continued to trade insults.

It was an unfortunate episode in the history of exploration of Newgrange, and a needless one at that. Both sides had contributed enormously to our understanding of the Irish megalithic culture. Indeed, the cosmology enthusiasts could not have made some of their discoveries had it not been for the diligent work of the archaeologists, while the archaeologists were perhaps dismissive of some of Brennan's claims. The lack of mutual recognition from either side seemed to add fuel to the fire, as Claire O'Kelly's letter indicates:

> Yet this book could not have been put together without the con-
> tributions of these same modern archaeologists, unacknowl-
> edged by Brennan except in the rarest cases and in the vaguest
> terms.[4]

Brennan left Ireland under a cloud in the mid-1980s and the episode obviously hurt him deeply because he didn't come back here for 25 years, until he was keynote speaker at a conference near Newgrange in December 2009 entitled 'Boyne Valley Revision', of which I was principal organiser.

I saw Brennan's return as an opportunity for healing, and to recognise the gravity of his contribution to our understanding of Newgrange and the other ancient passage-mounds. Thankfully, a great deal of healing did take place during that visit, and Brennan was gratefully introduced to a large number of people, including a couple of archaeologists with whom he had perhaps been less friendly in the 1980s. Afterwards, he described a meeting with Professor George Eogan as 'warm and genuine', and seemed very pleased at the friendly welcome he had received in the Boyne Valley.

Archaeologists are commonly faulted for describing Newgrange as a passage-tomb, and criticised for using this label without sufficient evidence. Author Chris O'Callaghan suggests the evidence does not support the use of the word 'tomb':

> There was no sign then, or later, that Newgrange had been used
> as a catacomb, a mortuary, necropolis, royal or otherwise, or a
> crematorium. Despite the assumptions, there is not the faint-
> est evidence that Newgrange had ever been used as any sort of
> dedicated repository for bodies, bones, burial artefacts or ash.
> Nor have the interpretations been able to show that any of the
> patterns carved into the stones signify death or burial in any
> way. Despite the mantra of modern academia, the application of
> 'grave or tomb' to Newgrange is unsupportable.[5]

*Archaeologists have been criticised for labelling Newgrange
a tomb without sufficient evidence.*

Perhaps there is a point here? He goes further by suggesting that laboratory testing of the Newgrange bones were unable to definitively date them. 'Certainly, no link was suggested, let alone established, between the human bones and the date when Newgrange was in use.'[6]

He points out that Edward Lhwyd, the first antiquarian visitor to Newgrange after its rediscovery in 1699, did not 'suggest the presence of human bones' in any of the four letters which he wrote about Newgrange.[7] The considerable evidence of burials and cremations that one might expect of a community of the size that built Newgrange has not been found in the three centuries since it was reopened. It could be therefore reasonably deduced that, 'while the Boyne Valley People obviously found an efficient means of disposing of their dead, cremation and or interment of bodies and bones within the Newgrange monument was not one of them'.[8]

But some defence of archaeology must be made here. How can generations of archaeologists have wrongly labelled Newgrange? And if there isn't enough evidence, why do they persist with the tomb ideology? One of the reasons is because similar monuments were found with significant bone deposits. At the Fourknocks passage-tombs, for instance, there was a great deal of bone material, burnt and unburnt, found, including the remains of at least 21 children in Fourknocks Site I alone.[9] The passage of this mound was stuffed almost to the top with a mixture of stones, clay

A recreation of the ceremonial bowl from Knowth's eastern chamber with bone fragments.

and human remains. In the eastern chamber of Knowth, a 'general blanket deposit of cremation, 3-15 centimetres deep, existed all around the sides' of the left recess.[10] There were a further six deposits in the right recess.

There are different types of tomb too, such as portal tombs and court tombs, and here evidence of burial in the Neolithic has been ascertained. At the Poulnabrone portal tomb in County Clare, the remains of at least 22 individuals were found, dating to between 4200 and 2900 BC.[11] At Ashleypark in County Tipperary, a Linkardstown-type tomb, the bones of a man of about 60 years of age were radiocarbon dated to between 3650 and 3350 BC.[12]

Archaeologists don't pluck ideas out of thin air. They have labelled Newgrange a passage-tomb because it is, comparatively, a 'best fit' for the evidence available to hand. 'Virtually every Irish passage tomb that has been excavated had within it human remains.'[13] In addition to all this is the fact that archaeologists readily admit that 'tomb' does not describe all the functions of Newgrange or similar monuments. They are open to questioning the idea 'that the structures that archaeologists usually term "megalithic tombs" only or always functioned as tombs'.[14] Neolithic expert Gabriel Cooney says it is now often suggested that megalithic tombs 'should be seen instead as repositories for select ancestral remains and as foci for ancestral rituals, as houses, temples and shrines for the ancestors'.[15] The term 'tomb' is retained by archaeologists, but they do recognise that the sites had a variety of functions.

This is reinforced by another archaeologist, Dr. Elizabeth Twohig, who acknowledges that, in some cases, there are very few human remains found in the so-called tombs:

> Careful consideration shows that the monuments cannot have been built solely or even primarily for burial. Many have very few burials in them, while in some instances the paucity of human remains may be due to tomb robbing (for example Newgrange), the overall impression is that only a very small proportion of the population can have been buried in the monuments. . . . The small number of burials demonstrates, therefore, that the func-

tion of tombs was not merely as a place for the disposal of the dead.[16]

Archaeologists also recognise that the deposition of the select ancestral remains might have included ritual activity that involved 'encountering the supernatural and/or the ancestral powers who are in charge of human destiny'.[17] In this way, encounters with the otherworld occur at sacred places that are 'liminal, between this world and the spirit world'.[18]

It is clear from the above that modern archaeologists are not stuck in some archaic, outmoded line of thought. Their own interpretations of various megalithic sites span the sacred and spiritual as well as the scientific realms.

In the minds of some archaeologists, Newgrange could be comfortably re-labelled a 'temple of the ancestors' or something similar. It really doesn't matter all that much. The vast majority of archaeologists who have studied the Neolithic will readily admit that the ancient stone monuments were more than just tombs. Chris O'Callaghan interestingly labels Newgrange a 'Temple to Life', which is the title of his book. It has variously been described as a 'spirit temple', a 'star mound' and of course a 'passage-tomb'.

The Lithuanian-born archaeologist Marija Gimbutas might have preferred the label 'passage-womb', because her study of many ancient European structures led her to conclude that many of them were shaped like the female body.[19] Newgrange is no different in this regard. It has been suggested that the ridge upon which it sits presents the 'impression of a large image of a pregnant woman'.[20]

It has often been said that the passage and chamber of Newgrange, cruciform in shape, also portray the female reproductive system. Chris O'Callaghan imagines the mound was created to represent the Mother Earth:

> Accordingly, the end chamber would represent the womb and the alcoves the ovaries – the basins in the alcoves ready to hold the symbolic 'eggs' chosen to be fertilised. During consummation, entry to the womb could only be reached via the Sun Window

and along the passage leading to the end-chamber, or more accurately, the nuptial chamber.[21]

The prehistoric monuments of Europe show that the process of death
and transition was viewed differently in ancient times, according to Gimbutas. In Neolithic religion, she wrote, 'the processes of death and transition were cyclical',[22] again reinforcing the view that the cosmic vision of
the Neolithic people held everything to be part of the grand cycles of
nature and the cosmos.

> As in the organic world, where new life grows from the remains of
> the old, birth, according to the Old Europeans, was part of a cycle
> that included death. Just as the goddess' womb obviously gave us
> birth, it also took us back in death. Symbolically, the individual
> returned to the goddess' womb to be reborn. Exactly what form
> this rebirth was imagined to take is unknown; what is clear is that
> Old European religion understood life and death as aspects of
> larger cyclic processes.[23]

Her study of monuments in Europe, in particular the early shrines
of Lepenski Vir in the Iron Gates region of Serbia and Romania, which
date to c. 6500-5500 BC, led her to suggest that such structures could be
considered wombs as much as tombs. 'Vulva and uterus images – both
natural and geometric – predominate. They can be found in the architecture of the tomb or as symbols of the tomb itself.'[24]

Many writers have pointed to the womb-like qualities of the design of
Newgrange. One suggested that Newgrange's interior was:

> . . . shaped like the female generative organs; a long narrow pas-
> sage resembles the birth canal, leading into the main chamber,
> like the womb with the two side chambers to resemble the ova-
> ries. Newgrange was constructed to resemble both tomb and
> womb.[25]

The same author suggests the purpose of Newgrange was 'both spiritual and cosmological'.[26] Some of the possible cosmological reasons for
its design will be explored in Chapter 14.

Christopher Knight, co-author of *Uriel's Machine,* also sees the similarities. Examining a plan of the Newgrange tunnel and chamber, it appeared to him 'to be highly reminiscent of the female reproductive organs'.[27]

In the artwork on the stones of Newgrange and its sister sites, Marija Gimbutas saw regeneration as being one of the main themes: 'There is a clear affinity in symbolism between the life column within the egg/cave/womb and the cupmark (or dot)-in-circle or concentric circle.'[28]

Newgrange has strong associations with the Tuatha Dé Danann, including the earth/moon/river/Milky Way goddess Bóinn, who gives her name to the river beneath the monument and to the cosmic river of the sky. Bóinn is the archetypal *mater dei,* one element of an ancient divine trinity that included the Dagda, the sun god, and Aonghus, the miracle swan child, and their stories are infused with miraculous imagery which may stem from a Neolithic preoccupation with themes that include creation, procreation, and the all-pervading idea of cosmic regeneration.[29] As a lunar goddess, her rhythm is strongly tied with the gestation periods of both humans and cows, and if Newgrange is to be considered her earthly womb, then perhaps a sacred union with the solar Dagda can be viewed in the context of the joining together of creative cosmic forces.

On the shortest days of the year, at sunrise, the sacred beam of light from the sun penetrates the vulva of Newgrange into the dark womb within, and there, in the winter light, the year is born again.

Some effort has been made by this author to suggest a link between the original name of Newgrange, *Brug na Bóinde,* and the word 'womb'.[30] The Early Irish word *brug* means many things, but all tied to the idea of an abode. It can mean a palace, mansion, house, an abode of fairies, a hillock, tumulus, or a fort. The Old Irish word *brú* is a different word, and means 'womb'. The two words are not, apparently, connected, being from different roots. The modern spelling of *Brug na Bóinde* is *Brú na Bóinne,* due in no small part to the fact that at some time in the past *brug* became *brugh* – in other words, the word was softened, and later the spelling changed to *brú.* But *Brú na Bóinne* still derives from *brug,* mansion, not *brú,* womb.

This does not detract greatly from the idea that Newgrange might have been constructed to represent or symbolise a womb. It is one monument of many, scattered across Ireland, and Europe, and indeed other parts of the world, which may have been built by devotees of 'an ancient rebirth ritual – wrapped up in sophisticated astronomical observations'.[31]

We have seen from Vallancey how there was a plethora of Irish terms and concepts representing the idea of patterns, cycles, returns, periods, revolutions, circles and rings. In the world view of a Neolithic farmer astronomer, it is not difficult to imagine that life itself was seen as part of the grand cycle of things.

The chamber of Newgrange – a womb, a tomb and a mansion of the gods.

The builders of Newgrange watched the sun grow and fade as it moved north and south along the horizon over the course of the year. They saw its strength dissipate as the year waned towards the solstice and, in the dim light of the stone womb, it died and was reborn, in one continuous movement. Is it possible that, by placing some remains of their recently deceased ancestors in the dark chamber on the night before the shortest day, their hope was that the soul of the deceased would be reborn into the next world, transported there by a beam of light from the new sun?

In Irish mythology, the otherworld is regularly seen as being underground, in caves and chambers and mounds. It is also perceived as being in the Atlantic Ocean, way out beyond the furthest western and southwestern coasts of Ireland. Regularly, is it also associated with the sky, and the entrance to *Tír na mBeo*, Land of the Living, was said to have opened when the sun was touching the earth, that is, at sunrise and, particularly, at sunset. Indeed, it is after the sun sets and the light fades that the stars begin to appear.

The apparent confusion between a subterranean otherworld and a stellar otherworld could be explained if one thinks of the journey to the afterlife as one that necessitates both. In this view, the spirit of the deceased must first encounter the night, returning to the womb-like darkness, mimicking what happened at the beginning of physical life. It was there, in the early darkness of life, that the foetus awaited in innocence the push of the labour pangs and the journey down the birth canal towards the light of a new life. That new life could not begin without first the long stay within the dark cocoon.

Given that so much of what was happening in the world was viewed to be cyclical, we should not be surprised if our Neolithic ancestors saw the beginning of physical life, the ending of physical life, and the dawning of a new spiritual incarnation as part of a cycle, much like the patterns which they saw repeating, over and over again, in the sky and in nature.

For surely a people who lived so closely with nature saw all the risings and fallings, the comings and goings, the birth and death, as natural rhythms in the pattern of nature, and by extension, life itself. They doubtless perceived that the rise and fall of the tide was connected with the movements of the moon, that the new crops they planted were nourished by the growing strength of the sun, that the migratory birds of the Boyne Valley arrived and departed at the same time each year, and that the leaves fell off the trees in the late autumn. A great deal of what they could see happening before their eyes in the valley was occurring as part of a pattern or cycle.

Why, therefore, should we be surprised to learn that the builders of Newgrange might have considered its chamber as a giant womb of the goddess, of Bóinn, from whom the valley and the monument is named? Bóinn was the great archetypal mother who was one of the divine race called the Tuatha Dé Danann who are said to have withdrawn into the mounds, waiting, perhaps in the stellar otherworld, to one day return to interfere once again in the affairs of humanity.

It is not at all beyond the realms of possibility that Newgrange was considered both a tomb and a womb by its builders. In this regard we must approach our study of Newgrange from an esoteric perspective as much as a scientific and logical viewpoint. After all, even Professor O'Kelly acknowledges that his archaeological work at Newgrange does not contradict the 'concept of Newgrange as a house of the dead and an abode of spirits at one and the same time'.[32] Why, therefore, should we not consider it a place of death and birth concurrently?

The ultimate truth of the matter is that archaeology recognises that Newgrange is much more than just a tomb, although whether all the latter day writers and theorists will acknowledge that it is a tomb at all is another question.

One more aspect of the interpretation of Newgrange is worth mentioning here, and that is the idea that interpretations change according to a person's own beliefs and social milieu. The many interpretations of Newgrange can 'say as much about their authors as they do about the tomb'.[33]

In general, archaeologists still refer to Newgrange as a tomb, and there is little deviation from this description, despite the many reservations that individual archaeologists might have about whether this term adequately describes the monument. Do they see it as a dead thing, and the people who created it as a people who have vanished, of whom no trace survives in any way?

A great deal of visitors and writers who are spiritual or esoteric in their outlook about Newgrange see it very much as a living thing, and many see a continuation, or a resurgence, of the old ways and beliefs. There is a very genuine conviction among some people that the place is spiritually 'alive' and for whom the description of Newgrange as a tomb is anathema. There are still a great deal of people who frequent Newgrange and the Boyne Valley, and other ancient and sacred sites such as the Hill of Tara, who feel a powerful aura, a great energy, at these places. Some archaeologists consider these people to be disconnected from reality. Others are more accommodating of the various beliefs and ideas sur-rounding Newgrange.

The open-minded visitor will perhaps sense and understand many of the feelings that Newgrange engenders in people. Those who are open to spiritual energy encounter sometimes profound experiences, and in general they will always thrive upon some deeper energy from unknown forces. I have seen visitors to the Newgrange chamber on the solstice mornings place their hands upon spirals in the recesses and meditate, as if they are literally drawing a mysterious force or energy from the stones. One person who recounted their experiences in Newgrange stumbled over words:

> This is all very overwhelming . . . Obviously this is a personal experience . . . It could be like a retreat . . . You can't help go to that place, I am sorry, if you can't go to this place at some level of spirituality, you need to see a shrink, there is a problem, a big problem.[34]

There is a word – *numen* – which comes from Latin, and is used to describe what people experience and cherish and desire about their ex-cursions to sacred and ancient places. Numen means 'a beckoning from the gods', and metaphorically it 'connotes a spiritual force or influence

The light of the winter solstice shines along the wall of the Newgrange passage.

that human beings associate with an object, a phenomenon or a place'.[35] The phrase 'numen-seeking' was coined by Rudolf Otto in his 1958 book *Idea of the Holy*. According to Otto, 'a numinous experience is a sort of religious rapture or ecstasy . . . a deeply spiritual effect that places and objects can have on us'.[36]

Those for whom Newgrange is a numinous experience might more readily accept the idea that it is a womb. In seeing the monument as a place of birth or rebirth, perhaps there is a recognition or belief that the spirituality of Neolithic times is returning. This should not be surprising in light of the spiritual crisis of modern times, and the enormous 'falling away' from the traditional church that has been hit by repeated scandals and an increasingly outmoded image.

People who feel a detachment from the religion they were brought up with, or for whom there is a spiritual emptiness in the traditional church, might feel more at home with a cosmic or natural spirituality such as that found in the Neolithic. With the political, economic and religious institutions and systems of modern Ireland in deep crisis, it is no wonder that people are turning in greater numbers to the shrines of the pre-Christian past for some sense of their personal spirituality.[37]

For those archaeologists who still believe Newgrange functioned primarily as a tomb, the monument is a dead thing, and its people long gone. There are stones, and bones, and implements, fragments of a story from the lost yesteryear. For those who might cherish the notion that Newgrange is a womb, they perhaps come to this great shrine to be reborn in the womb of the goddess, to encounter spiritual forces which are still very much alive . . .

People are returning to pre-Christian shrines in this time of spiritual crisis.

8.

TOWARDS THE LIGHT

WE ARE ALL GOING TO DIE. Every one of us, without exception, will perish from this world and pass to the great beyond, whatever or wherever that may be. Corporeal death is one of the great certainties of life, and there is not one among our number who can outwit it, or who can outlast it. In the words of poet James Shirley, 'there is no armour against fate'.[1]

Some day, our time will come. We will take our last breath of air on this beautiful planet and then we will succumb to 'death the leveller'. No king or priest or leader, no scientist or alchemist or magician, no politician or preacher, no peasant or farmer, has yet outsmarted death, and the multitude of processes and circumstances that lead to it, and it's doubtful that any human being ever will. It is as sure to happen to us as being born. It is the great inescapable reality that we cannot run from, and in the fullness of time every single human who now walks on this earth will be gone.

At some juncture in the future, hopefully a long time from now, these printed words might be read by a person yet to be born, and they will wonder what it was like to live in Anthony Murphy's time. This is what happens to us when we visit Newgrange, and look at its carvings and its giant stones, and behold its great mass, looming over the valley of the Boyne. We wonder what it might have been like to live in their time. For they, the builders, are vanished from the world; their time has been and gone, and they are lost to prehistory.

Death is the one fate that binds all of humanity, across all of time. From the remotest times to the remotest places, we all share this one destiny, this one doom. We are locked into a binding and irreversible contract with life, a treaty that insists upon death for every last one of us, with no exception.

If death is one of the great certainties of life, what happens when we die remains one of its enduring mysteries. In this enlightened age of science, which apparently has an explanation for everything, even science itself cannot decide what happens to us 'on the other side', if anything at all. It is this uncertainty, in part, that creates the intense mourning we feel for someone who has passed on. No matter how strong a person's faith or belief in a heaven, or an otherworld, or a good god who is compassionate, there is hardly anyone alive today who feels absolute certainty about the survival of the soul beyond bodily death.

The apparent finality of death, and the complete loss of the presence of a loved one, is something that those of us who are left behind must endure, with all its heartache, and its mourning, and its despair. It is felt most distinctly in those quiet moments when we realise our loved one has departed this life, not to return, and we will never be able to speak to them, or hold them, or hug them in this world again.

Being bereft means to be deprived of someone, and the loneliness and poignancy their departure leaves us with is something that most humans will have to deal with at some time in their life. This is another connection that bonds humanity across the ages. We have all felt loss, and we have all wondered what lies beyond the edge of death.

The otherworld, if it exists, is not a place most of us can visit or see or sense in any way. This makes it unfathomable to the conscious mind, something beyond what we have experienced in this life, and therefore we create a virtual heaven of our own liking. In ancient Ireland the otherworld was known by various names, many of which are connected with the idea of eternal life.

Winter Solstice sunlight in the passage of Newgrange.

This ancient Irish heaven was variously known as *Tír na nÓg*, the 'Land of Youth, *Tír Tairngire*, the 'Land of Promise', *Mag Mell*, the 'Pleasant Plain' and *Tír na mBeo*, 'Land of the Ever Living Ones', among other names. Some of these names imply that the otherworld is a place where there is immortality, or at least in the case of *Tír na nÓg*, eternal youth, which is fundamentally the same thing. Whether these names had their origin in the Neolithic, it is not possible to say. However, we can make an argument that some people in the Neolithic might have experienced death and crossed over to the otherworld, only to return back to life in this world.

Many people in modern times who have had what are termed 'near death experiences' (NDEs) have described extraordinary and fantastic occurrences on the other side of death. Some of these were people who had heart attacks and were resuscitated, others were involved in road accidents, and others still died on operating tables in hospitals and were later brought back to life. There are many common elements to their stories, and these elements appear to cross religious and ethnic divides, such that the near death experience can almost be described as a universal phenomena for those who have come back to this life from the great beyond.

Tens of thousands of these near death experiences have been documented around the world. Many people reported the sensation of leaving their body, of floating down a dark tunnel or void, of meeting deceased relatives and friends, of encountering a brilliant light, of having a 'life review' with a 'being of light', variously described as an angel or god himself. This last aspect of the near death experience seems to have the most profound effect on the individual who has passed to the other side and returned.[2]

Although no two stories of near death experience are ever exactly alike, there are many universal aspects to their accounts. A great deal of people who have encountered death have felt the sensation of floating down a dark tunnel towards a brilliant light.

The late Dr. Elisabeth Kubler-Ross was a Swiss-American psychiatrist who worked with thousands of terminally ill patients and who is credited as having been the world's foremost expert on death and dying. She describes some of the sensations a person will experience at the moment of death:

> . . . you will realise that dying is only a transition to a different form of life. The earthly physical forms you leave behind because you have no need for them anymore. But before you step out of your physical body in exchange for those forms which you will keep for eternity, you pass through a phase which is totally imprinted with items of the physical world. It could be that you float through a tunnel, pass through a gate, or cross a bridge . . . After you have passed this tunnel, bridge, or mountain pass, you are at its end embraced by light. This light is whiter than white. It is extremely bright, and the more you approach this light the more you are embraced by the greatest indescribable, unconditional love that you could ever imagine.[3]

Dr. Raymond Moody is another psychiatrist who has been studying the near death experience for decades, and whose book *Life After Life* continues to be a best seller. Moody describes fifteen 'components' of the near death experience which he assembled from the accounts of more than 100 people who had physically died and survived.

Although not all components are present in every story, and although each account is unique and no two accounts are ever precisely identical, the dark tunnel and the brilliant light are part of the experience for many people who have ventured to the edge of death and the afterlife:

> . . . people have the sensation of being pulled very rapidly through a dark space of some kind. Many different words are used to describe this space. I have heard this space described as a cave, a well, a trough, an enclosure, a tunnel, a funnel, a vacuum, a void, a sewer, a valley, and a cylinder.[4]

The encounter with a brilliant light is often the most profound part of the near death experience, according to Moody. The light is dim when it first appears, but it 'rapidly gets brighter until it reaches an unearthly brilliance'.[5] Despite this great indescribable luminance, the light does not dazzle the subject or hurt their eyes. In addition to this, the light is perceived by the subjects as a being, a 'being of light', who emanates love and warmth to the extent that the intensity of this love is beyond description.[6] One account given to Moody typifies the whole dark tunnel/bright light sensation:

> . . . I began to feel as though I were tumbling, actually kind of floating, through this blackness, which was some kind of enclosure . . . Everything was black, except that, way off from me, I could see this light. It was a very, very brilliant light, but not too large at first. It grew larger as I came nearer and nearer to it.[7]

If you've ever heard the phrase 'there's light at the end of the tunnel', this aptly describes the experiences of some people who have been on the verge of passing over to the otherworld.

An Irish author, Colm Keane, has collected dozens of accounts of near death experiences from people in Ireland. His books *Going Home* and *Distant Shore*, featuring these extraordinary accounts, were published in 2009 and 2010 respectively. Many of these stories feature descriptions of the sensation of being in a dark tunnel or void and moving towards a brilliant light.

One man who lost both legs in a bomb blast in Antrim during the Northern Ireland troubles described the tunnel and light experience:

> It was as if I was in a narrowing tunnel although I couldn't see walls. It was dark. Everything was dark except for the light. The tunnel was converging on the light. The light was the focus. I was drifting and all the time I was going towards it and it wasn't coming to me.[8]

A police officer who was badly injured in Belfast in 1981 had a similar experience while in the operating theatre, where, it later emerged, he had died for a time:

*Many people who have had a near death experience report
floating down a dark tunnel towards a light.*

> I was suddenly aware of being in a dark tunnel, with a light at the
> end of it. I was travelling along the tunnel and ending up in the
> white light. . . . I was aware of the bright light at the end of it. I
> was moving towards it.[9]

Another woman, born in Wicklow but living in the UK, described
being in a blue-coloured tunnel, and seeing her sister running up this
tunnel towards a bright light at its end.[10]

A Dublin woman who had been administered the wrong medicine
and was effectively poisoned while eight months pregnant described her
experience:

> I suddenly went through darkness like a tunnel. I was travelling.
> It seemed like I was moving pretty fast. Then I came from the
> blackness into a large area where there was a lovely brightness.[11]

The tunnel is not always black, and is not always dark. One woman described floating, not walking, down a dark brown tunnel towards a crystal-white light. 'The light was the goal. It was the place to go.'[12] She also described meeting her deceased grandfather at the end of the tunnel.

A Roscommon man recalled a near death encounter which happened in 1965 during which he 'went flying through a big black tunnel'. He said the tunnel was very dark and about eight or ten feet in diameter. 'I went through it very fast . . . I was going at an awful rate, really flying.' He described going through a big bright light, the width of the tunnel. 'It wasn't blinding or dazzling at all. I could see it approaching before I went through it. I flashed through it.'[13]

Colm Keane, a journalist by profession, was moved by the authenticity of these near death accounts, and he believes the tunnel and light elements are not the product of cultural conditioning.

> I'm not so sure that it necessarily would be cultural, because some of the elements, well, why should they be? Like the tunnel, and moving through the tunnel towards the light and things like that. There is no reason why that should happen. You might accept heavenly skies full of cherubic angels and choirs and all that, but not the specifics of this.[14]

A sceptic by nature and a non-religious person, Keane has come to believe that 'something continues after the point of death, whether it's the survival of the brain or the soul or the mind'.[15]

Dr. Elisabeth Kubler-Ross was a self-confessed 'skeptical semi-believer, to put it mildly', but having studied 20,000 people who had near death experiences, she came to believe in the survival of the soul after death. 'Death is but a transition from this life to another existence where there is no more pain and anguish.'[16]

Was the passage of Newgrange inspired, at least in part, by a near death experience? Does its long, dark, narrow tunnel, leading towards the light box above the entrance, replicate elements of the deathbed journey to *Tír na mBeo*? This is speculation, of course, but as a supposed repository for the bones of the dead, and a possible 'temple of the ancestors', as it has often been described, would this not be a fitting aspect of its design?

For this theory to hold any weight, we must assume that someone in the New Stone Age had experienced a brush with death, and had returned from a journey down the dark tunnel towards the light and a possible meeting with deceased ancestors to recount their extraordinary tale.

Is this so far-fetched? Not at all. The near death experience is much more commonplace than we would have believed. The stories related in Colm Keane's books were elicited largely through his letters to various newspapers around Ireland, asking people to recount their experiences. Although many people were nervous about recounting their apparently incredible near death experiences for fear of being ridiculed or branded as strange or unstable, the stories came in abundance. The newspaper appeals 'produced an outstanding response'.[17]

If the near death experience is such a widespread phenomenon today, then why not 5,000 years ago? One reason, of course, is that modern medicine has dramatically improved our odds of survival from serious illness or injury. However, it is still possible that a number of individuals in the Stone Age experienced an encounter with death, and came back to this world to tell the tale:

> We can imagine the scene, with our early ancestors enthralled by the extraordinary tales of tunnels, bright lights and a 'superior being' recounted by those who undertook the first near-death and out-of-body journeys. Those early stories, with their vivid afterlife images, found their way into the core manuscripts of various faiths. Where else did the first concepts of heaven originate than in the narratives identical to those being reported today?[18]

The passage of Newgrange, leading to the brilliant light of solstice, might have been intended as a physical replica of the tunnel described by some Neolithic farmer who had had a brush with death.

Colm Keane believes that the elements of the near death narrative:

... have been with us right back to the earliest time of man, right back to when the first unfortunate who fell over a cliff or got into a scrape with a wild boar came back to the tribe with a story of bright lights, a superior being, meeting dead relatives etc.'[19]

Keane recalls that:

One night ... I decided to go back and see how far these stories could be traced. Not only did I find them in vast swathes of medieval literature but also back in the stories of Saint Furza and Saint Adamnan, in St. Paul, in the Old Testament (Ezekiel) and in the New Testament also where there are so many references to the concept of life after death, something travelling from the body, the light, judgement, meeting those who passed on etc.[20]

It was particularly the Old Testament and right back to ancient Egyptian papyrus scripts, that one night, brought me a genuine revelation – it wasn't that various religions were influencing the telling of these stories; rather it was the other way around.

The problem is, of course, that there is only so far back that you can go in recorded time. However, it really was the Old Testament that swung it for me, preceding Christianity with all its allusions to another world, light, judgement etc.[21]

And crucially to our theory about Newgrange, he adds:

I have no doubt that your most clever presumption regarding Newgrange could well have a basis on the same fundamental I describe in my books. And I guess the word is really 'fundamentally' – I think I mention somewhere that the various religions are many different pieces of coloured glass in a stained-glass window, each reflecting its own interpretation of the fundamental light behind it. Indeed, the more I got to look at the near-death experience, the more closely I could see how all religions derive from it.

So I think you are on to something, although you can never prove it – nor can I prove that the near-death experience provides the origins of all religions. But it's a fair proposition and certainly

Solstice sunlight viewed from the Newgrange chamber:
the tunnel and light feature in the majority of near death experiences.

makes sense. As I have discovered, the light is everything and the
journey to the light is all that matters.

Interestingly, the tunnel and the light feature in the bulk of near
death experience accounts. 'These are the two most prominent elements,
by far,' Keane says, 'and either or both feature in the vast majority of narratives, well over 95 per cent.'[22]

It has to be pointed out that the near death experience is not the only occurrence where there is an encounter with the tunnel opening towards a bright light. Archaeologist Carleton Jones refers to the fact that people in a deep state of altered consciousness:

> . . . often experience the sensation of moving down a vortex or a tunnel which has a bright light at its end (the near death experiences of many people are described in this way).[23]

The authors of *Inside the Neolithic Mind* say that:

> . . . the near-death phenomenon is by no means the only context in which a vortex [or tunnel] is experienced . . . shamans around the world frequently use similar imagery to describe their out-of-body travels to the spirit realm, regardless of the way in which they alter their consciousness.[24]

Further intrigue is added by one interpretation of the spiral symbols which are to be found engraved onto certain key stones at Newgrange, including a triple spiral symbol in the end recess of the chamber. If, as has been suggested by certain archaeologists, the spiral motif is 'a vortex connecting two planes of existence or consciousness', we might ask what its purpose might have been in the context of the 'tunnel and light' experience:

> This motif is only illuminated by the sun's rays at the midwinter solstice and for a few days either side of the solstice. If it was envisaged as a connecting vortex by the Neolithic people, it is possible that it only 'opened up' for these few days each year. Who might have travelled along this vortex when it did open? Two likely candidates are shamans and the dead.[25]

The idea of a tunnel opening up into another realm is something that is 'wired into the human brain' and it has been suggested that spiritual or ritual specialists might have been able to enter through that mental vortex to visit the otherworld and return to the land of the living.[26]

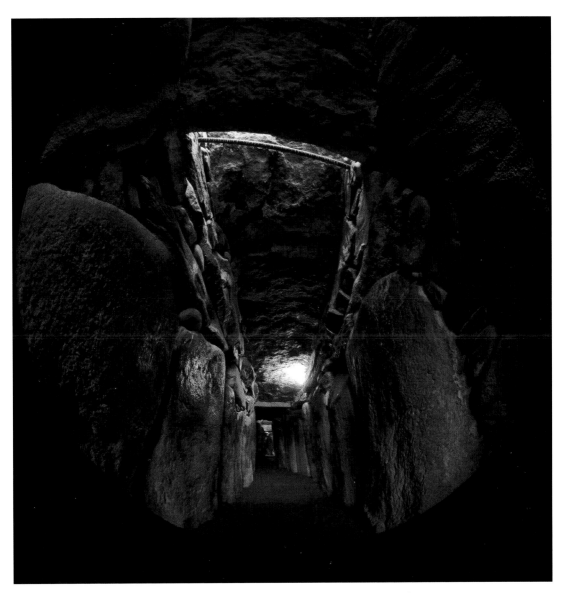

*A 'fisheye' view of the tunnel of Newgrange viewed from
directly underneath the roofbox.*

The notion that Newgrange might have been viewed as some sort of portal to the otherworld is certainly not a new one. As we will see in the next chapter, the gods of ancient Ireland, the Tuatha Dé Danann, were said to have retreated into the mounds and raths of Ireland, and are said to be residing there, perhaps in the otherworld, to await a return to this world at the end of time.

145

Some authors have suggested that Newgrange was used for an astronomical ritual involving the bright planet Venus, which shines into the chamber on the dawn of winter solstice once every eight years. They say this ritual involved the belief that the souls of the departed were transferred into the bodies of the newborn by the light of Venus.[27]

If there was a burial or funerary purpose to Newgrange, 'it was connected with the belief that the soul of the deceased could be transported to the otherworld out of the chamber, along the sky beam formed by certain heavenly bodies such as the sun, and on into the plain of happiness, the land of eternal youth of myth'.[28]

Even Professor O'Kelly, the excavator of Newgrange, who might well have been sceptical about such spiritual and ethereal notions, acknowledged that, as stated in the last chapter, he had no difficulty with the concept of Newgrange has a house of the dead and an abode of spirits.[29]

The so-called 'dramatic thresholds' of many passage-tombs, consisting of huge decorated kerbstones in the case of Newgrange and Knowth, suggest a system of communication between the exterior and interior of the monuments.[30]

> Exactly what or who was being led into or out of the tombs is not certain but given the elevated position of these stones and the association of Newgrange with the sun's rays, we might conjecture that it was spirits rather than people.[31]

Indeed, it is recognised that monuments such as Newgrange were places where ancestors and spirits, and perhaps even 'non-material tiers of the cosmos' could be contacted.[32] The presence of so much exotic white quartz, brought here from Wicklow, might also be significant in this regard. It is suggested that:

> . . . quartz, even as far back as the Neolithic, may have symbolized the soul; for the living, quartz may have represented 'the gateway to other dimensions through which they negotiate with the spirit world.[33]

Did the megalithic builders believe that the soul was transported out of the chamber to the otherworld along a beam of light from the sun?

The spiritual journey undertaken by the Neolithic shaman, or priest, or (heaven forbid!) druid, might have involved the descent into the hole, and the visit to the dark cave inside the earth. Here, perhaps in a state of altered consciousness which can, sometimes, be brought about by prolonged auditory and sensory deprivation, the shaman might have been facilitated 'a visual, experiential dramatization of spiritual journeys'.[34] Perhaps the ritually experienced Stone Age priest became accustomed to these journeys into the dark, and there, in the belly of the great Newgrange mound, he might have communed with long dead ancestors, or even the gods themselves.

Winter Solstice sunlight bathes the Boyne Valley beneath Newgrange.

9.

CAVE MYTHS

Deep in the womb chamber of Newgrange, beyond sight and sound, certain privileged elders of the community of the Boyne may once have held intimate ceremonies, during which they attempted to commune with the spirits of deceased ancestors. This is certainly one of the possibilities thrown up by our investigation into the likely purposes and uses of this grand monument. There, in the murky depths of the interior, cut off from their peers, they might well have encountered spirits of a different nature too.

If Newgrange was envisaged by its builders as some sort of device, a portal, connecting this world with another world, it might be possible to discern some implication of that in any mythology attached to the site.

Newgrange is known under various ancient names, one of which describes it as the *sídh* of the *Brugh*,[1] a *sídhe* being a fairy mound, and, 'by implication, the realm beyond the senses, the otherworld or, in oral tradition, the fairy world'.[2]

The fairies are a product of the folklore of much more recent times than when Newgrange was built. They are 'diminutive supernatural beings in human form' that like to live in caves and burrows and the ancient mounds of Ireland.[3] However, the first references to fairies don't appear until the twelfth century AD. The fairy folk are of little concern to our investigation, being as they are the product of medieval storytellers. It is to a much more original and ancient divine race of Ireland, the Tuatha Dé Danann, that we must now turn our attention.

There is a long-standing tradition in Ireland that the *sídhe* were the sacred retreats to which the Tuatha Dé Danann fled after they were defeated by the mortal Milesians.[4]

We first find mention of the Tuatha Dé Danann in the *Lebor Gabála Érenn*, known as the 'Book of Invasions of Ireland', which is described thus by Michael Slavin, an expert on the ancient books of Ireland:

> The *Lebor Galála Érenn* . . . is a fascinating document that tells of successive incursions of peoples onto our island from the time of the flood down to the millennium before Christianity.[5]

The Book of Invasions describes various forays on Ireland by a swathe of invaders, including the Parthalonians, the Fir Bolg, the Tuatha Dé Danann and the Milesians. Of all these, a greater part of the modern day reverence for our ancient myths is reserved for the Tuatha Dé.

This semi-divine race arrived into Ireland in spectacular and incredible fashion, but their departure from this world was controversial, embarrassing and downright submissive. They are said to have descended from the clouds just before the festival of Bealtaine, 'settling on an obscure mountain in the west, causing a three-day eclipse'.[6] This particular description of their arrival has led many theorists to propose or suggest that the Tuatha Dé Danann were in fact an extraterrestrial race who came here from another planet in prehistory. This author will make no such fantastic claims!

But their defeat at the hands of the Spanish invaders, the sons of Mil, known as the Milesians, was nothing short of a catastrophe, and the humiliated gods of the Tuatha Dé retreated underground, into the raths and mounds of Ireland,[7] where, apparently, they will remain, until some future calling.

It is not the *Lebor Gabála* that consigns their fate to the ancient stone chambers of Ireland, but rather 'more popular materials that describe them surviving as immortals in the ancient barrows and cairns'.[8] Following their humiliation, the gods become diminished, banished from the world, defeated by mortals, and in the long centuries between ancient and modern times, the mythical and folk boundaries have become confused, such that the old divinities and the fairy people are perhaps seen as one and the same thing. Indeed these fairy folk are said to be invisible to ordinary motrals, except at key festivals in the year, including Samhain (now celebrated as Hallowe'en) and Midsummer's Eve.[9]

Despite their apparent humbling and diminution, the Tuatha Dé Danann remain today the most revered of the ancient characters of Irish myth. Their association with some of the key sacred sites of Ireland gives them a special place in the hearts of those who love Ireland and its stories. Indeed for many people, the Tuatha Dé Danann are not diminished at all, and remain at the centre of our fondest tales.

Some of the leading figures of the Tuatha Dé include Dagda, Lugh Lámhfhada, Aongus Óg and Bóand/Bóinn, and while there are many more, all of the above are strongly associated with Newgrange.

Dagda, or Dagdae, was the chief of the gods, the principal deity of ancient times. His name may have meant 'good god' but he was very much a male sky deity.[10] His mighty cauldron was one of the mysterious artefacts that the Tuatha Dé brought with them upon their arrival in Ireland, the others being the Lia Fáil (Stone of Destiny), the spear of Lugh and the sword of Nuadu. Interestingly, there is a giant cauldron stone in the Boyne Valley, although not at Newgrange. This huge basin stone is located in the right-hand recess of Knowth's eastern chamber, so big that it must have been placed there before the recess stones themselves were put in place.

Dagda was said to have been the owner of Newgrange – at least up until the point that his son Aonghus managed to take it from him by cunning. The Dagda is seen as a progenitor, an ancestor god, the 'father of many'.[11] He is absolutely a sun god, with various epithets, including *Eochaidh Ollathair*, meaning 'horseman', the horse pulling the sun around the sky in some traditions, and *Deirgderc*, meaning 'red-eye'.[12] We saw

A painting of Dagdha, the chief of the gods by Jane Brideson.

in Chapter 5 how Vallancey referred to *Daghdae-rath* as the sun in Irish, although he failed to connect the prefix with the name of the chief god whose residence was Newgrange.

Lugh Lámhfhada, Lugh of the Long Arm, is one of the great heroes of the Tuatha Dé Danann. Another sky deity, Lugh's mythology is strongly associated with the constellation we know today as Orion.[13] He has another sobriquet, *Samhildánach*, meaning 'master of all arts'. He is adept in the use of a sling and a javelin, and often the cosmic symbolism wrapped up in his story sees him as a giant Orion, throwing the sun, moon and planets from his upraised hand along the ecliptic. Under whatever names it was known in prehistoric Ireland, Orion held a special place among the stellar pantheon, and was considered to be a great god or warrior in various stories. As a god of the 'long throw', Lugh guarded the ford of the sky – the *áth* (ford or crossing place) where the ecliptic passes the Milky Way, the heavenly Boyne river. Indeed, his offspring, Cúchulainn, did much the same thing, as described in the *Táin*:

> Rise mighty son of Ulster
> now that your wounds have been healed
> a fair man facing your foes
> in the starlit ford of night[14]

One of the many stories about Lugh connects him with Newgrange through his son, the great hero Cú-chulainn, originally named Setanta, who was conceived through a supernatural union of Lugh and Bóann at Brú na Bóinne. We will explore this conception in more detail in Chapter 10.

Bóann (also Bóand or Bóinn) is the archetypal mother goddess, whose mythology and symbolism echoes up and down the Boyne and its valley, from source to sea. She is a creator and life-giver, an earth mother and a sky goddess all in one. Her name is from *Bó Finne*, the bright or illumi-

A depiction of Bóann by Jane Brideson.

nated cow, and there can be no doubt that the cosmology of her lore sees her as a moon and Milky Way goddess.[15] Newgrange is her great belly or womb, sitting astride the ridge on a vast promontory formed by a great loop of the Boyne river which bounds the megalithic complex of Brú na Bóinne to the east, south and west. The Boyne is named from the Irish *Bó Fhinne*, meaning 'white cow', and indeed it was seen as the earthy equivalent of the great river of the sky, the Milky Way, which was known in Irish as *Bealach/Bóthar na Bó Finne*, the Way or Track of the White Cow.

There is a connection too with gestation and pregnancy. The gestation period of the cow – and the human – is almost exactly nine and a half synodic lunar months.[16] In Sanskrit literature, sacred rivers are seen as milk flowing from a mystical cow. And in the early Irish literature, a person who drank water from the Boyne was said to become a seer-poet.[17] Bóann is the wife of Nechtain, also known as Nuadu, but curiously it is the Dagda who impregnates her with the miracle child Aonghus, of which we will speak more in the next chapter.

The Tuatha Dé Danann are generally held to be Celtic deities, from a time much later than Newgrange. The western migration of the Celtic culture eventually brought settlements to Ireland, as early as the fifth century BC, where the newcomers encountered the great megalithic remains which had been built at least two and a half millennia earlier. It is said that the incoming Celtic communities learned about the importance of these sites from the locals and, 'using their own imagination, the newcomers associated the structures with mystical otherworld beings'.[18] In this scenario, all of the stories of the Tuatha are imports, and the original myths – if there were any – are either lost, or, at best, mingled with the deities of the European newcomers.

But we must be missing part of the picture. A significant case was made in *Island of the Setting Sun* that the cosmology of some of the Tuatha Dé Danann stories relates to the Neolithic. The supposedly later Celtic mythology seems to describe cosmic events of earlier times. Did the Celtic incomers merely adapt the existing myths to their own tastes? Is there something in the Tuatha Dé Danann tales that is a true echo of the original Neolithic mythology?

If we accept that Dagda is a sun deity, and that Newgrange is the womb/uterus of Bóann, the cosmic intercourse of the Winter Solstice makes great sense. Aonghus, their offspring, had taken the form of a swan for his swan maiden lover, Caer, and the great swan constellation of the sky, which is cross-shaped, was thus transferred into the cruciform-shaped Newgrange chamber. The architecture of the Neolithic echoed the cosmology of the Neolithic.[19] How much of this could have been known in Celtic Iron Age times, when the true nature and function of Newgrange could not have been discerned, owing to its passage and chamber being completely blocked up?

The sacred eminence attached to Newgrange throughout the ages is something of a quandary in light of the cairn collapse. Why, for instance, were Roman offerings of 'high value' deposited at Newgrange during the early centuries AD? Fourth century gold coins and pendants, along with four third century coins and even two first century coins were found at Newgrange during excavations, either on the mound or near the Great Circle. The largest concentration of coins was outside the three standing stones opposite the entrance.[20] It is obvious from all this that the entrance and kerb were covered over during this late Iron Age period. The earliest Roman coin dated to 81 AD.[21]

The exceptional value of the Roman offerings indicates the high reverence surrounding Newgrange. How had this reverence been kept alive over the period of three millennia from the time Newgrange had collapsed and been abandoned to the visit of the Roman pilgrims? The answer, according to archaeologists, lies in the ancient legends:

> It is difficult to imagine stories being passed down about a place for over seven hundred generations, but how else can the maintenance of the special place accorded to Newgrange right into the historic period be explained?[22]

Professor O'Kelly agreed that the Irish myths were bound by a 'Celtic strait-jacket'.[23] In his time at Newgrange, archaeological dating techniques had shown the monument to be a thousand years older than had

Some of the Roman coins found during excavations at Newgrange by Professor O'Kelly.

been thought, and he wondered whether a similar 'lengthening of per-spective' was overdue in relation to the myths:

> One cannot help feeling that the richly accoutred warriors of the
> Irish Bronze Age are far more convincing prototypes for the dra-
> matis personae of the Irish heroic cycle than the shadowy figures
> revealed by archaeology for the centuries immediately before
> and after the start of the Christian era. If this were the case it
> would not only free a great deal of early Irish tradition from the
> Celtic strait-jacket in which it has hitherto been confined, but
> it would also bring it nearer in time to the people who built the
> Boyne tombs. Can it have been they who planted the first seeds
> of Irish oral literature and should one begin to think of this not
> as a window on the Iron Age but as one on the Late Neolithic?[24]

The quandary of what was Celtic and what was older has been ac-knowledged for a long time now. Thomas Rolleston, writing in *Celtic Myths and Legends* in 1911, asked: 'Can we now, it may be asked, distin-guish among them what is of Celtic and what of pre-Celtic and probably non-Aryan origin?'[25]

When the Celts arrived, they found in Ireland a people who were al-ready intensely spiritual. Being a 'spiritually sensitive' people themselves, the Celts did not depose the beliefs and rituals of the indigenous popula-tion, but rather 'honoured them and gradually absorbed them into their own culture.'[26]

There is a story in the *Dindshenchas*, the book of place name lore, about a king called Bressal, who commanded the men of Ireland to build the great mound of Dowth. The story apparently dates to the Iron Age, and yet an interpretation of the cosmology of the legend clearly describes the astronomical function of the monument, which is contemporary with Newgrange and therefore much, much earlier than the Iron Age.[27]

What are we to make of the tradition that the Tuatha Dé Danann retreated into the mounds of Ireland – including the great monuments of the Boyne Valley – even though Newgrange has been blocked up since the Bronze Age?

Are the myths of Newgrange Celtic, or much older?

There are, in Ireland and Britain, stories of heroes who are said to be waiting to 'return to interfere again in the affairs of this world'.[28] John Rhys refers to these, and other legends in Wales of hidden treasure guarded by sleeping warriors, as 'cave legends'. This description fits the story of the Tuatha Dé very well. They may not be sleeping warriors guarding treasure, but tradition holds that they will return to this world from the *sidhe* at some juncture in the future. Their defeat by the mortal Milesians saw them withdraw from this world into the mounds, caves, barrows, hills and raths of Éire.

> The marvellous palaces to which the Tuatha Dé Danann retired when conquered by the race of Mil were hidden in the depths of the earth, in hills, or under ridges more or less elevated. At the time of their conquest, Dagda their high king made a distribution of all such palaces in his kingdom. He gave one síd to Lug, son of Ethne, another to Ogme; and for himself retrained two – one called Brug na Bóinne, or Castle of the Boyne, because it was situated on or near the River Boyne near Tara, and the other called Síd or Brug Maic ind Oc, which means Enchanted Palace or Castle of the Son of the Young. And this Mac ind Oc was Dagda's own son by the queen Boann, according to some accounts, so that as the name (Son of the Young) signifies, Dagda and Boann, both immortals, both Tuatha Dé Danann, were necessarily always young, never knowing the touch of disease, or decay, or old age.[29]

Indeed, it was also said that mortals could live in the world of the sidhe for ever, and that the Tuatha Dé Danann had the ability to 'take beautiful mortals whom they loved, and . . . confer upon them fairy immortality'.[30]

The retreat of the Tuatha Dé to the otherworld, through the so-called fairy mounds, is fascinating. They dwell there, says the folklore, in *Tír na mBeo*, the Land of the Living, 'a place of everlasting life, one of several distant lands settled by the semi-divine Tuatha Dé Danann after their defeat by the mortal Milesians'.[31] But the Tuatha Dé Danann are not regarded as being dead. They are very much alive in the otherworld, and there is a notion, expounded in various Irish literature, that they 'live on side by side with the human inhabitants of Ireland'.[32]

Further to this, a long-standing prophecy of folklore states that they will come out of the *sidhe* once more, at some time of great need or calamity, at some unspecified point in the future. In this way, the awaited return of the ancient gods can be said to be a messianic myth, and perhaps even an apocalyptic one. The stories of the awaited return of the gods from the otherworld are 'just one form of a very old and universal folk theme, that of the enchanted hero reserved for a future day of deliverance'.[33]

The story of Garrett's Fort at Hacklim, some ten miles or so north of Newgrange, speaks of a sleeping army underground, with Garrett, the eighth Earl of Kildare, at their head, waiting for the last great battle to ride out to win Ireland's freedom.[34] This Earl Garrett is confused in local folklore with Fionn MacCumhail, who is also said to have had a castle at Hacklim.

Tales such as the sleeping army of Garrett's Fort may be 'a memory of the tales of Angus Og and the other mighty lords invisible who are to come thronging out of Brugh and join Lugh Lamh Fada in his triumphant return from Tír na N-og'.[35]

Of course such tales might also have been the product of the imagination of the downtrodden, stories that stem from imperial oppression and the desire to be free once more. It is in this light that we can certainly view some of these narratives, which were no doubt woven during the long period of occupation by Britain.

Thus far we have seen that the divine Tuatha Dé Danann were considered gods, that they were immortal. We learned how they were defeated by the invading Milesians, and that they retreated into the otherworld, where they live on to this day. They accessed this realm of immortality by entering into the raths and mounds of Ireland, which we take to mean the prehistoric monuments, especially those with passages, chambers, caves or other subterraneous structures. And they will emerge once again from their paradise otherworlds, returning to this world in hordes, emerg-

Newgrange, the greatest of the mounds, was reserved as the residence of the chief gods.

ing from the passage-mounds of Ireland once again. The greatest of the ancient passage-mounds, Newgrange, was reserved as the residence of Dagda, the greatest of the gods, and later his son, Aonghus.

If Newgrange was sealed up since the early Bronze Age, as archaeologists believe, then stories suggesting that the Dagda and/or Aonghus reside in it are interesting because apparently no-one knew there was a passage and chamber in Newgrange since the time that it was blocked up, which we now know to be a period of roughly 4,000 years.

One author suggests that the tomb might have been accessible in the eleventh century AD, describing how at Hallowe'en, 'one Gilla Lugán entered the megalithic tomb of Newgrange in 1084 seeking oracles from the immortal Oengus Óc'.[36] However, the original source, Whitley Stokes' nineteenth century translation of the *Annals of Tigernach*, does not specify knowledge of a passage and chamber. The annals describe a great pestilence which killed a quarter of the men of Ireland, the cause being demons which came from the northern isles of the world breathing swords of fire, 'as Oengus Óc, the son of the Dagda, related to Gilla Lugan, who used to haunt the fairy-mound every year on Halloween.' Because the annals do not mention a chamber or tunnel, we can only suggest that the manuscript's authors assumed that there was one, as was the case with many prehistoric cairns and mounds.

Do the cave myths preserve an ancient memory, going back to the late Neolithic or early Bronze Age, that there is a chamber within Newgrange? And thus, does this mean that the story of Dagda and Aonghus is at least Bronze Age in date? Or was it that the chamber and passage have been open at some point in the past, between the Bronze Age cairn slip and the 1699 rediscovery?

Or it it just that the legends of the Tuatha Dé Danann retreating into the mounds are so widespread that the Newgrange story just became part of that tradition at some stage in more recent history? It is, perhaps, just a case that it is a 'good guess' that Newgrange is a passage-tomb, and that many unexplored mounds dotted around Ireland, as mentioned previously, may yet be found to be passage-tombs?

If that is the case, how come Newgrange retained the great significance it did during the long ages when it was sealed up? Even the archaeologists admit this is something of a mystery.

Over time, the great heroes of the Tuatha Dé Danann became diminished, their grand stature in the psyche of the Irish people gradually replaced with stories of the fairies, a diminutive and sometimes mischievous race who were also known as the 'good people'.[37] The fairies inhabited the otherworld, like the Tuatha Dé Danann, and simultaneously they were able to inhabit this world, although they were generally invisible to humans. They accessed the otherworld through their 'secret places in hills, in caverns, or underground' and, as discussed in Chapter 6, their folklore protected many an ancient monument from vandalism.

There is so much in common between the folklore of the fairies and that of the Tuatha Dé Danann that it would not require a great stretch of

*Newgrange and its sisters were considered the
sanctified entrances to a tranquil otherworld.*

the imagination to suggest that fairy lore is just a later incarnation of the
older cave myths.

> In oral tradition the story of the Tuatha Dé Danann's defeat and
> migration underground becomes a means of accommodating
> international fairy lore. The old divinities become the áes side
> [people of the fairy mound], invisible to most mortals at most
> times, Samain and Midsummer's Eve being the chief exceptions.[38]

The fairies are, there is no doubt, 'the discarded gods and diminished
heroes of the old native religion'.[39] It is somewhat ironic that, in the past
century, belief in the fairies has diminished to the extent that they are
hardly spoken of at all any more. The electrification of rural Ireland during the first part of the twentieth century seems to have been a major
contributory factor to the decline of the fairy faith. The fairy lights which
often described as being seen in the vicinity of a ringfort or rath were no
longer being reported.

At roughly the same time as fairy stories were starting to disappear, and overlapping with their gradual demise in folklore, came a rising interest in the Tuatha Dé Danann and the many characters and myths of Ireland's pre-Christian heritage, due in no small part to the Irish Literary Revival, led by such luminaries as William Butler Yeats, Lady Gregory, Douglas Hyde and others.

The lore of the Tuatha Dé is as rich and popular today as it as ever been. A Google search of the term 'Tuatha Dé Danann' yields over one million results.[40] It's almost as if they never left us, such is the fascination with their story. Their mythology suggests that they were not defeated as such, being allowed to live on in the otherworld by the Milesians, while at the same time ceding their power to these mortal newcomers. Their residences were the great Stone Age monuments including Newgrange, and countless other ruins around Ireland, which were considered the sanctified entrances to a tranquil otherworld. This otherworld was known by various names, as we have seen, and the Tuatha Dé continued to live on, not in some sort of dire purgatory, but in fact they lived in 'idyllic realms'.[41]

They never really left us, and nor were they ever supposed to. The Tuatha Dé Danann are considered by many to be the original gods of Ireland, the earliest divinities who watched over human affairs since the far-off days when we used stones as tools. No invasion – whether it be a purely mythical one, a religious incursion or a culture-changing imperial assault – could drive the Tuatha Dé Danann completely from the Irish psyche. They were not allowed to suffer the ignominy of a complete humiliation, being as they were both immortal and supreme. They were allowed to live on, our mythical protectors during the long years of occupation, both spiritual and imperial.

The *Lebor Gabála* speaks of various waves of mythical invasions, starting at the time of the great Biblical Flood, during which Noah's granddaughter, Cessair, came to Ireland to flee the coming deluge. Whether or not any of these invasions were related to real influxes of peoples from different lands, it is clear that Ireland has been under various forms of invasion for millennia. In the days of Newgrange, it was the influx of Neo-

Our monuments have endured the passage of millennia.

lithic farming methods and technology from the continent that wrought the first major changes in the social dynamic. Then, we are told, came the Celts, although their influence on matters spiritual and mythical cannot be fully ascertained. The Romans never invaded Ireland, although they did leave offerings at Newgrange, an indication of its sacredness, despite having been blocked up for three millennia. Christianity came to Ireland, apparently with Saint Patrick in the fifth century, and although there was never a military invasion from Rome, the religious and spiritual Roman invasion is something that has, up until recently, shaped much of the recent Irish story. The Norman invasion, followed by the Protestant English occupation, eventually saw the indigenous Irish deprived of land, of food and of dignity. During the Great Famine, one million people died, and another million fled these shores for the hope of a better existence in other lands. Even today, in the era of peaceful relations with our old enemies next door, we have ceded power again, to a new invasion, that from political and economic Europe. Will we ever stand on our own two feet?

None of these invasions could significantly diminish or undermine the most precious gift of the people of Ireland – our heritage. During all the long centuries that have passed since the lowly days of prehistory, we have retained many of our ancient monuments, a vast body of mythology and folklore, and the majority of our old place names, although anglicised in most cases, are still in existence today. That's not to say we haven't lost anything, for we have lost a great deal. Countless monuments were vandalised or destroyed, and it's impossible to know what stories have been erased from memory, especially in light of the fact that our most ancient myths came down to us from our early ancestors by word of mouth.

But all of the material which remains – that immortalised in the pages of medieval manuscripts, or in the books of countless libraries, or on the tongues of many rural dwellers who continue to propagate the stories of old – is tantamount to one of the greatest literary and mythic collections of any nation in the world today. The student of Irish folklore and mythology has enough material to keep them busy for many lifetimes, be it from the *Metrical Dindshenchas*, the *Lebor Gabála*, the Folklore Commission archives, the Ordnance Survey Letters, the archaeological journals, the *Táin Bó Cuailnge*, or the countless other sources which remain to this day.

So long as people kept telling stories, whether it be in hushed corners or in gatherings around the hearth, the Tuatha Dé Danann could never

The Tuatha Dé Danann are said to inhabit Newgrange
and other ancient monuments.

die. They were with us all throughout those long years when we might have felt abandoned or forlorn. They are part of our story, and our collective consciousness. While they were in their caverns and underground passageways, we were also, metaphorically, in our own caves, awaiting the coming of the light.

The survival of Newgrange down the cold centuries coupled with the endurance of the legends of the Tuatha Dé Danann is no coincidence. Today, under a barrage of assaults from various political, religious and economic forces, we seek the retreat of the fairy mounds for solace. Our revived interest in the dwelling places of the gods should come as no surprise. We wish to enter the sanctuary of the stone womb, to commune with and seek solace from our most ancient deities, and to re-emerge as children of light, ready to overcome any threat. That is why the Tuatha Dé Danann never died.

> the truth was not known beneath the sky of stars,
> whether they were of heaven or of earth.[42]

Kerbstone 52 at Newgrange may depict the belt stars of Orion pointing at Sirius.

10.

THE DIVINE CHILD

IN 1897, SEVENTY YEARS BEFORE Professor O'Kelly first observed the winter solstice sunlight illuminating the inner chamber of New-grange, a most extraordinary fictitious tale which appears to describe the phenomenon was penned by a self-claimed psychic called George William Russell.

Russell was one of those credited with the so-called Irish Literary Revival, which saw a renewed interest in the ancient heroic and mythical sagas and Irish music and culture in general. He had taken the pseudonym Aeon, the name of a mythical figure, and often shortened it to AE. In his story entitled 'A Dream of Angus Oge', no doubt inspired by the early Irish saga called 'Aislinge Oenguso', the Dream of Aongus, he describes in astonishing imagery and language what appears to be an experience of the winter solstice illumination of the Newgrange chamber.

> As he spoke he paused before a great mound, grown over with trees, and around it silver clear in the moonlight were immense stones piled, the remains of an original circle, and there was a dark, low, narrow entrance leading within. He took Con by the hand, and in an instant they were standing in a lofty, cross-shaped cave, built roughly of huge stones.

Aengus Óg, a painting by Jane Brideson

'This was my palace. In days past many a one plucked here the purple flower of magic and the fruit of the tree of life.'

'It is very dark,' said the child disconsolately. He had expected something different.

'Nay, but look: you will see it is the palace of a god.' And even as he spoke a light began to glow and to pervade the cave and to obliterate the stone walls and the antique hieroglyphs engraved thereon, and to melt the earthen floor into itself like a fiery sun suddenly uprisen within the world, and there was everywhere a wandering ecstasy of sound: light and sound were one; light had a voice, and the music hung glittering in the air.[1]

The character who takes Con into his palace soon reveals his identity. He is none other than Aonghus of the Tuatha Dé Danann.

'I am Angus,' Con heard; 'men call me the Young. I am the sunlight in the heart, the moonlight in the mind; I am the light at the end of every dream, the voice for ever calling to come away; I am the desire beyond you or tears. Come with me, come with me, I will make you immortal; for my palace opens into the Gardens of the Sun, and there are the fire-fountains which quench the heart's desire in rapture.' And in the child's dream he was in a palace high as the stars, with dazzling pillars jeweled like the dawn, and all fashioned out of living and trembling opal. And upon their thrones sat the Danann gods with their sceptres and diadems of rainbow light, and upon their faces infinite wisdom and imperishable youth.[2]

While the Newgrange passage had been opened by Campbell's labourers in 1699, it is highly unlikely that anyone had witnessed the solstice phenomenon before O'Kelly's time, mainly due to the poor structural condition of the aperture which had ceased to function because of the settlement of some of the roof slabs closest to the roofbox.

The reconstruction of this part of the passage did not begin until 1964. Up until that time, any light shining into the shallow aperture of the roofbox would have been obstructed by the sloping lower surface of the lintel known as RS2 (Roof Slab 2).[3] The passage orthostats upon which the lintels rested, with the help of some smaller slabs, had progressively leaned inwards over time, lowering the ceiling height and cutting off the light. It was only after O'Kelly's reconstruction work in the 1960s that the passage orthostats were returned to the vertical and the roofbox was able to function properly again, as it had done when the monument was first constructed.[4]

This adds further intrigue to Russell's essay about 'Angus Oge'. How could he have known about the solstice illumination of the interior of the chamber when it was not possible to witness the phenomenon taking place? Was Russell really psychic? Or was this just an embellished account of someone who had seen sunlight in the passage and not necessarily the central chamber? Or perhaps had he seen the sun shine into some other stone chamber somewhere, and assumed the same thing occurred at Newgrange? Russell later explained how the dialogue came into his head in the first place:

> To one who lay on the mound which is called the Brugh on the Boyne a form like that the bards speak of Angus appeared, and it cried: 'Can you not see me? Can you not hear me? I come from the Land of Immortal Youth.' And I, though I could not be certain of speech, found the wild words flying up to my brain interpreting my own vision of the god, and it seemed to be crying to me . . .[5]

There might be a clue to the inspiration behind Russell's vision of the solstice event in other works from long before the O'Kelly reconstruction. As long ago as the late eighteenth century, Charles Vallancey had hinted at the astronomical function of Newgrange. He wrote that the druids:

> ... directed their worship to Saman [the sun] in caves and darkness. Such I take to be the cave of Newgrange.[6]

In 1909, astronomer and Solar Physics Observatory director, Sir Norman Lockyer, stated that Newgrange was orientated towards the winter solstice sunrise, in his book *Stonehenge and Other British Stone Monuments Astronomically Considered*.[7] In his 1911 book *The Fairy-Faith in Celtic Countries*, W.Y. Evans-Wentz implied the same thing:

> It is well known that very many of the megalithic monuments of the New Grange type scattered over Europe, especially from the Carnac centre of Brittany to the Tara-Boyne centre of Ireland, have one thing in common, an astronomical arrangement like the Great Pyramid, and an entrance facing one of the points of

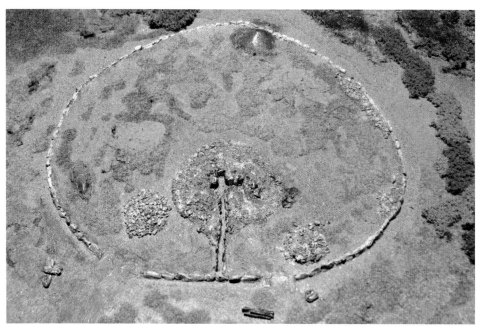

A model of Newgrange under construction from the Visitor Centre.
Its passage was orientated towards the Winter Solstice sunrise.

the solstices, usually either the winter solstice, which is common, or the summer solstice.[8]

Evans-Wentz had visited Ireland and Brittany in the years 1909-1910. There is no implication that he directly witnessed the solstice illumination, nor was there any evidence that either Lockyer or Russell had seen it either. And yet, during a period when the condition of the sunken passage ceiling could not have admitted light into the chamber, the winter solstice alignment was being implied, and, in Russell's case, described spectacularly in a visionary manner.

The ever powerful folk memory, which has preserved many an ancient tale and belief over the long centuries, was at work in the Boyne Valley too.

The American writer and world mythology expert Joseph Campbell had recorded a folk myth in the Boyne Valley which suggested the Morning Star, Venus, would shine into Newgrange once every eight years, as we saw in Chapter 4. Campbell cited this as a 'good example of the durability of local tradition'.[9] It has since transpired that this assertion of folklore is indeed true, and it would be possible for an observer hunched down on the floor of the central chamber to see Venus through the roofbox in the early twilight of winter solstice once every eight years.[10]

Before the reconstruction works at Newgrange, it had been said that there was a belief in the locality that the rising sun shone into the chamber and illuminated the three-spiral carving in the end recess of the chamber 'at some unspecified time'.[11] This was acknowledged by O'Kelly, before his reconstruction of the roofbox, but he claimed it was a modern tradition, 'or at least more familiar in modern times'.[12]

Could the same have been said for the legends of the Tuatha Dé Danann, the chief among whom were those who were said to have resided in Newgrange? The Literary Revival certainly helped to put the ancient gods back into the popular conscience. Writers such as Russell and Evans-Wentz, and a whole plethora of others, were restoring the prestige of the early race of deities in the minds of the natives.

*There was a belief that the rising sun shone into the chamber
and illuminated this three-spiral symbol.*

These popular writings were putting the names of the Tuatha Dé Danann back on the tongues of ordinary folk, if indeed they had ever left. Chief among the characters associated with Newgrange and the Boyne complex, as we saw in Chapter 9, were the Dagda, Bóann and Aonghus, who form a very early holy trinity of sorts.

Aonghus' appellation, variously given as *mac Óg, mac Óc, mac-ind-Óg, Óengus Óc* and so on, is commonly held to mean 'son of the young' or 'son of the youth'. But the word óg is not grammatically correct in this context. It has been argued that Aonghus' true epithet might be 'son of the virgin', *Mac na hÓige*, and that this may be a reference to the nature of his conception, being as he was the supernatural offspring of a miraculous divine union.[13]

Aonghus is the divine child, the son of a sun god father and a moon goddess mother, although Dagda and Bóann were not husband and wife. Bóann's husband was Elcmar, also known as Nuadu Airgetlám, Nuadu of the Silver Arm. The Dagda desired Bóann, and thus sent Elcmar on a journey which seemed to last just a day and a night but in reality lasted nine months, during which time The Dagda became Bóann's lover and they conceived the child Aonghus. Elcmar returned from his journey, knowing nothing of the miraculous birth. In one version of the tale, Bóann then asked Elcmar to become Aonghus's foster father, 'as a means of hiding the adultery from her usual husband, Nechtan'.[14] Aonghus thus becomes the prehistoric antecedent of the universal Son of the Virgin, Jesus, and his story describes an immaculate conception in which he was 'begotten at the beginning of a day and born between that and the evening'.[15]

One author says that the story of Dagda, Bóann and Aonghus represents the 'Myth of the Eternal Return'.[16] Sean Ó Duinn says that at the winter solstice, Dagda and Bóann mate, and overnight the young son, Aonghus, is born. Aonghus represents the young, growing sun, whose power and strength grows with the length of day. When summer solstice arrives on June 21, Aonghus realises that he is no longer youthful. As the year wanes from summer to winter, Aonghus Óg becomes the father figure, the Dagda, the old sun god. And inevitably, Dagda reaches the final day, winter solstice, again, and 'the process of alternation proceeds for ever and ever'.[17]

While it was the Dagda who originally resided in Newgrange, it was his son Aonghus who eventually became its owner, after dispossessing his own father by tricking him out of his tenure. The mythology suggests that the Dagda was responsible for distributing the various *sídhe* among the Tuatha Dé Danann, but that the young Aonghus was absent when the allocations were being made. Upon returning, Aonghus demanded a *sídh* but his father had to tell him there were none left. Aonghus begged his father to allow him stay in 'the sídh of Brugh-na-Boyne (Newgrange) for a day and a night'.[18] The Dagda agreed, but when the day and night had passed, he found, upon reminding the boy his time was up, that Aonghus refused to budge. Aonghus gave the logic behind his refusal:

> He had been granted, he claimed, day and night, and it is of days and nights that time and eternity are composed; therefore there was no limit to his tenure of the sídh.[19]

While such logic might not satisfy a similar claim to rights today, nonetheless Dagda ceded Newgrange and 'abandoned the best of his two palaces to his son, who took possession of it'.[20]

At this point the Dagda fades from the limelight, and although the Tuatha Dé Danann hold a council to elect a new ruler, Aonghus is not among the candidates. Elected as the new leader is Bodb Dearg, Bodb the Red, who is said variously to be either a good friend of, or the eldest son of Dagda.[21] Aonghus shuns the responsibilities of king in favour of a life of freedom, and soon falls in love with a mysterious maiden who appears to him in a dream.

An account of the love sickness of Aonghus is beautifully told in an ancient story called *Aislinge Oenguso*, the 'Vision or Aonghus', a story preserved in a sixteenth century manuscript in the British Library.

A mysterious woman appeared to Aonghus in a dream. He tried to embrace her but as he put his arms around her, she disappeared. During the next day, Aonghus refused to eat, and the following night, the mysterious maiden appeared again, playing music and singing to him. The day after that, Aonghus fasted again.

That's how it went for a whole year, with Aonghus fasting and wasting away with love sickness. The Tuatha Dé Danann physicians warned that his ailment could prove fatal. Aonghus called for his mother, Bóann, and told her of his plight, imploring her to help him. She in turn begged The Dagda to help find the dream maiden, lest Aonghus languish away for her love and become sick beyond the help of the Tuatha Dé Danann magicians and healers.

Dagda enlisted the help of Bodb the Red, the new king of the Tuatha Dé,[22] who in turn enlisted the assistance of other gods in the search for the maiden. Eventually, after a whole year had passed, the disconsolate Aonghus received word that the maiden had been sighted, at the side of a lake known as Dragon's Mouth, in Tipperary.

The mystery maiden was revealed by Bodb as Caer Iobharmhéith, an otherwordly maiden whose residence was Sídh Uamhain in Connacht. Caer's father, Eathal Anbhuail, revealed to the Dagda that his daughter was a swan maiden, who took the form of a swan every year when summer was over.

> But, refusing to be thus put off, Angus waited in patience until the day of the magical change, and then went down to the shore of the lake. There, surrounded by thrice fifty swans, he saw Caer, herself a swan surpassing all the rest in beauty and whiteness. He called to her, proclaiming his passion and his name, and she promised to be his bride, if he too would become a swan.[23]

Aonghus agreed and they embraced before flying around the lake three times and then they flew together as swans to Brug na Bóinne, where the story says they put the dwellers of that place to sleep with their enchanted singing. Caer remained with Aonghus at Newgrange after that.

The story has a fascinating cosmology, as revealed in *Island of the Setting Sun*. The magnificent swan constellation of the heavens, which we know today as Cygnus, dominates the northern hemisphere of the sky, and has done since time immemorial. This great swan of the heavens is embedded in the glittering array of stars which form the cosmic river,

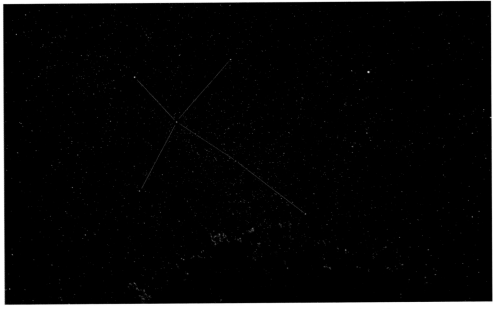

The constellation Cygnus, the swan, is cross-shaped,
like the chamber of Newgrange.

the Milky Way. It could be said the swan appears to glide down the river in stellar flight.

The Aonghus-Caer love story was no doubt inspired by the cosmos. The passage and chamber of Newgrange form a cross, just like the great swan constellation. Furthermore, the passage points in the direction of another small passage-tomb some 15 kilometres southeast of Newgrange, called Fourknocks. The passage of Fourknocks in turn is oriented towards the far north eastern horizon, where the bright star of Cygnus, which we call Deneb but which probably had a different name in ancient Ireland, would have been rising after a brief scrape along the horizon during the Neolithic period.

Further to this is the fact that Newgrange is, and probably has been since ancient times, an important wintering ground for the whooper swan, which arrives into Ireland from Iceland in great numbers every October. The number of whooper swans at Newgrange regularly exceeds 50, and they winter here along the floodplains of the Boyne until March, when they make the journey back to Iceland.

Aonghus was the divine child, the 'son of the virgin', the supernatural offspring of a union of sun father and moon mother, born as the result of an immaculate conception of sorts. His symbol was the cross, copied from the sky into the architecture of Newgrange, which was his abode. These are certainly characteristics that mark him out as a prehistoric forerunner to Jesus.

Many connections have already been explored between the Boyne river and the Milky Way, and it has been suggested that the milky white quartz which fronts Newgrange might have represented the great starry band of heaven, which, at the time Newgrange was built, could be seen to sit on the entire horizon from north to east to south to west and back to north again, something it does not do today due to the wobble of precession.

In the story of Aonghus and Caer, we are told that when Aonghus found his mystery dream maiden at the shore of Dragon's Mouth Lake, she was in the company of 'thrice fifty' maidens all linked together by a 'silver chain',[24] and Caer herself was adorned with a silver necklace. Is this the silver chain of the Milky Way, the silver chain that Lugh Lámhfhada wore around his neck?

The northern area of the sky containing Cygnus and other constellations which were circumpolar – that is, they never set below the horizon – might have held a special significance as the 'final resting place of the soul of human beings'.[25] *Cygnus Mystery* author Andrew Collins thinks this area of the sky has been sacred since the earliest times:

> Today we can accept that there was once a worldwide proliferation of interest in Cygnus as a symbol of cosmic life and death. What is more, situated at the northern extreme of the Milky Way – universally seen as an astral road or river to the sky-world – it marked the entrance to the realms of light, the abode of the gods and the place of the afterlife, a belief that could well go back to Palaeolithic times.[26]

Did the people who built Newgrange see the majestic whooper swans depart from the valley each spring, and think perhaps that they were transporting the souls of the deceased to the land of the living in the northern regions of the sky?

> Folklore frequently describes the newly-born baby as having been brought by the stork/swan from the otherworld and presented to

A flock of whooper swans not far from Newgrange in December 2009.

the new mother and similarly, at death, the soul is often depicted as making its exit from the mouth of the dying person as a bird and taking off on its flight to the Otherworld.[27]

The story of Aonghus is interesting. He shuns power, instead seeking the love of a mysterious dream lady. He is miraculously born of an illicit union in which a spell is cast upon his father so he knows nothing of what has taken place. He takes the form of a swan and lives in Newgrange with his swan lover, Caer. He is known as 'Mac ind Oc, *Mac na hÓige,* the son of the virgin, whose symbol is the cross, the prehistoric crucifix, immortalised on the ground by the shape of the Newgrange chamber, and in the sky by the arrangement of stars which we know today as Cygnus, the swan. The celebration of the new sun/new son at Newgrange takes place at Winter Solstice, the ancient Christmas.

In his wide-sweeping look at pagan and Christian beliefs, Edward Carpenter[28] examined the deities of the Mediterranean and wider area in the centuries up to the time of Christ, and found several common attributes which are of interest to our assessment of Aonghus. The deities of the Greeks, Romans, Persians, Syrians, Phrygians, Egyptians, Babylonians and Carthaginians had ten shared attributes, of which we will list those most relevant to Aonghus:

* ***They were born on or very near Christmas Day.***[29] Although the myths do not explicitly state that Aonghus was born on the Winter Solstice, which is the prehistoric festival tied most closely with Christmas, it is nevertheless implied. The mating of the Dagda/light shaft/ phallus with Bóann/womb-tomb/vulva at the solstice creates the new sun/son, and the Neolithic holy trinity comes into being. It differs from the Christian Holy Trinity in that there is a female present. The mother figure is absent from the Christian Trinity which is made up of father, son and holy spirit. In Catholicism, Mary the mother of God is outside of the trinity, although she is viewed as a co-redemptrix alongside Jesus. In the Neolithic trinity, Bóann is an intrinsic element, and in some ways the prehistoric trinity is a more natural one, reflecting the reality of human family, where new life is created with the coming together of a man and a woman, father and mother.

* ***They were born of a Virgin-Mother***. Aonghus is the *Mac ind Oc*, the Son of the Virgin, created in a mystical and magical union of the Dagda and Bóann. His gestation in the womb of the divine mother is made by magic to last just one day, and his real father, Elcmar, who is akin to the Joseph of the biblical story, is unaware of the passage of nine months. While Joseph is told explicitly by God what has happened to Mary, the truth about Aonghus is concealed from Elcmar, who, in one version of the myth, is asked to become the child's foster father.[30]

* ***[They were born] in a Cave or Underground Chamber***. This needs little explanation, other than to say that Newgrange is both a cave, albeit manmade, and an underground chamber.

* ***They were, however, vanquished by the Powers of Darkness***. As one of the Tuatha Dé Danann, Aonghus and his kin were vanquished by the Milesians, who had come to Ireland from Spain to take the country from the ruling gods. As to whether we could describe the Milesians as the powers of darkness is a subjective matter. They were driven here by a jealous longing for Ireland, which they had confused with the 'clouds of heaven'[31] and which was described as a beautiful country: 'From the setting to the rising sun there is no better land'.[32] Although some of the Tuatha Dé Danann were said to have been killed by the Milesians,[33] the majority retreated to the otherworld, into the barrows and cairns, and thus 'the world is divided in two, the surface going to the ordinary, mortal Milesians and their progeny while the Tuatha Dé live underground . . .'[34]

* ***And descended into Hell or the Underworld***. The invisible realms into which the Tuatha Dé Danann retreated can hardly be described as hell, especially as they were portrayed as 'living in idyllic realms'.[35] The *sídh* were seen as gateways to the otherworld, so the Tuatha Dé had to descend into the earth before accessing the realms of *Tír na mBeo*, the

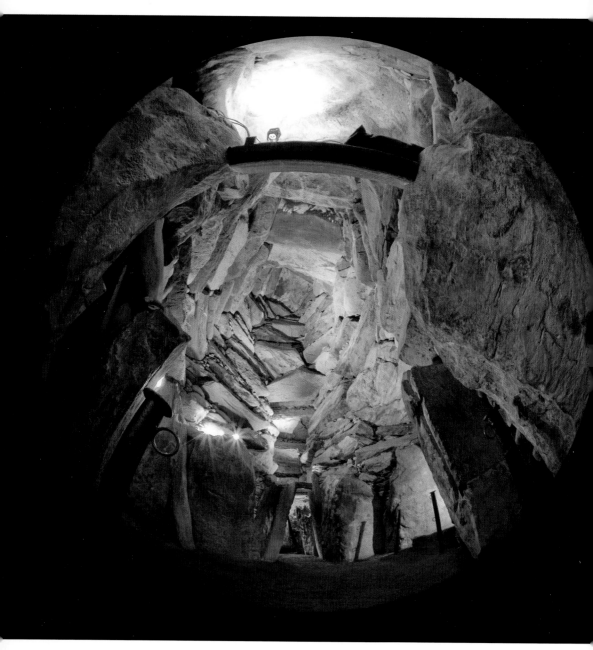

Aonghus, like many early gods from around Europe,
was born in a cave or underground chamber.

Land of the Living. It has been said of the Tuatha Dé that they have the
power of *féth fiada*, a magical mist or veil, which enables them to wander at will through this world without being seen by ordinary mortals.

180

* *They rose again from the dead, and became the pioneers of mankind to the Heavenly world*. Aonghus and the Tuatha Dé never died according to popular folklore, and have lived on in their *sídh* since defeat by the Milesians. They reside in the otherworld, beyond the sight and sound of ordinary humans, but it could be said that they are indeed pioneers of mankind to the heavenly world.

There are other aspects of Aonghus and his companions that are similar to the Biblical stories. There is a messianic aspect to the story of the Tuatha Dé Danann, which was explored in Chapter 9. Like Jesus, they are prophesised to return at some point in the future, to save humankind from some great tribulation. While Jesus died and was later resurrected, Aonghus and the Tuatha Dé were never thought to have died in the first place. Jesus emerged from the stone tomb after three days, perhaps a structure akin to Newgrange, and a giant stone was rolled away from the entrance. Such a door stone is present at Newgrange, one probably intended to seal off the passage and chamber either during sacred ceremonies or perhaps afterwards. Like Jesus, Aonghus will, according to prophecy, some day emerge from the stone tomb. Indeed, he has done in the past, according to legend: 'And as to Angus Og, son of the Dagda, sometimes he would come from Brugh na Boinn and let himself be seen upon the earth.'[36]

Aonghus is not the only miracle child whose conception occurs magically at Newgrange. The child Sétanta, who later became Cúchulainn, the warrior hero of the *Táin Bó Cuailnge* epic, is said to have been conceived at Brú na Bóinne through a magical union, again involving birds, most likely swans.

Deichtine (also known as Deichtire), the sister of Conchobar mac Nessa, the King of Ulster, was getting married to Sualtam, an Ulster chief. At the wedding feast she unwittingly swallowed a may fly which had landed in her cup of wine. Later that afternoon, Deichtine fell into a deep sleep, and in her dream Lugh Lámhfhada appeared to her, and related how it was he whom she had swallowed. Deichtine later disappeared with 50 other maidens. The Ulstermen spent three years seeking the vanished ladies without success. Eventually, Deichtine and the maidens returned to Emain Macha, the capital of the Ulster kingdom, in the form of a flock of birds, where they proceeded to destroy all the crops and laid waste to the vegetation there. This greatly vexed the Ulstermen, who decided to harness nine chariots to drive away the birds. The birds were driven off the plains of Emain Macha but lead the hunting party eventually to New-grange, the magic mound of Aonghus, overlooking the Boyne.

At Brug na Bóinne they encountered a grand palace and a handsome man who was accompanied by fifty maidens, and there was a great feast laid on for the Ulster warriors. The man was later revealed as Lugh Lám-hfhada and the maidens were Deichtine and her consorts. During the night, the warriors heard the sound of a new-born child, who was later revealed as Sétanta.

There are various adaptations and variations of this story, which differ either slightly or perhaps more significantly in certain particulars, and in Thomas Kinsella's translation of the *Táin* the episode where Deichtine swallows a tiny creature in a drink comes after the birds are driven to Brú na Bóinne.[37]

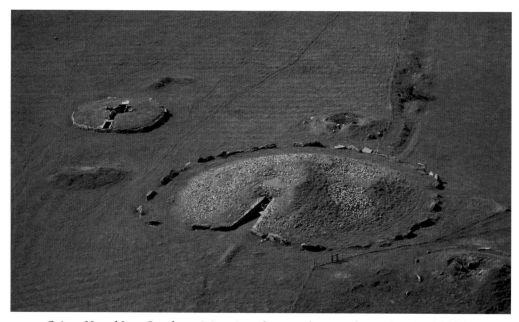

Cairns H and L at Carnbane West, Loughcrew. The cruciform chamber of Cairn H shows that the cross was a sacred symbol in Ireland long before Christianity.

The details which remain constant can be summed up as follows: A flock of birds is driven from Emain Macha to Newgrange at winter time, and Deichtine becomes the mother of the supernatural boy hero Sétanta through a miraculous conception by the Tuatha Dé Danann god Lugh Lámhfhada, also known as Lugh mac Ethnenn.

> She slept that night and dreamed that a man came toward her and spoke to her, saying she would bear a child by him – that it was he who had brought her to the Brug to sleep with her there, that the boy she had reared was his, that he was again planted in her womb and was to be called Sétanta, that he himself was Lug mac Ethnenn . . .[38]

We can surmise that the birds driven from Emain Macha, whether Deichtine was one of them or not, were in fact swans, because they are joined together with a silver chain, just like Caer and the other swans at Dragon's Mouth Lake.

> There were nine scores of birds with a silver chain between each couple. Each score went in its own flight, nine flights altogether, and two birds out in front of each flight with a yoke of silver between them.[39]

There are similarities in the stories of Aonghus and Sétanta/Cúchulainn. They are both conceived in miraculous circumstances of Tuatha Dé Danann fathers, one the Dagda and the other Lugh. Both conceptions are associated with Newgrange, and both stories contain references to swans.

But for all the parallels, the stories of Aonghus and Cúchulainn are otherwise in stark contrast. Aonghus is the young lover, who shuns power for romance. Cúchulainn is the lone warrior, who defends Ulster against the onslaught of the Connacht army quite murderously and viciously. Their tales may reflect the differing concerns of the times in which they were first told.[40] If the story of Aonghus does indeed go all the way back to the New Stone Age, which is not an implausible suggestion, given the strength of the oral tradition in Ireland, then it can be said that the fundamentals of the Jesus story – the virgin birth in the cave, the divine parentage, the connection with Christmas day and so on – were first devised at least three millennia before Christianity.

Aonghus was the archetypal son of god, who had as his symbol the great cross, and whose immense monument, Newgrange, was seen as a gateway to the next world. He was the prehistoric antecedent to Jesus, one of many, a messiah of ancient times. And, like Jesus, he is prophesised to return again, at some unknown point in the future. But there was no last supper, no requiem for Aonghus. For he lives on, in the magical abodes beyond sight and sense, the mythical realms where the gods and ancestors reside in eternal peace . . .

A mute swan on the Boyne near Newgrange. Mute swans are present at Newgrange all year long, while the whooper swans come here in October and leave again in March.

11.

INSIDE THE CHAMBER
OF LIGHT

THERE IS A GREAT PILGRIMAGE which takes place at Newgrange at the time of Winter Solstice. Hundreds of people gather at the monument to greet the dawn on the shortest day of the year. They come here no matter what the weather, and the vast majority will watch outside the mound when the sun rises while the select few wait and hope that the magic happens within.

This is very much how it must have been in the Neolithic. The chamber is not designed to hold a crowd, and any more than 15 people makes for an uncomfortable ensemble. Those who were within the stone vault were the special ones, the chosen few, while the greater community participated in whatever ceremonies were held outside to greet the dawn, and the coming of the new sun.

Today, if you wish to be one of the chosen few inside the chamber of Newgrange at winter solstice, you must enter a 'winter solstice lottery', held every October at the nearby Brú na Bóinne Visitor Centre. The popularity of this competition for ringside seats at the light show which is still happening after 5,200 years continues to grow every year. There were 31,500 applications for the lottery in 2011.[1] Only 50 names are drawn, ten for each of the five mornings on which the illumination of the chamber is open to the public. A reserve list is drawn in case some people can't make it.

Before the archaeologists came to the Boyne Valley, there was a very limited interest in the passage-mounds, or 'the caves', as they were popularly known in the area and in nearby Drogheda, from where many couples came to Newgrange, Dowth and Knowth for 'courting' purposes on a regular basis!

In those days, Newgrange was a sad shadow of its original glory. It was overgrown and forlorn, with huge trees growing out of its flattened mound, and cattle grazing upon its crown. But it held a mystique for many people over the years. Peter Kavanagh, a journalist and former newspaper editor, recalls an adventure to Newgrange when he was a much younger man:

> Since I was a boy I have always had a great interest in the Brú na Bóinne sites and can boast that I crawled into the Newgrange underground passage before the now famous 'light box' was discovered. I can thank my oldest friend Richard Martin, who now lives at Blackrock, for that great adventure, as it was he who first told me about that great prehistoric mound which was probably built over 5,000 years ago. This was long before the site was opened to the general public. He got the keys to a padlock that secured the entrance gate to the tomb from a nearby house and we only had the light of a bicycle lamp to illuminate the timeless wonders carved into the living stone. It required quite a bit of courage, mainly on his part, to enter that dark world but not as much as it did for the persons who first re-discovered the tomb more than two hundred years earlier.[2]

The O'Kelly excavations and restoration did much to broaden the appeal of Newgrange. However, for a number of years after the work was completed, the phenomenon that the winter solstice is today had not yet taken hold.

Archaeologist Elizabeth Twohig was at Newgrange to take measurements in the 1980s, when the solstice event did not have the popularity it holds today. Twohig was there 'when there wasn't nearly as much hype about it. I was specifically trying to check if the light beam was highlighting any particular carvings, so was more engaged in observation than the 'experience'. I don't think there were any, or only very few, observers outside, and the whole thing was quite low-key'.[3]

For a long time after the excavations, those who wanted to see the solstice illumination of the chamber had to put their names on a waiting list. This waiting list eventually grew so long that the authorities decided upon a lottery as the fairest chance of allowing people the opportunity to witness the spectacle first hand.

There is nothing low-key about modern day celebrations at Newgrange. There have been recent solstices during which a couple of hundred spectators have descended upon the monument, just to be there for the sunrise, to be present at Newgrange on the day, even though none of them were going to be inside the chamber at sunrise. Many people are content to stand outside the front of the monument and watch the sunrise over the hill of Red Mountain on the opposite side of the valley.

The Irish state broadcaster RTÉ has transmitted live footage of the event from Newgrange in recent years, bringing the phenomenon to a new digital audience around the world. Clearly, there is an appetite for Newgrange today that simply didn't exist up until recent times. For years, I have been one of the enthusiastic witnesses content to stand outside the mound at sunrise while the select few were huddled inside the chamber, waiting for the creeping sun shaft that sometimes arrives in glory and other times doesn't happen at all. There have been lots of solstices at Newgrange in recent years when the dawn was completely shrouded in cloud, but this generally doesn't dampen the enthusiasm of the gathered crowd, many of whom come for deeper reasons.

While I had always wondered what it would be like to experience the solstice illumination of the Newgrange chamber, I was able to imagine it quite well from all the photographs I'd seen in newspapers and on the internet over the years, and indeed from the many descriptions I had heard from those who had seen it first hand. In addition, there are other opportunities to see similar events, for instance the winter solstice sunset illumination of the southern passage of nearby Dowth, and the twice-yearly equinoctial illumination of Cairn T at Loughcrew.

In 2010, I was contacted by a British filmmaker, Grant Wakefield, who was working on a new film to be called *Ancient Skies*. I agreed to be interviewed at Newgrange by Grant for his film, which was to be shown in planetarium domes. Obviously, it was going to be a very special film if the imagery was to fill an entire planetarium dome. The topic was, of course, ancient astronomy, something close to my heart, and Grant was interested in hearing from the author of *Island of the Setting Sun*, a book he said he had enjoyed immensely. Of course, even at that time, four years after the book had first been published, I still hadn't witnessed the solstice sunbeam in the chamber of Newgrange. But all that was about to change, thanks to this enthusiastic and diligent filmmaker from England.

Grant planned to be at Newgrange at the time of winter solstice, to shoot time-lapse photography for *Ancient Skies*. But the weather intervened. The winter of 2010-2011 was one of the worst in living memory, with below freezing temperatures and heavy snow, something which

*British filmmaker Grant Wakefield and the author
at Newgrange in October 2010.*

is relatively rare in Ireland. Coming up to the time of the solstice, and knowing that he required to make the journey by road and ferry because he needed to bring all his equipment in his van, he knew it would neither be safe nor sensible to travel.

Knowing that photography was one of my passions, Grant phoned me to see if I would agree to deputise for him, as a last-ditch attempt to get some footage from the solstice, knowing that missing this one would mean waiting a whole year for the next opportunity.

I can remember the phone call. Grant explained how the snow was grinding things to a halt on the English roads, and it was looking like he would have to abandon his trip. But he suddenly started asking me what type of camera I had, and asked if I had ever done time lapse photography. I said no, but he explained that if the camera had an interval setting in the menu, it would be easy for me to learn. Very quickly he was talking about asking the Office of Public Works (OPW) permission to allow me deputise in his place, if I would be willing.

If I would be willing? As he spoke, the excitement grew within me. I knew he had permission to take interior photography at Newgrange, and that his plan would give me the possibility not only to be inside Newgrange on the solstice, but to be there on several mornings in a row. I jumped at the chance. Anyway, I love being at Newgrange. Some might think it a strange thing to say, but the place gives me energy. I always come away from Newgrange with a heightened vigour, as if the place allows me to plug into some mysterious cosmic energy. Given the chance, I would spend many more days there.

By 16 December 2010, Grant had agreed with the OPW that I would be his stand-in. I did not have the sort of camera equipment suitable for what he called a 'Full Dome' fisheye format, but nonetheless I had a camera capable of producing high quality stills, and for time-lapse sequences. Access was agreed for me on several days, starting on 18 December. That was a Saturday, which made things easier as I would not have to leave Newgrange early to get to work.

Newgrange covered with snow in winter 2010.

There were two spells of snow during December 2010. The first was early in the month, with significant snowfall on the east of the country, where Drogheda and the Boyne Valley took the brunt of the snow. We hadn't seen anything like it in over two decades. The second spell of snow occurred on the week around the time of the solstice. By 18 December that year, the first day of my photo shoot for Grant Wakefield at Newgrange, there was already snow on the ground, and it was to get worse day by day before Christmas. Of course, all this unusual weather gave us photographers a rare opportunity, to capture Newgrange and the other Boyne Valley monuments covered with snow, so the bad weather did have its up side! Another even greater boon was the fact that the snow meant I was going to be at Newgrange for several days.

Every year at the time of the solstice, the OPW allows those who have won places in the Winter Solstice Lottery to be present in the chamber of Newgrange. This occurs over five or six days centred on the actual day of solstice. Because the sun shines into the chamber on several days before

The author at Newgrange pictured just before entering the mound on Sunday, 19 December 2010.

and after the solstice, this allows for the phenomenon to be viewed on numerous mornings. Each lottery winner is assigned a specific day. If the sun shines on that morning, the lucky group gets to see the sun lighting up the chamber. If it's cloudy and the sun doesn't shine, it's tough luck, because the winning ticket only allows you access on one day! And then your only option is to enter the lottery again and hope for another chance . . .

I arrived early on the morning of Saturday, 18 December. It was very cold, and there was snow on the ground. I live on the western edge of Drogheda, just 4.1 miles or 6.6 kilometres from Newgrange as the crow flies, so although the journey was a slow one, I was able to get there in reasonable time without too much danger to myself.

On that morning, I was allowed permission to place my camera carefully on a passage orthostat not far from the entrance of the passage, pointing up the passage in the direction of the chamber. The idea was to get a sequence showing the sun lighting up the stones as it shone into the chamber beyond. I had to wait until the lottery winners were inside the chamber before placing the camera, starting the sequence and exiting the passage again. The whole sequence was shot over a period of about 20 or 25 minutes.

While the camera was clicking away inside, I remained outside, taking some shots of the exterior of the monument. There were about a dozen hardy souls outside. The sky was blue, streaked by high wispy cirrus clouds, and the air temperature was below zero. The light dusting of snow made for some beautiful photos of the monument.

The next day, Sunday the 19th, there was more snow on the ground. There had been some falls during the night and the valley was even whiter than the day before. This was the big day, and my moment had arrived. I was getting into the chamber of Newgrange to witness the solstice illumination – but only if the clouds didn't obscure the sun. Unfortunately, the

The tripod was left at knee height. Even with a
small group the chamber is quite crowded.

morning of the 19th was not as clear as the previous day. There was some cloud. I felt a deep sense of trepidation that my one chance to see this event might be spoilt by the Irish weather, and not typical weather either.

I was allowed to have a camera on a tripod in the chamber, as agreed with Grant and the OPW. I was worried that having the camera in the chamber clicking away throughout the event would detract from its enjoyment – for me and for the others, some of whom had travelled long distances to be there. Leontia, our guide that morning, was brilliant. She put everyone at ease. As is always the case when groups are being brought into Newgrange – whether on the solstice or any other day of the year – those who might suffer from claustrophobia are advised to enter the passageway last, so in the event that they have an attack of panic they can just turn around and walk out of the passage unimpeded. All of the other members of the group were brought in first, while I was advised to wait till last because I was carrying camera equipment.

Having been in the chamber of Newgrange on many, many occasions throughout the past thirteen years, I should have been fine with the whole experience. Yet I found myself anxious, and it was with a measure of trepidation that I entered the doorway of Newgrange with camera on tripod in hand. I knew I would be in there, in the chamber, in complete darkness until sunrise. Somehow that daunted me, even though I had been in the chamber in darkness on other occasions.

Thankfully, when I arrived into the chamber the lights were still on! Leontia had kept a spot for me at the rear of the chamber, at the threshold of the end recess, the one with the beautiful triple spiral symbol carved into one of the side stones. Having been present in the chamber on so many solstices, she was experienced at dealing with press photographers and their needs. I slotted into position.

At that point, I decided there was only one way I was going to be able to make the photography work without spoiling things for everybody. I would leave the tripod at a fixed height, at about knee level or slightly higher, pointed towards the passage. I had a shutter release cable with me which meant I would not have to keep getting down on my knees to

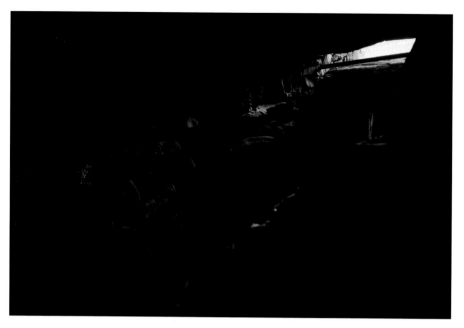

A view of the first glint of sunlight coming in through the roofbox.

operate the camera. Before Leontia turned off the lights, I focused the camera and left it ready to operate.

When the lights went off, my anxiety returned. I suddenly felt uncomfortable, as if trapped, stuck in this confined space with a dozen or so others, not able to see an inch in front of my face. Within a short time though, the ambient light reaching into the deep interior of the structure from the pre-dawn sky outside had begun to allow us to see, even if it was still very murky in there.

I found that I was able to operate the camera with ease, and without much disturbance to the gathering. The shutter is not generally noisy, although in a hushed enclosed atmosphere such as the Newgrange chamber, it does sound louder than normal. I could change a few settings on the top of the camera without having to hunch down, and was able to release the shutter standing up, with the cable release held in one hand.

Within a short time, we began to see light coming into the chamber. It was not a vivid beam of light, but rather a somewhat anaemic streak of pale sunlight that shone onto the floor of the chamber. Leontia explained that what we were seeing was the result of the sun being partially

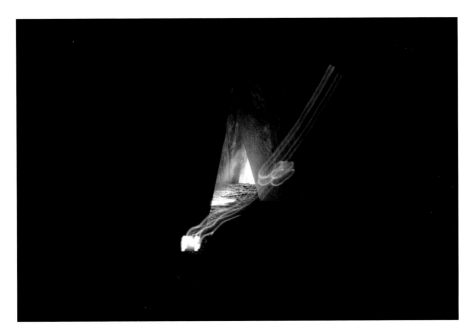

*As this exposure was taken, someone else was using a
mobile phone to capture an image.*

obscured by cloud. We were not seeing the event in its full brilliance,
nor were we thwarted completely by an overcast sky, as so many disap-
pointed lottery winners have been over the years. What was important at
that point was that we were seeing much the same thing as our remote
Neolithic ancestors had done, aeons previously, not long after these huge
stones had been hauled into position to create this wonderful astronomical timepiece.

Seeing the light coming into the chamber filled us all with a sense of
arcane warmth. Where initially I had felt uncomfortable and anxious, I
now felt calm and restful, almost snug, as if I had wandered off into some
wondrous dream. There wasn't enough light to set the whole chamber
aglow, but the real illumination was taking place within. I kept clicking
away with the camera, but my mind was in distant realms. I found myself
thinking about Lugh, and Dagda, and Bóann, and Aonghus, and long lost
ancestors and relatives who had lived in this valley in the centuries and
millennia previously and whose corporeal lives had been exhausted at
some remote moment in the past.

I might have preferred to be alone with my thoughts, and to have this moment to myself, such was its power. Some of the others in the chamber began using camera phones to try to capture the event. All this new light and activity did distract from the event somewhat, but I cannot blame them for their excitement. We were here, in the chamber of Newgrange on the midwinter dawn (or a couple of days before it!), just as our Stone Age ancestors must have been, sharing an experience which had been first encountered by people at this very spot more than 5,000 years previously.

A feeling of calmness came over me. I was completely relaxed. It was if the light had shone into my very soul, comforting me from some long-held distress. I had been on a spiritual journey, a long and lonely pilgrimage out of the bondage of my previous religious shackles, a journey which had lasted for many years up to this point. My wanderings up and down the Boyne Valley, to sites historic and prehistoric, Christian and pre-Christian, had imbued me with a sense that the religious foundations upon which my spiritual existence had been built were questionable to say the least. Here, at Newgrange, in the stone womb dedicated to the great cosmic mother, Bóann, I felt alive, invigorated, renewed. A rebirth

The sun at full strength shining through the roofbox on 18 December 2010.

*Tour guide and Newgrange.com website author Michael Fox places
his hand into the sunbeam in the passage of Newgrange.*

had occurred. I had become the divine child, born into the light of a new
spirit, a new self, free from the bizarre rituals of a foreign religion brought
to these shores from a distant Roman capital.

My struggle to find my own spiritual truth had begun in earnest in
September 2001, when the horrors of 9/11 drove me to the Bible to find
hope, and to find answers. In a world where such enormous dreadful-
ness could be visited by human against human, I felt sick, alone and in
despair. I suffered from acute depression at that time. In the pages of the
Bible, I found only contradictions, mystery and confusion. One question
only led to several more questions, with no real answers coming forth,
and with no feeling of succour at all. It genuinely felt as if I was moving
further and further away from the truth with every page that I read. After
some time – months and months – praying and hoping and struggling
to find my place in a spiritual spaghetti junction, I suddenly gave up.
Looking back at that time in my life now, it is obvious that I had realised
I was looking in the wrong place for answers. I stopped praying, I stopped
reading the Bible, and I started questioning everything that I had ever

accepted as being true. Needless to say, this period shook me to my spiritual core. Everything was stripped away. I was essentially starting on a brand new journey, and I became a spiritual initiate, a child in the eyes of the cosmos.

An intense period of investigation of the monuments of the Boyne Valley was well under way at that stage with my friend Richard Moore, which culminated in 2006 with the publication of our book *Island of the Setting Sun*. During that time, I became aware of what I refer to as the prehistoric 'cosmic vision' which had been realised by the builders of Newgrange over 5,000 years ago. The great monuments of the Boyne represented a grand endeavour, where science and spirituality combined on a massive scale to create these exceptional cosmic edifices. The people who created these structures were surely a very spiritual people, a community in touch with nature, the cosmos and the spirit world. How then, I wondered, could such a people be deemed damned and lost by Christianity, having lived before Christ and been unable to share in the everlasting glory promised by a profession of belief in him? This, for me, represents one of the single biggest contradictions of Christianity. If you lived before Christ, you cannot share in the afterlife. You are damned for living in the wrong time!

It was also during those years of research that I came to realise that Aonghus was a prehistoric Christ of sorts. His story might not have precisely echoed that of Christ, but there were several stark similarities, which were outlined in the previous chapter. Perhaps the story of Christ had always existed, in various forms, since the first stories had been told by human beings?

In the chamber of Newgrange on 19 December 2010, I felt no fear about thinking any of those thoughts, or asking any of those questions about my religious upbringing. I felt completely at home with myself. It seemed little wonder to me at that point how George Russell had once claimed that Aonghus was more real to him than Christ.[4] The stark truth, if I am able to express it without fear of reproach, is that Christ and Aonghus are equally mythical – they are both as genuine or as imaginary as

The sunbeam retreats out of the chamber down the passage as morning grows.

anyone wants them to be. The stories told by some of those who have died and returned to this world seem to suggest that faith is of little consequence to our ultimate fate. Colm Keane says anyone can have a near-death experience:

> . . . incorporating all cultures, races and creeds. Christians have them. Buddhists and Hindus have them too. Atheists also have them. Even those with no interest in religion have them as well.[5]

And some of those who come back from their encounter with the other side have no major desire to rush off to mass. Their experience transcends religion and belief.

Within a short time, the light was retreating from the chamber of Newgrange, withdrawing back down the passage. The witnesses began to file out of the chamber. I waited until last so that I could get photographs of the light in the passage, which I did. A short time later, perhaps only a minute or so, I was outside the mound in the cold winter air again. I met Clare Tuffy at the top of the steps. I told her I had communed with my ancestors. They might not have heard me, and I might not have heard them, but I felt I had connected with them, and in doing so, I had repeated a very ancient ritual, begun here more than five millennia previously. I hope those ancestors are happy now, in a new eternal existence. Is this not what every community of people hopes for those relatives and ancestors who have gone before?

The feeling of a rebirth or ascension to a new life is one that other people have encountered during the solstice at Newgrange. Dolores Whelan, a writer and expert on Celtic spirituality, had a significant experience in the chamber at winter solstice in 1986.

> Never having been to Newgrange before, I was very excited and went with a huge sense of anticipation. That morning, I had the privilege of being present when the sun entered the central chamber or womb, and I was allowed to take part in a 5,000-year-old ritual. I was completely overwhelmed and awed by the experience and knew that something significant had happened. Although at that time, I did not have the conscious awareness or the language to fully express what had taken place, some part of me knew that a doorway had been activated or opened.[6]

Maggie McDonald was present in the Newgrange chamber on winter solstice 1978, and described a sensation of being reborn during that event. Much like my own experience, Maggie found herself feeling uncomfortable and 'slightly claustrophobic' initially, and in the pre-mobile phone days of the 1970s, it was the spark of cigarette lighters that caused her to wish she was alone to experience the event. Seeing the beam of light on the chamber floor was a 'hugely emotional' event for Maggie, and one that was to live with her for the rest of her life.

> There is a sense of endless time inside the tomb, the entire world outside . . . seemed not to exist. I felt overwhelmed by a sense of being born again in a very strange way, and I felt extremely vulnerable and awed. It was almost as though we were inside some kind of time capsule and when we finally emerged from the inside, pulling tarpaulin sheets aside and avoiding the supporting structures of the restoration, I was actually disappointed

Looking up the passage of Newgrange in the direction of the chamber.

to find myself 'back in the real world' again. I actually found my-self wishing I could travel back thousands of years and leave the world I had been born into behind. The entire experience for me was almost a spiritual one, and stories of Messiah figures laid in tombs and rising again was very prominent and whirling in my mind as I tried to clarify and process my feelings and thoughts.

Inside the tomb was, for me, a place where death and life meet in the most highly symbolic way and yes, the experience had a deeply long lasting effect on me. So much so that I have spent many years since visiting the ancient sites and tombs of Éire in an effort to establish both an understanding and connection to those who have walked this island before me and who knew the skies as well as themselves.[7]

Artist Jeremiah Keogh had what he describes as an 'epiphany' when he visited the Newgrange chamber back in 1992.

As I entered the chamber I felt very heavy as if I was walking through thick bog up to my knees and I had to put my hands on the wall of the chamber to support myself along the passageway.

A beautiful image of the highly-adorned kerbstone 67 at Newgrange, on display at the Brú na Bóinne Visitor Centre.

As I reached the inner chamber I felt relieved and elated, and my mind took off on a wonderful flight of imagination. It was like stepping from the visible to the invisible worlds of ancient realms and all the stories of Irish mythology that I had listened to as a child came flooding back to my mind in psychedelic pictures. I felt an amazing thirst, both physically and mentally, and the experience opened up a whole new way for me to capture a dreamlike quality in my paintings. After this experience I went on to paint a series of Irish mythological stories.[8]

Not all those who visit Newgrange, either on the solstice or afterwards, experience any profound spiritual episode or rebirth. But many come away feeling a sense of connection with something arcane, something ancient, something liminal.

Martin Dier recalls being in the chamber on the solstice morning a number of years ago, before the introduction of the lottery system. It was cloudy outside and there seemed little chance of anything happening, but while huddling with the group inside the darkness of the interior, the light suddenly burst forth. The sun had found a gap in the clouds:

Suddenly the sunlight was on the floor of the chamber, fully formed, a vivid orange light with a radiance that bathed the entire chamber and the people in an exquisite, soft golden light. The guide said that if anyone wanted to place anything into the beam they were free to do so. With that the tension was broken and everyone started rooting in pockets and promptly several crystals were being illuminated along with wedding rings, a special poetry book and a photo of a loved one. People's hands hovered in this holy of holies. They were dipping their hands into the light beam with a reverential tenderness. There was a silence, an electric atmosphere and a palpable sense of the sacred. A sense that the spirits of those who had orchestrated the experience thousands of years ago were somehow basking in pure delight. There was a sense of arrival, fulfilment, completeness and joy close to tears.[9]

The majority of those who come to Newgrange on the solstice have to remain outside the mound, but many are happy to do so. They enjoy being present at the event, without necessarily having to witness the illumination of the chamber to feel a connection, as one visitor commented in 2005:

> I like to make the connection with all those who have come before me. It brings me back to my roots. For me December 21 is my new year.[10]

Few people come away from Newgrange on the solstice without having felt some connection with the past. There are some who fantasise, of course, about what their Newgrange experience means to them. Many of us have been guilty of an episode or two of numen-seeking in our visits to this sacred monument. Perhaps we go there seeking some sort of spiritual comfort, some sense of belonging, and a feeling that we are connected with ancient and cosmic forces. Maybe it is the lack of spiritual and divine fulfilment in our ordinary daily lives that drives us to visit such places. Whatever the forces that move us to visit this very special monument, they are largely benevolent and related to existentialism and the cosmos. Newgrange is a calming and benign influence on our minds and souls. In some cases, this influence is quite dramatic. In my own case, and in the case of others who have been in the chamber of light, it has renewed us, in a way that is difficult to describe.

I went there to commune with my ancestors. I felt at peace, and felt renewed. I no longer felt like a pilgrim on strange paths. On that winter's morning at Newgrange, I came home.

12.

WHAT CAME AFTER NEWGRANGE?

THE THOUSAND YEARS OR SO between about 4000 and 3000 BC was one of the most exciting periods in the history of the people of this island. In that space of time, people had evolved socially and technologically in ways that would change our system of living forever. Men and women who had scraped and foraged a delicate and burdened existence of hunting, fishing and scavenging for whatever morsels would keep them alive were, in a short period of time, bestowed with new expertise which would allow them to live very different lifestyles.

That was the era we call the Neolithic. Some might call it a period of enlightenment. It was the age of the megalith, during which men and women living much more sedentary lifestyles than they had done in the Mesolithic, turned their hands to creating vast memorials to the gods and the ancestors.

Monument building had reached a zenith in the Boyne Valley. Earlier, smaller, cruder passage-mounds towards the northwest – in places like Loughcrew in County Meath and Carrowmore and Carrowkeel in County Sligo – although beautiful and spectacular in their own right – paled in comparison to Newgrange and its sisters. As the builders progressed in their skills and the scale of their exertions, there seemed no limit to their capabilities.

The Boyne Valley passage-tombs represent the apex of this gargantuan temple building project. They were larger and more ornate than their predecessors, and the experience of constructing cairns on hilltops such as Knocknarea in Sligo and Sliabh na Caillighe in Meath – information about which was probably communicated down through the generations – gave the Boyne builders insights into engineering and construction methods which might have made the task of building Newgrange easier.

The Boyne sites were bigger than those in Loughcrew and Sligo, but they were not built on the tops of hills and mountains. And therein lies a crucial trade-off for the builders of Newgrange, Knowth and Dowth. They were able to construct larger monuments, containing much greater quantities of stone than previously, by virtue of the fact that they didn't have as far to climb. Even the fittest people today have to exert themselves to walk to the summit of Knocknarea or Carnbane East at Loughcrew. Imagine having to repeat this task many times over, carrying quantities of rocks and boulders!

Cairn T and Carnbane East at Loughcrew. Many cairns were built on hilltops.

Carnbane West, Loughcrew. The Boyne sites were bigger than those in Loughcrew and Sligo.

In any case, if the archaeologists are correct in postulating that the large stones were transported to Brú na Bóinne by sea and river from places like Clogherhead, the proximity of the Boyne would have been critical to the construction project. It would have enabled the builders to use larger stones than those used at Loughcrew or Sligo, and this logistical detail, combined with the increase in construction expertise over the generations, meant that Newgrange could be grander and more lavish than anything that had come previously.

But, just as they reached a pinnacle, when it seemed that there was no limit to what these incredible people could achieve with such primitive technology, the era of passage-mound construction came to an end. Newgrange was, it seems, the last great Stone Age structure to be completed. After its completion, it appears that the Neolithic astronomer farmers of Ireland laid down their tools. Precisely why this happened remains a major mystery today.

There might not have been an abrupt end to passage-tomb building. Some smaller mounds were built after Newgrange. These might have included a small satellite mound to the southeast of Newgrange, known as Site Z, and perhaps some of the satellites at Knowth. Conor Brady says there is 'good stratigraphic evidence to show that Site Z was built on top of material that slipped from the main mound at Newgrange'.[1] However, even though there are examples of smaller mounds that were built after the completion of Newgrange, they are few and far between, and there can be no doubt that the golden era of the passage-mound was coming to a close.

> We cannot establish which were the first Irish Passage Graves, although we can say with reasonable probability that the Boyne Valley tombs were not the beginning of the series but its zenith – after which came a period of comparative decline, represented by the Mound of the Hostages on the Hill of Tara, among others.[2]

As the Neolithic period drew to a close, and the Bronze Age dawned, there was a period where there seemed to be a considerable respite in monument building, and perhaps a more generalised lull in activity. This is not to say that the great monuments went out of use. There is evidence for later burials at Knowth, and none of the Neolithic mounds was destroyed, at least not to the knowledge of archaeologists.[3] But what happened to bring about the end of the great stone temple construction is shrouded in obscurity.

> . . . a general 'standstill' occurred in the middle of the third millennium, c 2500 BC. Archaeologists' reports from some regions sound more like a setback. Explanations differ. But the megalith builders slowed down. Tombs were blocked up and camps abandoned.[4]

In parts of England:

> . . . fields dating from the Bronze age that had been cross-ploughed for generations with the Neolithic ard, or 'crook plough', reverted to waste. Elsewhere, woodland returned to the valleys cleared earlier.'[5]

There are differences of opinion as to whether something similar occurred in Ireland, and in particular in the Bend of the Boyne. While the construction of passage-tombs and giant cairns ground to a halt, the creation of new types of monuments began, the only great mystery being when the tomb building stopped and when the new phase began. Perhaps they even overlapped?

It has been acknowledged that there 'is a relatively low visibility of Early Bronze Age material within Brú na Bóinne'.[6] So what happened at that time? Was there some catastrophe, an environmental disaster perhaps, that obliterated large parts of the population that had built Newgrange?

This seems unlikely. The new monuments associated with the Bronze Age included enclosures and timber circles, and also standing stones and stone circles. Some of the enclosures in the Boyne Valley are massive, particularly the one archaeologists ingloriously call Site Q, which is lo-

Bronze Age monuments included timber circles, such as this one immediately southeast of Newgrange, as shown in a model at the Visitor Centre.

cated some distance to the east of Dowth. At 175 metres in diameter at its widest point, it is an incredible structure, and one which no doubt required many hands to build.

The end of the passage-tomb phase, although the reasons for it are obscure, was followed by an apparent dearth of passage-tomb construction. But the lull in monument construction, if there was one, did not last long. Within a few centuries, there was an apparent revival in construction activity, although the monuments of the Early Bronze Age were much different to the enclosed stone vaults encased in giant cairns of stone which had gone before.

The areas around the passage-tombs, and most notably their entrances, became foci for renewed activity and outdoor ritual. 'Large ceremonial enclosures were constructed from stone, timber and earth for great public assemblies'.[7] At Newgrange, new monuments were being built in its immediate vicinity. These included a huge circle of clay-lined pits and post holes on the south-eastern side of Newgrange, which had been partly excavated by David Sweetman in the early 1980s. At 67 metres in diameter, this impressive structure consisted of several arcs of post holes

The so-called 'Great Circle' of stones around Newgrange were erected in the Bronze Age.

One of twelve surviving stones of the Great Circle,
pictured on the morning of Winter Solstice.

which had supported timbers and clay-lined pits where there had been intensive burning and in which were found cremated remains of animals. This curious structure, dating to about 2000 BC, has been compared to the Aubrey Holes at Stonehenge in England. The exact function of the site is not known, and indeed it may have had astronomical alignments, although this has not been investigated.

Other structures which appeared in the vicinity of Newgrange subsequent to the passage-tomb phase include the giant circle of stones which formed a ring around the mound. These stones, known as the Great Circle, were found to have been built on top of the remains of the aforementioned pit circle, and therefore the Great Circle was a Bronze Age construction, coming perhaps a millennium or more after Newgrange was built. There are only twelve surviving standing stones, but there might originally have been as many as 38. Curiously, the 'missing' members of the stone circle might never have been erected in the first place. There is a lack of evidence from excavation of the areas around these apparent missing stones suggesting that they ever existed,[8] so it is plausible to sug-

The Great Circle might not have been a complete circle.

gest the Great Circle was never completed, or indeed that it was never intended to be a complete circle in the first place.

An investigation of the Great Circle by Frank Prendergast revealed that the shadows of some of its stones crossed the three spirals on the western side of kerbstone 1, the entrance stone at Newgrange, at significant calendar dates around 2000 BC. The shadow of stone GC1 crossed the lower part of the three spirals at winter solstice, while the shadow of GC-2 crosses the spirals at equinox.[9] Other alignments were found. The prehistoric interest in astronomy and determining major calendar dates had obviously continued from the Neolithic into the Bronze Age.

Another feature to emerge in the era following the passage-tomb construction phase was the Newgrange cursus. This curious U-shaped ditch, which may have been some sort of ceremonial avenue, is located to the east of the monument.

If there was a catastrophe at the end of the Neolithic which brought the great era of passage-mound construction to a halt, perhaps it was a social or ideological event rather than one which impacted upon the population.

The U-shaped cursus is partly visible on the right
of this aerial image of Newgrange.

Conor Brady of Dundalk Institute of Technology suggests that perhaps the passage-tomb idea had run its course.

> We need to realise that the ideology over the passage-tomb period was not static. There is evidence in the art and the settings, the architecture of the tombs, that indicate that ideas were shifting and changing all the time. At the end of the period, new ideas had developed or taken root, probably due to influences from outside, from Britain and the continent. The time may have been ripe for a new idea.[10]

In fact, Brady says there are similarities between the passage-tombs of the Neolithic and the enclosures of the Bronze Age. Both monument types are circular, he points out, and burial is an element in both, 'as far as we know'. The move away from enclosed vaults deep within cairns of stones towards large outdoor spaces in the interior of enclosures suggests a more inclusive and democratic ideology had developed.

> Passage-tombs are enclosed and access is restricted. This may
> have served to reinforce the social position of an elite group of
> leaders or priests. Certainly, the whole population would not
> have had access to the interior. I wonder how many people did
> have access to the interiors at any time. Enclosures seem to be
> more democratic in that they can accommodate larger groups.
> The interiors have restricted visibility in and out. Their position
> in the landscape of Brú na Bóinne suggests landscape design on a
> massive scale – they are carefully positioned relative to each other
> and the earlier (?) passage-tombs.[11]

In addition to the above, there is some indication that the embanked
enclosures of the Bronze Age might also have been oriented towards significant astronomical events, just like some of the passage-tombs were.
For instance, Site Q has been shown to have two openings which are
aligned towards sunrise on the summer solstice.[12]

The cursus monument to the east of Newgrange is an 'intriguing element within the monument complex', one which suggests processional
movement, according to Brady. A number of similar possible avenues
have been identified on LIDAR surveys, including one at Dowth heading
north from the monument and another at Crewbane, heading west away
from Knowth.[13]

Brady is not convinced that there was any population decline, or indeed any lull in activity, at the end of the Neolithic and into the Early
Bronze Age.

Archaeologists are unsure when the construction of the enclosures
began. There are four earthen enclosures in the Bend of the Boyne, part
of a larger group of thirteen in the lowland river valleys of Meath which
have been studied and documented by Geraldine Stout.[14] One of these
encircles a satellite mound on the slopes to the southeast of Newgrange,
known as Site A. Another example, at Monknewtown, is the only one
in the area where archaeological excavation took place. A 1971 'rescue
excavation' found a good deal of Late Neolithic and Early Bronze Age
pottery and flint and stone tools.[15] Radiocarbon dates at Monknewtown
indicated a construction date of c. 1860 BC.

Conor Brady thinks it's possible there was some overlap between construction of the later passage-tombs and the earlier enclosures, and he does not believe there is any evidence for a fall-off in population.

> Certainly, after this period, there is less emphasis on the construction of grand monuments in the Brú na Bóinne area. This doesn't automatically mean a decline in population. Rather, the ideology shifted again to leave the area alone – perhaps where the landscape was preserved as a sacred area but without new monuments. In more recent times less visible monuments like ring ditches have been identified from aerial photography and geophysics, so people were still being buried in the area and were also presumably living there too.

Indeed, recent development has revealed what could be 'a concentration of Middle/Late Bronze Age funerary monuments' in the townlands of Oldbridge and Sheephouse, which would be outside the Bend of the Boyne, in an area which would be described as peripheral to the core Neolithic monument complex.[16]

Brady says that, based on his own work and glancing through various excavation reports from the area, there was no indication of a decline in population into the Bronze Age, during which period settlement is well represented. In fact, he says that the lithic scatter data suggests an increase in activity.

> The evidence as far as I can see doesn't suggest decline. The Brú na Bóinne area may have declined in importance during this period, it probably did. What we are seeing is a more 'normal' level of activity for a typical Bronze Age landscape in eastern Ireland. There are still people in the area – Hill of Rath cemetery, Keenogue, Slieve Breagh, Mound of the Hostages – but people no longer seem to feel that they must focus on Brú na Bóinne.[17]

Interestingly, Brady adds that the sacred and monumental focus on Brú na Bóinne wanes at the end of the Neolithic and in the Early Bronze Age. 'It is interesting to note,' he says, 'that all subsequent activity in the area from survey and excavation, related to settlement rather than large-scale ritual.'[18]

For reasons yet to be discerned, just when the community of the Boyne Valley seemed to be at the peak of their capabilities, and with three major passage-mounds completed and a smattering of smaller ones constructed here and there, some in the vicinity of the main mounds and others further away, they stopped building. It was as if, with the last stone at Newgrange in place, they had completed what they had set out to do. Granted, there might be a handful of smaller mounds which were erected after Newgrange, but by and large the project was complete. Was this how it was intended before they started? Did they plan to build only three main mounds, each serving slightly different astronomical, ceremonial and ritual functions? And thus, when Newgrange was completed, was their mission concluded?

Towards the end of the Neolithic period new forms of pottery were introduced to the Boyne Valley, and elsewhere. The first was what archaeologists call Grooved Ware, a style of pottery which was adopted from Britain, c. 2900-2700 BC.[19] The other was Beaker pottery, an 'important and novel ceramic style'[20] which was introduced shortly after 2500 BC. Both pottery styles were found during excavations at Knowth and Newgrange. Beaker pottery in particular is now strongly associated by archaeologists with the birth of metallurgy in Ireland. The Beaker phase at Newgrange can be categorised as straddling both the Late Neolithic and also Final Neolithic/Early Bronze Age. This is one of the facets of the archaeology at Newgrange that makes it difficult to discern when the Neolithic ended and when the Bronze Age began. The tomb building stopped, but life did go on . . . and even archaeologists admit that the lines between Neolithic and Bronze Age are blurred:

> . . . one of our difficulties in looking at the Late Neolithic is the extent to which traditions and practices continue into the Early Bronze Age and this indicates the reality that life went on. For the people involved there was no such thing as 'the end of the Neolithic'. We can see this reflected in the history of continued

episodes of use during the Final Neolithic/Early Bronze Age of sites that were first constructed in the Neolithic and in the continued creation of rock art. It is important to remind ourselves that this concept of an end to the Neolithic is an archaeological convention.[21]

The demarcation of the end of the Neolithic can broadly be said to have come with the end of passage-tomb construction, and the beginning of the Bronze Age can similarly be roughly marked with the appearance of bronze weapons and tools, and the construction of new types of monument. 'While there is continued use of certain passage tombs and a continued focus on the area of these earlier monuments, the change in monument styles is dramatic and may signal significant social developments.'[22]

With the Bronze Age also came new implements, most notably weapons, including blades and daggers, halberds and later spearheads. The relatively peaceful coexistence enjoyed in the Neolithic gave way to a society based on settlement, not ritual, and one during which the first

New types of monument, including embanked enclosures, were appearing in the Bronze Age.

major skirmishes over territory likely developed. It could be said that the Bronze Age was the period when mankind's troubles really began to manifest. Men and women declared ownership of lands and territories, and fought over these rights. As the Bronze Age progressed, more defensive structures were erected, indicating an increase in violence in society.

We should not necessarily paint a rosy picture of the Neolithic period either. There is evidence to suggest there were some killings in the Neolithic, and the perception that the Stone Age was an entirely peaceful period in which humans lived happily side by side is not entirely true. Forensic archaeologists have revealed evidence of violent assault and aggression during the New Stone Age, involving clubs, axes and arrowshot.[23]

However, it can reasonably be postulated that a society which built the huge passage-mounds of the Boyne needed to work as a unit and that, by and large, the community of the Boyne Valley probably lived together in relative harmony. There was a common goal, a cosmic ideal, to which they were all striving, something which transcended the banalities of their ordinary everyday existences and the petty squabbles

which they might have been caught up in from time to time. They were involved in one of the single greatest construction projects in prehistoric Europe, one which represented a confluence of spiritual zeal, cosmic awareness, memorial creation and the desire for transcendence to otherworldly realms.

Precisely why this incredible community achievement came to a dramatic halt after Newgrange and Knowth and some of the satellites were finished is difficult to comprehend. The societal and ideological changes which came with the Early Bronze Age no doubt contributed to a move away from the combined community effort required to bring such vast endeavours to fruition. But the relatively abrupt termination of the passage-tomb phase is hard to fathom unless there was some other dramatic change in circumstances in the Boyne Valley.

Perhaps, as suggested in Chapter 6, the great mounds of Brú na Bóinne were designed as very permanent landscape features, and therefore no more were needed to be constructed. If they were intended to last

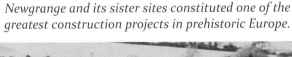

Newgrange and its sister sites constituted one of the greatest construction projects in prehistoric Europe.

through the centuries and millennia, and if the vast effort required for their construction had pretty much exhausted the community, maybe the time had come for the builders to take a break from their labours and enjoy the fruits of their endeavours.

Conor Brady says:

> At the time, I am sure they were considered to be very permanent statements on the landscape. The act of creating monuments is profound – it is an expression of ownership and control of the elements of the land, memorialising the ancestors. . . . [T]hey envisaged their way of life continuing ad infinitum, although there was also a degree of constant change. However, I do not think that they had the same concept of the future in terms of a technologically different world that we do today.[24]

Geraldine Stout, another archaeologist who has worked in and studied the Brú na Bóinne complex in great depth, suggests that the exhaustive effort required to build Newgrange, Knowth and Dowth and the many satellite mounds could not continue unabated:

> The people who created the tombs in the Bend of the Boyne were not conquered by a superior force, nor is there evidence that the construction of the tombs led to a marked degradation of the landscape. Most probably, the societal energy which resulted in the unprecedented outpouring of construction and artistic endeavour simply could not be sustained. The tombs, or the massive artificial mounds with the strange symbol-decorated stones as they would have been known to subsequent peoples, continued to exude a magic which maintained this area as a focus for ritual activity.[25]

Whatever the circumstances which led to the demise of the passage-tomb phase, it can be said with certainty that the world changed after that, and that it has been a very different place since then. The Neolithic marked a period of transition, from the time-intensive hunting and gathering lifestyle of the Mesolithic, to the more materialistic and territorial

Newgrange, one of the most impressive monuments in the world.

lifestyle of the Bronze Age which saw the rise of ownership of property, implements, fine jewellery and weapons.

Modern society owes at least some of its foundations to each of these periods. Ideologically, we all desire the freedom of the Mesolithic, where men and women could roam the riverbanks, the forests and the uplands relatively unimpeded, but with the benefit of a more readily available food supply, such as that offered by the new farming methods of the Neolithic. And we all desire the possession of property, and fine goods, similar to what was first enjoyed in the Bronze Age.

Newgrange, and its great sister monuments of Knowth and Dowth, are some of the most intriguing and impressive monuments in the world, and certainly the greatest achievement of human beings on this island up until recent times. Nothing that has been built in Ireland from that time up until the last century or two could match the uniqueness and impressiveness and the permanence of the great Boyne mounds.

We have been bestowed with the most incredible archaeological treasures, surpassing many of the great monuments of the world in age and in human endeavour. They are our pyramids, mysterious and ancient, wrapped up in arcane cosmology and the lost rites of a society obscured by the mists of time.

Now, with the advantage of a much more sophisticated technology than our distant forebears, we are investigating the nature of these giant structures, and trying to peer into the ancient minds that conceived them. That has not been an easy task. We rely on the material finds of archaeology to interpret long lost lives, but we dismiss the folklore and mythology of the monuments, and indeed the astronomical and cosmic alignments, at our peril.

There might be much more prosaic answers to some of the questions we pose about our prehistoric ancestors. There might yet be a simple explanation as to why they stopped building passage-tombs. But the mystery is part of the enjoyment, and revelation is part of the journey of discovery. And that is one of the common bonds that unites us with our hoary ancestors, for we are all striving for greater things. We are human, after all. We have our frailties and our faults, as well as our initiative and our genius. We all want to leave our mark on this world, and, thankfully, we all want pretty much the same things: love, peace, happiness and a long life. The ultimate goal of humanity is to achieve some certainty about death and the nature of the soul, some solace and comfort in the knowledge of a heavenly afterlife. This is what drove our ancestors to build Newgrange, just as it drove our much more recent ancestors to build the enormous cathedrals of stone, dedicated to the modern Aonghus and his divine parents. We want to know that our ancestors are safe in Tír na nÓg, and we want to enjoy the thought that some day we will meet them there, in eternal happiness.

13.

WHAT HAVE WE LOST?

There is a power, a force, a magic about Newgrange that defies the discernment of archaeologists and eludes the perspicacity of historians. It is a very ancient and eternal force, one which captivates the human spirit, and one that entangles the mysterious and austere aspects of the human soul with the unseen fabric, the ethereal mesh of the cosmos.

Lots of people who come to Newgrange today can sense this force. They understand that this sacred monument is much more than a neatly organised pile of stones. It is a place where the bewildered pilgrim, feeling a sense of alienation and detachment from the frenetic boisterousness and the incongruous machinations of a twenty-first century world, can come and connect to a different energy matrix.

It is patently obvious to anyone who studies Newgrange that its people possessed an innate cosmic wisdom, and that they maintained a worldview in which they appreciated the divine sense of the connectedness of all things. This is what we call 'cosmos', the divine and sacred order of the universe, and the 'cosmic vision' that is memorialised in stone in the Boyne Valley represents a unique moment in the human story of this island when men and women truly realised their place in the grand scheme of things.

A place of magical energy – bean draoí *(female druids) at Newgrange.*

The Neolithic might not have been the perfect era, and no doubt there were challenges and struggles, but if there is one period in the history of this island when we seemed to be setting out on the right path, it was the New Stone Age. A social and spiritual programme that would unify a people was put in place, with the agreement of all, and a community of human beings worked together and laboured long and hard towards a very noble and eternal cause.

The forces and factors that underlined the monumental stone temple construction project were undoubtedly many. Here was a people who wanted to give thanks to the cosmos, to the great forces of nature, to pay homage to the great mother who provided all that they needed, to celebrate the death of the old sun and the birth of the new, to assist the transition of the souls of their deceased to the next world, to immortalise and memorialise their ancestors, and to enshrine a unique moment in celestial time when very special things were happening in the heavens. And these are just a few of the factors behind the creation of these magical monuments.

The mystical energy of Newgrange, and other sacred ancient stone sites in Ireland, is something that is recognised by some, and derided as fantasy and hogwash by others. But who among those who have been at Newgrange on a solstice cannot say they have been instilled with the magical energy that permeates the very landscape? Is the notion of a cosmic energy, an unseen aura, a universal force, anathema to the modern logical mind? Was it purely scientific endeavour and curiosity that drove the builders of the great monuments to study intricately the machinations of the heavens?

> Perhaps it may be a bit too far-fetched – perhaps not – for Francis Hitchings to suggest in his book *Earth Magic*, that megalithic man needed all this astronomical and geometric knowledge to enable him to place the stones in a circle 'so that at certain key moments in the rhythms of the cosmos, his magical sites were imbued with a supernatural energy that renewed and enhanced life on earth.[1]

Perhaps one of the reasons we understand Newgrange so poorly, and the people who created it, is that we are disconnected from the cosmos today. We wandered far from the natural paths when we created territories and boundaries, concrete buildings, artificial light to banish the night, and all of the manifold technology which dislocates us from a cosmocentric world view and places us instead in the realm of individualism, materialism and cosmic ignorance.

A definition of cosmocentrism helps us understand what it is we might have lost on our journey towards technological and material mastery: Cosmocentrism denotes a:

> . . . way of viewing universal life and nature as more than just a backdrop to our lives, but as an integral part of who we are. It is seeing both ourselves and the source of life as being at one with nature... it is learning to live in harmony with the universal rhythms of life.[2]

A cursory perusal of various aspects of the design of Newgrange indicate a sense of cosmocentrism among its builders. It was constructed in the shape of a natural hill, so as to represent a part of the earth, with largely unworked slabs of stone, in a somewhat circular shape, which is a very cosmic form. It represents both the tomb for the interment of the deceased, and a womb for the rebirth of the soul to the next wonderful realm. It is oriented towards the winter solstice sun, when the great source of light and heat has waned to its weakest point, calling upon the sky's rhythms to renew the cycle of the year and to bring back growth so that the valley can become lush again with the fruits of the harvest.

As early as the Bronze Age, we began to lose our cosmocentric view. We began to make metal objects, including weapons, and we started to mark out the boundaries of our own territories. We started to place value on material possessions, and to become jealous of those who had more possessions than us. Our jealousies drove us to conflict, to skirmish, to battle, to murder. We were no longer the innocent children of the sacred mother earth. As we learned more knowledge of the sciences and developed keener skills in metallurgy, weaponry and defence, we saw that we could perhaps forge our own individual destinies on the earth without

recourse to the consequences for the future sustainability of our way of life and our planet.

This is not something that happened overnight. It had its origins in the Neolithic, when we stepped out of the forests and began the first clearances for farmland, but took hold to a much greater extent from the Bronze Age onwards, when populations began to grow to the extent that resources had to be guarded more zealously than before. In many ways life has continued in this vein since then, and the individual ownership of wealth and property – especially in a fashion that is so inequitable – can be said to be the cause of much modern conflict. There is a sense too that our technology, while advancing and enriching our lives in some ways, has led to us feeling detachment from real community, and of course from nature.

> Was the 'Primordial Vision' of the Ancients, in which they saw themselves as integral parts of the vast complex of the Universe, the great 'Health Design' now threatened by 'Alienation' in which man feels himself alone in the world, cut off from people and from nature?[3]

A view of Red Mountain from Newgrange.

In her wonderful and beautiful study of Celtic spirituality, *Ever Ancient, Ever New*, author Dolores Whelan alludes to this modern day alienation:

> We live in a society that understands little about meaningful relationships with the earth or with the many non-human species with which we share this planet. Our present way of living is creating a wasteland, not only of the earth, but within the human heart and human soul. . . . This results in a society that is out of touch with its mother, the earth, and so we are like motherless children, searching everywhere for a sense of relatedness and for a sense of home.[4]

It is interesting, in light of this pervading sense of estrangement with nature and disconnection from the sacred, that so many people are flocking to consecrated and revered ancient sites such as Newgrange. Although visitor numbers have been fluctuating in recent times due to global economic uncertainty and a serious recession in Ireland, up to a quarter of a million people will visit Newgrange in the space of an average year. Hundreds will turn up on the solstice, while tens of thousands more will enter the annual Winter Solstice Lottery in the hope of winning a place in the chamber on those special days of midwinter.

This fascination with Newgrange, and with other sacred centres, is a relatively new phenomenon. As Elizabeth Twohig reported in Chapter 11, even in the 1980s the solstice event was a low-key one, with precious few visitors. Undoubtedly, the archaeological excavations and part restoration of Newgrange spurred a growth of interest in the site. The publicity surrounding the solstice phenomenon in particular has been unrelenting over the years, leading to increased awareness of the sophistication of the monument. The opening of the new Brú na Bóinne Visitor Centre in the mid-1990s led to a greater ability to accommodate visitors to the site, and the capacity to bring people quickly and easily to the monument was increased almost exponentially. In the space of two decades or less, the number of people coming to Newgrange grew from a trickle to a torrent,

Many visitors are inspired by Celtic and prehistoric spirituality.

resulting today in the proud boast that a multitude of people – several millions – have been to the site to behold its wonders.

Coupled with the almost explosive growth of interest in ancient and sacred sites and monuments is the massive expansion of the so-called 'New Age' movement. Diverse movements and beliefs have cropped up, some inspired by Celtic and prehistoric spirituality, others by paganism and shamanism, and others still by druidism and witchcraft. There is a cacophony of spiritual voices in this divinely inspired fugue, and while many groups are peaceful and seek the betterment of humanity, there are some malevolent forces at work too. But generally, these are movements and groups of people who believe that the older forms of spirituality – mainly pre-Christian and therefore largely prehistoric ones – are purer and better than what we have today.

Personally, I don't fit into any one particular grouping or category. I am very much the spiritual pilgrim, finding my feet on a meandering path that leads – hopefully – from the darkness of the cave towards the divine light of Tír na mBeo. Spirituality is, for me anyway, a very personal thing. I do not feel the need to express it widely, to convert anyone, or to convince others of its merits. I feel no need to thrust it upon others. Nor can I precisely define what my spirituality or set of beliefs is at this moment in time. Right now, I am happy to continue the journey of enlightenment and discovery, and there is no doubt that Newgrange and the Boyne Valley have helped me on the way.

The Boyne river rises in County Kildare. Mythology says its source is Nechtain's well, which is today known as the Trinity Well, near the village of Carbury. Very close to that well, within a few feet, is a small bubbling brook, a tiny stream no more than a couple of feet wide, that can be easily stepped over. This tiny rivulet, this puny, insignificant and almost imperceptible flow of water, meanders and flows, and finds a cutting through the landscapes of Kildare and Meath, and grows and grows until it becomes the mighty Boyne, the great river flowing eternally beneath the great stone shrines of Brú na Bóinne.

The Boyne is a metaphor for the growth of interest in Newgrange, and the intensification of curiosity about the people who built it and their spirituality. It started in the eighteenth century as a trickle, and by the time of the O'Kelly excavations in the 1960s and 1970s it was still only an insignificant stream. Now, it has become a forceful torrent.

But while one river flows, another ebbs. There is a significant undercurrent to the growth in popularity of Newgrange and the surge of interest in ancient spirituality. And this is the spiritual, economic and political crisis which has developed in Ireland (and further afield) over the past number of years.

Our religious institutions are in turmoil. The church, which for so long has been a major foundation of Irish life, faces a crisis of (to borrow a Biblical term) apocalyptic proportions. The traditional church has been dogged by scandal and a constantly dwindling congregation, bewildered by an aloof and out-of-touch hierarchy. The Roman church has lost its footing, and to a great extent, its relevance, in modern Ireland. This is, without doubt, at least one of the factors inspiring the growth of alternative religions, including those with a focus on prehistoric spirituality.

Our political institutions are in turmoil. Irish politicians, having lost the run of themselves, allowed a massive overheating of the economy driven significantly by greed, speculation and a ravenous finance sector. The result of this, from a political viewpoint, is that Ireland has ceded significant control of her affairs to European bureaucrats. And so, the latest in a long line of invasions is currently taking place, this one an invasion of our sovereignty – and indeed our national dignity – from the European mainland. There is a considerable element of personal culpability involved here, and while it is easy to point fingers at seemingly hapless leaders and crooked politicians, we must acknowledge that our own desire for property and personal wealth – our weakness since at least the Bronze Age – was in some ways partly to blame for this unsavoury situation.

Our financial institutions are in turmoil. The wild exuberance of the so-called 'Celtic Tiger' years and the crass ambivalence to the sacrosanct rules and regulations of basic economic common sense were, to a great extent, the undoing of the modern Irish success story. The boom in this country was so expansive, and the spending and borrowing so extensive, that for a time the people of this small island began to think the good times were going to last forever. We borrowed so much money, as individuals, that the level of personal indebtedness reached levels that defied belief. For a nation that had been so poor for so long, and where thriftiness and frugality were part of the Irish psyche, we got completely carried away on a tide of growth and personal prosperity.

In this last regard, we were displaying a very ancient human weakness. We thought, and perhaps continue to think, that material wealth and possessions can bring us happiness. We are all guilty of this, including me. Which of us would sell all his possessions, and give the money to the poor, as Jesus proposed we do in order to achieve perfection? It could be suggested that we attempted to fill the spiritual vacuum created by the crisis of faith in the traditional church with material wealth. No wonder we are lost in a sea of uncertainty.

The average Irish person can tell you right now what the price of petrol is, how much a pint of alcohol costs, who the top scorer in the English premiership was this season, and how many Facebook friends they have. But how many people could tell you, without having to look, what the phase of the moon is right now?

What does that even matter, you might ask. It matters greatly. We have replaced cosmos with chaos. We have replaced spirituality with materialism. We have replaced the divine with the earthly, and the community with the individual. We have forsaken the earth, and endangered the future survival and prosperity of our species. And these are not the words of a lecturer. I understand my own frailties, and I acknowledge that my own desire for personal wealth contributes to this situation. How much has that recognition moved me to change my ways? Not enough.

In the Neolithic, humanity finally emerged from the bondage of what we call the 'hunter gatherer' lifestyle, which had sustained us, but in some ways trapped us, for tens, perhaps thousands of years. We had been slaves to the system. We were required to spend the majority of our time looking for food. We had little time for anything else, although I suspect that we always told stories, since the earliest archaic languages were first uttered by human mouths. During all that time, when we roamed the expansive forests of Europe and hunted its game, and fished its lakes and rivers, and foraged for morsels in the scrub, there was some sense of balance between mankind and the earth. That's not to say we didn't exhaust resources in a particular area before moving on to the next. But because population sizes were modest during the long years of the Mesolithic, we never truly threatened the earth, and it continued to supply us with what we needed, in abundance.

Our emergence from the forest was, initially, a glorious one. With more time on our hands due to new methods of agriculture, we turned our hands to monumental endeavours. We gave thanks – in a truly spectacular manner – to the earth and the cosmos, to the great female, the great mother who was seen as the provider of all things. In the Boyne Valley, she is revealed as Bóann, the benevolent cosmic mother who is

This is what we do to the landscape today. This giant limestone quarrying operation for the cement factory at Platin is located just 3.5 miles (5.75 kilometres) from Newgrange (see arrow).

seen in everything – in the river, and in the sky, and in the very monument of Newgrange itself, which is her womb of creation. Newgrange, and its sister mounds, also express the balance of the genders, and the equal importance of male and female in cosmic equilibrium. What some might see as a 'fertility cult' among the ancients, others might see as the recognition of this cosmic gender balance. The sun is male, the earth is female. A union of the two creates new life.

One author suggests that it was the great earth mother who supplied all the basic needs of humanity, and it was apparent to early man that it was the female who produced offspring and who was seen as intrinsic to the continuation of all life. The same author says that, 'Early man must have been dumbfounded by the awesome power of the female'.[6] Furthermore, he suggests that Newgrange is a theatre for an annual drama – the 'Sacred Marriage of the Sky God with the Earth-Mother, at Winter Solstice'.[7]

Has the power of the divine earth mother not now been greatly diminished? Has her significance waned to the point that our material culture no longer recognises her awesome power, and her fundamental role in the scheme of things? In our drive towards materialism, and perhaps away from cosmocentric spiritualism, are we not now adrift on an ocean of chaos, floating aimlessly and rudderless towards some great doom of our own making?

The power of the male, in all its malevolent and destructive forms, looms large in the world today. It is the male force that drives the creation of skyscrapers and cities, growing ever larger and higher, spreading out constantly, consuming forests and fields and natural landscapes, altering the earth for ever and annihilating ecosystems on the way. The skyscraper, the aeroplane and the rocket are all examples of the phallus, the potent symbolism of the young adult male, setting out to make his mark on the world. Cities and countries build bigger and higher skyscrapers, reaching further into the sky, each proclaiming how much bigger and better it was than the last. We would build a skyscraper reaching to the moon if we could, exhausting all steel resources in the process, and not think

There are many paths we could have chosen on our journey out of the forests of the Mesolithic.

twice about the folly of such a task. The commanding officer of one country's army who pushes a button or lifts a phone ordering missiles to be fired upon another thinks little of the consequences for those who might become civilian casualties of his dastardly act. The CEO of an aircraft manufacturing company likes to think that quieter, more fuel efficient, 'eco friendly' engines will help reduce pollution and will go towards saving the planet in some way. But what does the saving in emissions really mean if there are more and more aircraft flying in the sky?

As we gobble up the earth's resources in our ever increasing desire for dominance in the human fugue, we act in a way that is discordant with the cosmos, and we do so knowingly, with an intrinsic understanding that what we are doing is ultimately erroneous. Yet we persist with this patent foolishness, in the vain hope that our technological supremacy will somehow allow us to heal the world's ills, that it will ultimately empower us to restore the things we have destroyed, and to enable billions of humans to live together side by side in harmony on this planet, sharing its resources equally. This is nothing short of idealistic incongruousness.

There are many paths we could have chosen on our journey out of the forests of the Mesolithic. We chose to travel down the road of land ownership, of territorial conflict, of material culture, of spirituality and religion based on the power of a few over the weaknesses of the many, and of a way of life that was to gradually disconnect us from cosmos. If we could somehow magically transport a man or woman from the Neolithic into today's world, would they not be shocked and horrified by what they saw? Or would they, like us, become mesmerised by the awesome power of our technology? This is no trivial question. It is key to understanding the reasons we are where we are today.

Is this not how things were destined to turn out? What other conclusion could be reached, within the confines of human weakness and the frailties of our condition, than the chaos we now find ourselves in? Given our desire to own material possessions and land, it is not futile to suggest that we were destined for conflict, and as the population of the world grew, so did the amount and voracity of contention.

Perhaps a Neolithic time traveller, taking a plane trip over the Boyne Valley, would want to go back to his own time, to relate with childish excitement the thrill of the ride, and how wonderful it was to be closer to the sky, looking down on their grand creations. Perhaps not. The leap straight from Neolithic to twenty-first century might be too wide a chasm to jump. After all, our current world scenario developed and evolved, slowly and painstakingly at times, over hundreds and thousands of years. We did not suddenly find ourselves out of touch with the cosmos, although certainly our detachment from nature occurred relatively recently, largely in the past century and a half.

The signs of this detachment are, in some cases stark, and in others subtle. Climate change, brought about in part by our insatiable appetite for material resources, is one of the greatest effects of our modern developed world. But its effects can be seen in the Boyne Valley, and elsewhere in Ireland, by those who are still in touch with the natural rhythms of nature. The local impact of climate change is very real, according to an *Irish Times* report in January 2012. Leaves are appearing on trees earlier in the year, which suggests a warming of the climate, and bird patterns are changing, with earlier nestings and in some cases summer migrants now staying in Ireland for the whole year.[8]

But this climate change is also affecting the whooper swan, which has probably been coming to the Boyne Valley for thousands of years. Dr Alison Donnelly of the School of Natural Sciences at Trinity College Dublin said, 'we know that at least one large bird, the whooper swan, that comes in October and leaves in Spring, is now departing from Ireland earlier in the season to return to Iceland.'[9]

If, as previously suggested, the builders of Newgrange considered the whooper swan to be a sacred bird, transporting souls to the otherworld, they would undoubtedly have been greatly disturbed by a change in its migration pattern. We, however, hardly notice it. Only the ornithologists and the academic specialists with an interest in these things, and perhaps a few of the people living in the valley, will notice.

We are, unlike the builders of Newgrange, detached from cosmos.

We now stand at a threshold. For the first time since we emerged from the forests, we find ourselves capable of destroying our planet, and of wiping out a great deal of the human population of the world with weapons that are the stuff of nightmares. We find it difficult to resolve territorial contention peacefully – although the Northern Ireland conflict has definitely been an exception to the rule, and a very welcome one at that. We have developed and discovered all manners of nasty ways to injure and maim and kill each other. And all for a few possessions and the opportunity to own land that can never really belong to us. Some day, we will die anyway, and we cannot bring our wealth with us to the other side.

So where do we go from here? It is obvious that we have reached a point where we see that our present system no longer functions for the benefit of all humanity. We no longer trust the institutions that were previously considered the corner stones of modern society and civilisation. Is this not now a glorious opportunity, to create balance in an imbalanced world, to create a new society, based on much older principles?

We are reaching out for something. Our hunger for fulfilment is driving us back to the ancient, to the sacred, to the prehistoric. Newgrange is a symbol of something that worked, and that made sense. We want to go back, to a time of human innocence, and a time of peaceful interaction with the cosmos, and to a fairer system. As we stand at the crossroads, the question now is not so much, 'how do we go forward?' as, 'how do we go back?'

14.

HOW CAN WE GO BACK?

ALL IS NOT LOST. So long as there are people walking this earth who yearn to reconnect with the ancient and the sacred and the cosmic, there is hope. There is much about the story of humanity that is admirable and meritorious, and we have a precious value in the cosmic mesh, because we are the only creatures who are capable of understanding its nature.

Right now, we live in fascinating times from a cosmological viewpoint. If our Neolithic ancestors could join us in the twenty-first century, they would be very excited about the things that are happening in our skies, events that were not happening in their time.

The builders of Newgrange were accomplished astronomers. There seems little doubt about that. For them, the solstices were uniquely important days, being the times of year when the sun was at its strongest and its weakest.

The sun's path through the sky forms an imaginary hoop, which modern astronomers call the ecliptic. This is also, roughly, the path followed by the moon and planets. There is a second great hoop in the sky, the giant ring of light formed by the bright band of our galaxy, the Milky Way, the heavenly Boyne river. These two hoops are offset to each other, and intersect at two points in the sky. In other words, on its journey around the sky the sun, and by extension the moon and planets, cross over the cosmic river, the Milky Way, at two locations.[1]

One of these crossing points is located above the great warrior/ hunter/god constellation, Orion. In fact, the sun and planets appear to pass through, or slightly above, his outstretched hand, which seems to reach upwards, as if he is trying to control their movements. At this point the Milky Way runs down through the feet of Gemini the twins on one side and Taurus the bull on the other. The other crossing point is located between the constellations of Sagittarius, the archer and Scorpius, the scorpion, where the Milky Way appears to part into two separate streams, caused by a dark nebula or rift.

It is no insignificant coincidence that today, in the modern epoch, these two crossing points correspond with the location of the sun on the solstices. On the summer solstice, which usually occurs on June 21st, the sun is located above the outstretched hand of Orion.[2] Summer solstice marks the highest point of the sun in the sky over Ireland, and also the longest day.

The cosmological and astrological imagery is compelling. Here is the giant god of the sky grabbing the sun on its most powerful day, when it cannot be higher or stronger in the sky. Orion is Nuadu of the Silver Arm, the Tuatha Dé Danann king who was miraculously restored to glory after having his arm chopped off at the first Battle of Moytura. He is also Lugh Lamhfada, Lugh of the Long Arm, who threw the *tathlum*, the giant 'brain ball' at Balor, vanquishing his foe. Lugh is a god of light, who is identified with the 'guide of souls, Mercury'.[3] Orion is also Sétanta/Cúchulainn, showing off his skills with his hurl and *sliotar*, which he used to kill the great hound of Culann. This great constellation is also Fionn Mac Cumhaill, who appears to throw the sun and moon around the sky, and who is credited with throwing many of Ireland's ancient standing stones to the spots where they stand today. Orion is also Amergin Bright Knee, who planted his foot on the shores of the Boyne and declared, 'Who but I knows the ages of the moon?'[4]

Precession causes the stars to apparently drift slowly
out of position over many years.

Because of the slow wobble of the earth's axis, and the resulting precession of the equinoxes, the crossing point of the ecliptic over the heavenly Boyne is gradually moving, regressing westwards through the zodiac. While the phenomenon of Orion holding the sun on the day of summer solstice will continue to occur for perhaps the next number decades, it will gradually drift out of his upraised arm towards the horns of Taurus, the bull, on that day. On the timescale of a full cycle of precession, which lasts 25,920 years, this occurrence is but a fleeting moment, a brief instant in the vast chasm of cosmic time. Precession causes the sun's vernal position, i.e. its location on the vernal equinox, to regress westwards by one degree – approximately two moon widths – every 72 years. On the day of summer solstice, the sun will progressively shift to the west, out of Orion's hand, although it won't be situated firmly between the bull's horns until about the twenty-fourth century. That's how slow precession is.

To get an understanding of the significance of where we are in celestial time, you would have to go back to the early Neolithic, all the way back to around 4500 BC, to see the crossing points coincide with noteworthy solar days. Back then, before any of the great monuments of the Boyne had been built, and perhaps before the first agricultural practices had established themselves on this island, the sun was traversing the great ford of the sky, the *áth* or crossing point above Orion, on the day of the spring equinox. At that time, the other great fording point of the Milky Way, between Sagittarius and Scorpius, was crossed by the sun on the autumn equinox. Although 65 centuries have passed since then and now, and mankind has developed from the days of stone and bone to the days of space travel and the mobile phone, this huge chunk of time represents just one quarter of a full precessional revolution.

If you were to travel further back in time, all the way back to 11000 BC, towards the end of the last Ice Age, you would see the two crossing points coinciding with the solstices again, except this time the winter solstice sun would be positioned in the hand of Orion, while the summer solstice sun would be located between Sagittarius and Scorpius. And back then Orion did not rise above the horizon. The only part of this great constellation that was visible in that remote frozen epoch was his upraised arm. It is hard for us today to comprehend that there once was a time – and there will be again – when Orion was not a feature in the night sky over Ireland. In fact his period of hibernation, so to speak, was considerably longer than one can imagine. As early as 15000 BC the stars marking his feet or knees, known today by the Arabic names Rigel and Saiph, were no longer visible above the southern horizon, and he gradually sunk lower and lower until his entire frame except his elevated arm was invisible in 11000 BC. He didn't become completely visible again until around 4800 BC, meaning that Orion was only partly visible from Ireland for over 10,000 years. Perhaps the builders of Newgrange knew this. Certainly knowledge of precession seems to be inherent in their myths and monuments. There is no doubt this aspect of celestial movements fascinated and gripped early peoples, and given the strength of the oral transmission of knowledge in more recent history, it seems apt to suggest

*The Milky Way appears to split into two separate streams
as it runs down towards Sagittarius and Scorpius.*

that knowledge of Orion's emergence from the underworld might have been passed down over many generations.

We have arrived at a uniquely significant moment in cosmic history. Orion, the great god warrior of the heavens, holds the sun aloft on the longest and strongest day of the year. Like an Olympic torch bearer, he proclaims something truly momentous. Does this incredible astrological symbolism hold a message for humanity? Are we supposed to read it as a sign?

There is, undoubtedly, a messianic aspect to this celestial occurrence, something that might have been long foreseen by people in ancient times. Is this the moment that the ancient myth makers of Ireland yearned for, when the Tuatha Dé Danann, whose chiefs were represented by this huge anthropomorphic star grouping, finally seize their moment to return from the otherworld and restore their unquenchable power? Is this the once and future king, coming back from the dead to proclaim his everlasting presence?

The mesmerizing symbolism of this exceptional moment in cyclical time is immense. If one was looking for a sign from the heavens, this is just about the most momentous sign you could yearn for. It just so happens that the return of the sun to the crossing points of the Milky Way coincides with the end of the so called Mayan Long Count, the thirteen-*baktun* cycle which ends on 21 December 2012, this year's winter solstice. Many writers and researchers see this as the termination of the current cycle of the world, and perhaps marking either a period of unprecedented turbulence in the world or an era of great development.

Is this a sign of the coming enlightenment of mankind, marking a significant evolution of the human mind and spirit to a higher plane, heralding a golden age when humanity lives in a more altruistic and sustainable manner? Or is it a requiem for humanity, a lament for the fallibility of mankind, and for the sorry path we have beaten out of the forests of prehistory?

We are standing at a crossroads in the human story, that much is clear. How we proceed from here is the big question. Does the Olympic torch

Summer Solstice 2012. Orion grips the sun. (Image made with Stellarium).

bearer represent the illuminated aspects of the spirit of man, seeking light and virtuous paths? It might, conversely, represent the malevolent aspect of the male, whose aggression is often expressed through the use of dastardly weaponry, unleashed upon his fellow humans with rampant fury and little mercy. Is it a gloomy portent of impending calamity, an apocalypse of unprecedented scale that will burn out and wash away humankind from the narrative of life on earth?

Martin Brennan, the pioneer who discovered the solstice alignment of Dowth and the equinox alignment of Cairn T, Loughcrew, came back to Ireland in 2009 at my invitation to address a conference called the Boyne Valley Revision in the Newgrange Lodge. In recent years Brennan has been living in Mexico and has become somewhat of an expert on the Mayans. He was dismissive of the doomsday scenario painted by so many writers and researchers, and urged people to 'take off the blindfold' in relation to the doomsayers who are predicting calamity and disaster for the human race.[5]

He said we needed to move away from the doomsday mentality, warning that we are co-creators, and if we think about something long enough, we might make it happen. It might become a self-fulfilling prophecy. Brennan believes that winter solstice 2012 will be an enormously positive event, marking a 'beautiful evolution' for humanity, ushering in a time when there will be advancements in science and medicine, and also social progression which will bring peace, prosperity and happiness to the world.[6]

Without doubt winter solstice 2012 is a profound worldwide event,' Brennan said in a pre-conference press release.

> But it's not about doomsday, quite the opposite. It's about the light and the truth and the truth is in the glyphs. There is no doomsday scenario in the Mayan writings.[7]

He pointed out that Newgrange was built when the Mayan calendar began, adding that:

> Our job is to show that Newgrange has been here for 5,200 years and that it's going to be here for another 5,200 years. There's no need to panic whatsoever.

While the summer solstice, when Orion grabs the sun, is a very significant day, the winter solstice might be even more significant. This year, as the sun rises over Red Mountain and its light reaches into the vault of Newgrange (weather permitting of course!) it will be positioned in a very interesting part of the sky, where the heavenly river diverges into two separate streams. This area of the Milky Way is known as the Great Rift, and is caused by an elongated dark area of nebulous gas and dust which lies between us and the stars of the Milky Way which it obscures.

The ancient Egyptians perceived that the sun was reborn every day as an egg from the body of a great sky goddess. Archaeoastronomer Ronald A. Wells speculates that the goddess, Nut, can be seen as the personification of the Milky Way, and that the galaxy has the appearance of a female 'in the thinnest of gauze robes'.[8]

The great dark rift in the Milky Way, known to the Mayans as the 'Road to Xibalba', is envisioned by some writers as a great 'cosmic birth canal' from which the new sun will emerge on winter solstice 2012.[9] This celestial birth canal is formed by the separating streams of the Milky

The Great Rift in the Milky Way, pictured at Newgrange.

Way, which is just a visual phenomena, caused by a dark cloud of gas and dust which lies between us and the bright band of the galaxy, thus obscuring some of its stars.

Cygnus Mystery author Andrew Collins thinks the position of Cygnus in relation to this cosmic birth canal is very significant:

> If one were to extend the analogy of the birth canal further, and see the divided branches of the Milky Way on either side of the Great Rift as female 'legs', then Deneb and Sadr fall precisely in the vicinity of the 'uterus'.[10]

Collins suggests that the Mayans might have thought that the new sun emerged from a cosmic egg which had been 'dropped down the Milky Way's Great Rift by a celestial bird'.[11]

All of this is fascinating in light of the structure and design of Newgrange. The monument has a cruciform chamber and passage, replicat-

The position of Cygnus at the opening of the cosmic birth canal could be significant.

ing the shape of the swan constellation, the symbol of the magic lover birds, Aonghus and Caer. This chamber is the womb of Bóann, the great mother goddess from whom the Milky Way is named – *Bealach na Bó Finne*, the Way of the White Cow. Of further interest is the great milky quartz wall in front of Newgrange, which sweeps away from the entrance on either side like giant swans' wings. Was this parting of the quartz wall intended to replicate the diverging streams of the Milky Way as it ran down from Cygnus towards the galactic centre, which lies in the direction of Sagittarius and is located approximately 26,000 light years from earth? Perhaps so. We saw in Chapter 6 how the Newgrange quartz was associated with the word *brecshous*, meaning 'speckled light'. If the quartz represented the many stars of the Milky Way, then the passage of Newgrange could represent the Great Rift, the celestial birth canal, and its chamber represents the womb, corresponding with the stars of Cygnus. The miraculous conceptions and births at Newgrange of the supernatural offspring, Aonghus and Sétanta, take on a new light in such a cosmic milieu.

Newgrange might have been built to commemorate a very unique moment in cyclical time, when the bright star of Deneb was setting towards the north, or, at the very least, vanishing briefly as it swept down along the northern horizon. This is immortalised by the alignment of Newgrange with Fourknocks, and the orientation of the chamber of Fourknocks towards the point on the northern horizon where Deneb would reappear after its brief stint below the horizon. That was the only period in the entire 25,920 year cycle of precession, when the bright star of the swan constellation disappeared from view at this latitude. It is clear that Cygnus occupied a special place in the hearts and minds of the ancient astronomers.

A further compelling and utterly fascinating notion emerges from all of this. What if Newgrange was built not just to commemorate one significant moment in cosmic time, but two, one in the Neolithic, and one today? Was Newgrange designed to last until the early twenty-first century, when the current 25,920-year precession rotation is coming to and end, and the next cycle is about to begin?

A substantial argument has been made suggesting that the chamber and corridor of Newgrange were built in the shape of the swan constellation. Its owner took the form of a swan and came to Newgrange with his swan lover to stay there forever. A further contention has been put that Newgrange is as much a womb as it is a tomb. In addition to this, the white quartz fronting the monument might have been put there to imitate the bright band of the Milky Way. Now if we take Collins' suggestion that the stars of Cygnus represent a celestial uterus, and that the Great Rift in the Milky Way which opens at Cygnus is the birth canal, then we could be persuaded by the proposition that Newgrange was designed to celebrate a future moment in cosmic time, a very crucial moment, a spectacular ending of one cycle and the renewing of another, coinciding with the birth of a new sun from the heavenly mother on winter solstice 2012.

The monument's structure is inherently cosmic in design. Its fabricators were very intuitive people, in tune with cosmic movements, adept in the pursuit of astronomy and astrology, and knowledgeable of the great cycles of the sky. It is not at all beyond the realms of possibility that they foresaw the spectacularly exceptional 'end time' which lay five millennia beyond their lifetimes. Newgrange continues to function today, albeit in part thanks to restorative work, 53 centuries after it was put in place. Someone watching the illumination of the chamber this coming winter solstice will be seeing the same phenomenon that was first witnessed here by distant ancestors around 3150 BC. That's an incredible testimony to the skills and toils of the builders of this remarkable monument, the diverse purposes of which continue to mesmerise us today.

There is a further aspect of the celestial imagery that is interesting in light of the possible changes that these unique events might presage. Orion is the great male of the sky, and is at the point of his greatest height and strength. From this point on, he will be waning again, gradually, slowly, sinking in the sky over the next 13,000 years. Conversely, the area of the sky representing the female, including the stars of Cygnus and the Great Rift, will be in the ascendancy. The recent rising to dominance of the giant male coincides with the drift away from matriarchal religion

The monument's structure is inherently cosmic in design.

that has occurred over the past few millennia, in particular the last two thousand years. Back in the Neolithic, the two were in balance, located at the equinox points, sharing the same declination and therefore the same height in the sky. The Neolithic equinoxes were a time of balance, when male and female were in equal strength, and the day and night were of equivalent length.

Perhaps this is something the world needs right now – a return to the balance of the genders, in every sense, not just gender balance in the workplace. The feminine life-creating and nurturing and sustaining energy must be allowed to return.

The wasteland we have made of the earth, and of the human heart and soul, mentioned in Chapter 13, is something we can recover from if we embrace the archetypal energy of the female, according to Celtic spirituality expert Dolores Whelan:

> I believe that there is a way back from this place of destruction. I believe that the archetypal energy of Brigid – the embodiment of the divine feminine present within the essence of the Celtic culture – has the capacity to lead us from death to life and from war to peace, within ourselves and the world. For this to happen, it is necessary for us to understand that the archetypal energy that Brigid represents is an aspect of the human psyche that has been largely dormant over the past few hundred years but is now ready to re-emerge. And it is we who must begin to awaken this

Brigid energy present within ourselves so that she can help us to courageously and safely face the demons of this time and be our agent of transformation, the one who can breathe life into the mouth of dead winter as it is expressed in the soulless wasteland at the heart of western society.[13]

She adds that we must be willing to awaken to our senses, and that part of us that instinctively knows we are on the wrong path, that we are harming the earth and its species, and drastically reducing the future sustainability of not just human life, but all life on this planet.

We need to reboot the computer, to reset the system, and load entirely new software. We should look upon 21 December 2012 as a significant rebirth, a renewal of all things. Just as Newgrange is not merely a tomb, but also a womb, the coming solstice is not merely the death of one cycle, but the birth of another.

How can we go back?

Dolores Whelan believes that it is 'neither possible nor desirable to re-inhabit previous ages'.[14] Our nostalgia for the ancient past is born out of our regret for the present, and for the harm that we have wrought. But we can only inhabit one time, and that time is now. If the present is neither desirable nor pleasant, we must endeavour to make it so.

In any case, while we now view time as being linear, cosmic time is in many ways cyclical. Just as the earth is renewed from the harsh lifelessness of the winter as the days strengthen and the sun grows, our time can bring a healing and a renewal for humanity and for all life on this fragile planet.

A new era of humankind could be dawning, presaged by remarkable heavenly events. In addition to the harmony of the solstices with the Milky Way, the vernal sun is moving towards Aquarius, heralding the so-called 'Age of Aquarius', which many see as an era of enlightenment bringing positive developments for the people of the earth.

As I am writing this, NASA's *Curiosity* rover has just landed on the surface of Mars. We have come a long way since the days of moving huge stones around to build astronomical timepieces such as Newgrange. We are now able to put spacecraft, carrying advanced science and technology, onto distant planets and to receive images and data from those spacecraft back here on earth. Who could have imagined this even a century ago?

But what are the reasons for our curiosity about space, apart from our natural propensity for exploring new realms and our fascination with the cosmos? No doubt mineral exploration and resource exploitation are at least some of the factors driving the whole space program. There is constant chatter on the internet about possible future manned missions to the moon and Mars. The stark truth of the matter is that we have made a shambles of the earth, and we would wish that when we have exhausted all its resources, and created a wilderness of the planet, we can just hop on to the next planet and do the same thing there.

We must acknowledge that our hope for the survival of the human race lies on this planet, not any other. If we cannot get it right here, how can we hope to do so elsewhere? The people who constructed Newgrange long ago in the Boyne Valley peered out into the vast chasm of night and wondered why it was that some of the stars seemed to wander through the sky, something they might have referred to as the 'dancing cattle' of night.[15] Now, we know that those dancing stars are – the planets – and we know what size they are, what distance they lie from earth, and even what they are made of and what sort of atmosphere they have. But how much have we learned, if we cannot live in harmony with the cosmos that we would wish to conquer and have as our own property? We have removed some of the magic and the mystery of the night sky, but all the time in doing so we have been creating the rampant urban sprawl that not only consumes the earth, but blots out the wonders of the heavens from our view.

We must go back, and recover something of what we have lost as we departed the forests and woods of the Mesolithic and awakened to the new cosmic and spiritual dream of the Neolithic. Since then, we have become detached from cosmos, isolated from our inner spirit, immersed in materialism and technology, and bereft of direction and a sense of belonging. Dolores Whelan believes that it is 'essential that we now recover those nuggets of spiritual wisdom hidden for so long in the mists of time'.[16] The wisdom of ancient traditions and spirituality could contribute to 'a new life-sustaining spiritual vision for twenty-first century people living in western society'.[17]

In the true spirit of cycles and cosmos, and the return to the beginning that the renewal of a cycle represents, I will repeat some words from the first chapter of this book, the beginning of our exploration of Newgrange.

Can we yet recover something of the past? Is all of the glorious yesterday gone, forsaken, lost to the ether of time? We are all children of the cosmos. We share a common origin, we live on the earth and breathe its air, we behold its beauty and its awful tragedy, we grow old, we die. We all yearn for the same things – for a happy, fulfilling and peaceful life, for the flourishing of our offspring, for the safety of the world, and for a happy and peaceful passing into the next life. Are these not also the things for which the people of Newgrange yearned?

The builders of Newgrange understood the nature of the human spirit.

We must mend the broken path that brought us on our journey out of the amnesia of prehistory. We must reconnect with that which is old and arcane and sacred. 'The old that is strong does not wither, deep roots are not reached by the frost.' Something of who we really are, a part of that ancestral foundation we hold to be so special, remains. It has never been truly lost. We might have forgotten who our Neolithic ancestors really were, or what they looked like, and what their names were. But we are, and we remain, one and the same people, living in vastly different times and circumstances.

The builders of Newgrange might not have known the true nature of the stars and planets that they watched so diligently on the banks of the Boyne so long ago. But they did understand the nature of the human spirit, and the cosmic genesis of all life. We were born of the world, we are some of its constituent parts, and when we die we will return the matter of our bodies to the earth, in the true spirit of cosmic cycles and regeneration. Our souls, however, might survive our earthly death, to be brought to another realm, an afterlife beyond the comprehension of our worldly minds. This is something the Stone Age astronomers of the Boyne un-

derstood, and perhaps some of their own people had died and journeyed down the dark tunnel towards the light, and then come back again to relate their remarkable experience of the Land of the Ever Living Ones. They might have been among the first people of the earth to truly understand that while bodily death marked the end of this life, the journey of spirit was an everlasting one, and that ultimately the soul is immortal.

Despite our scientific and technological mastery, we are still in awe of Newgrange. We can put spacecraft on Mars and see pictures from the surface of remote planets, and yet we fail to see the true meaning of a heap of stones and earth wrought by an apparently primitive society of farmers. That carefully crafted stone monument acts as a cosmic time-piece, eternally watching the passing of the years, and the renewal that each new year brings. Its builders are dead, but not gone. We might get the chance to meet them again someday, in the afterlife, the magnificent realm of *Tír na nÓg*.

The reality is that Newgrange is not just a cairn of stones, it is not merely a tomb. It is something much greater. It is a monument to immortality, the eternal quest of the human spirit.

Newgrange is much more than a cairn of stones.

ENDNOTES

Chapter 1

1. I don't wear fine cloth, but in his eyes modern clothing would look very fine!

2. Tolkien, *Lord of the Rings*.

Chapter 2

1. Meehan, Robert T. and Warren, William P., *The Boyne Valley in the Ice Age, A Field Guide to Some of the Valley's Most Important Glacial Geological Features*, Geological Survey of Ireland, 1999.

2. Ibid., p. 8.

3. Hill, Dr. Emmeline, More About Genes – The Irish Really are a race apart, http://www.insideireland.com/sample19.htm, retrieved February 6th 2012. Dr. Hill works at the Department of Genetics, Trinity College, Dublin.

4. Ibid.

5. Harbison, Peter, *Treasures of the Boyne Valley*, Gill and MacMillan (2003), p. 100.

6. Ibid.

7. Cooney, Gabriel, *Landscapes of Neolithic Ireland*, Routledge (2000), pp. 12-13.

8. Ibid., p.13.

9. O'Kelly, Michael J., *Early Ireland – An Introduction to Irish Prehistory*, Cambridge University Press (1997) [1989], p. 33.

10. Cooney (2000), p. 13.

11. O'Kelly (1997), p. 29.

12. Ibid.

13. Ibid.

14. Hill, op cit.

15. Very early dates of between mid 5th to mid 4th Millennium BC for the Carrowmore megalithic complex in Sligo derived from carbon dating of charcoal samples are currently being contested. A new project by archaeologists at NUI Galway attempts to more securely date the period of actual use of Carrowmore by carbon dating bone and antler pins from two monuments there. Initial results of this project suggest a more recent date of occupation of Carrowmore than the dates previously suggested. A publication on the project is forthcoming. See http://www.nuigalway.ie/archaeology/Research/Ritual_and_Place_in_Prehistory/Bone_Pin_Dating_Project/bone_pin_dating_index.html for more. Retrieved February 8th 2012.

16. Stout, Geraldine and Stout, Matthew, *Newgrange*, Cork University Press (2008), p. 64.

17. Davies, Norman (2000) [1999], *The Isles: A History*, Papermac, p. 11.

18. Metrical Dindshenchas, Volume III.

19. Bennett, Isabel, The Archaeology of County Kerry, *Archaeology Ireland*, Vol. 1, No. 2 (Dec. 1987), p. 48.

20. Brady, Conor, Earlier Prehistoric Settlement in the Boyne Valley: A Systematic Ploughzone Survey, UCD School of Archaeology (2005). An abstract of this PhD paper can be found at: http://www.ucd.ie/archaeology/research/previouspostgraduates/conor_brady/

21. Ibid.

22. Ibid.

23. Stout and Stout, op. cit., p. 62.

24. Galor, Oded and Moav, Omer, *The Neolithic Origins of Contemporary Variations in Life Expectancy* (2007), p. 1.

25. Ibid.

26. Garnett, Jacqueline Ingalls, *Newgrange Speaks for Itself: Forty Carved Motifs*, Trafford Publishing (2005).

27. O'Kelly, Michael J., *Newgrange – Archaeology, Art and Legend*, Thames and Hudson (1998) [1982], ps. 112-3.

28. Cooney (2000), p. 200.

29. O'Kelly (1998), p. 195.

Chapter 3

1. Stout and Stout (2008), p. 103.

2. Stout (2002), p. 32.

3. Eogan, George (1963), A Neolithic habitation-site and megalithic tomb in Townleyhall townland, Co. Louth, *Royal Society of Antiquaries of Ireland Journal*, Vol. XCIII, pp. 37-81.

4. Stout (2002), p. 22.

5. Brady, Conor, personal communication, March 2012.

6. The UNESCO World Heritage Site of Brú na Bóinne, which includes Newgrange, Knowth and Dowth.

7. Brady, Conor, personal communication, March 2012.

8. Ibid.

9. Ibid.

10. Ibid.

11. Stout and Stout (2008), p. 9.

12. Corcoran, Mary and Sevastopulo, George (2008), The Source of Greywacke Used in the Passage Tombs at Brú na Bóinne. This was a presentation for the Brú na Bóinne World Heritage Site Research Framework Seminar held in Slane on March 11th 2008.

13. Smyth, Jessica (editor), (2009), *Brú na Bóinne World Heritage Site Research Framework*, The Heritage Council, p. 29.

14. Smyth (2009), pp. 29, 69; Stout and Stout (2008), p. 11. Clogherhead was part of the strand known in ancient times as Traig Baille (Murphy and Moore (2006), p. 7).

15. Meighan, Ian, Turkington, Phyllis and Cooper, Mark, Detective Work on the ancient stones of Newgrange, *Earth Science Ireland*, Issue 9, Spring 2011, p. 9.

16. Mitchell, Frank (1990), *The Way That I Followed – A Naturalist's Journey Around Ireland*, Country House, p. 245.

17. Meighan, Turkington and Cooper (2011), p. 9. It was Frank Mitchell who first pinpointed Rathcor as the source of the Newgrange wall granite.

18. Stout and Stout (2008), p. 6, suggest the boats which transported these cobbles might have been made of hazel and willow rods, covered with cattle hide.

19. O'Kelly (1998), p. 75.

20. Stout and Stout (2008), p. 11.

21. Conor Brady (personal communication, March 2012) says transportation by boat would have been the 'least cost' method of moving the large stones.

22. http://news.nationalgeographic.com/news/2011/12/111222-stonehenge-bluestones-wales-match-glacier-ixer-ancient-science/# Extracted 13 August 2012.

23. Ibid.

24. Burl, Aubrey (2001), Stonehenge: How Did the Stones Get There?, http://brian-mountainman.blogspot.ie/2011/03/stonehenge-how-did-stones-getthere.html, extracted 13 August 2012.

25. Ibid.

26. Ibid.

27. O'Kelly, Claire (1971) [1967], *Illustrated Guide to Newgrange*, John English and Co. Ltd., pp. 111-2.

28. Stout and Stout (2008), p. 11.

29. Ibid.

30. Stonehenge builders 'used ball bearings to move giant slabs of stone into position', Daily Mail online, 19 November 2010. http://www.dailymail.co.uk/ sciencetech/article-1330917/Stonehenge-builders-used-ball-bearings-giant-slabs-stone.html, extracted 13 August 2010.

31. O'Kelly, Claire (1971), p. 112.

32. And some, obviously, weighing a lot less.

33. Brady, Conor, personal communication, March 2012.

34. Lewis-Williams, David and Pearce, David (2005), *Inside the Neolithic Mind*, Thames and Hudson, p. 254.

35. Ibid., p. 255.

36. Stout and Stout (2008), p. 11.

Chapter 4

1. O'Kelly (1982), p. 124.

2. See chapter 6 for further discussion of this idea.

3. Murphy, Anthony and Moore, Richard, *Island of the Setting Sun: In Search of Ireland's Ancient Astronomers*, The Liffey Press (2008) [2006], p. 235

4. They are called quarter moons because the illuminated part of the moon visible to us represents just one quarter of the total surface area of the moon.

5. Murphy and Moore, p. 121 etc.

6. Murphy and Moore, pp. 236-7

7. Murphy and Moore, pp. 16-17

8. Ibid., p. 57

9. Dinneen Foclóir, pp. 1283-4.

10. Hadingham, Evan (1983), *Early Man and The Cosmos*, Heinemann, p. 62.

11. Even the aurora is linked to an 11-year cycle of sunspots!

12. Murphy and Moore, pp. 195-7

13. Murphy and Moore, chapter 11

14. Campbell, Joseph (1959), *The Masks of God: Primitive Mythology*, vol. I, Chapter 9, 'Thresholds of the Palaeolithic'.

15. Knight, Christopher and Lomas, Robert (1999), *Uriel's Machine: The Prehistoric Technology that Survived the Flood*, Century, pp. 281-5.

16. Murphy and Moore, p. 167.

17. Murphy and Moore, p. 170.

18. I am grateful to the ever-probing mind of Gillies MacBain, a member of the Irish Stones list at http://groups.yahoo.com/group/irish-stones who dis-

cussed this idea in detail. Gillies suggests the possibility that the 97 kerb-stones of Newgrange could relate to the fact that there are 97 leap year days in the modern calendar during a period of 400 years.

19. Allen, Richard Hinckley (1963) [1899], *Star Names: Their Lore and Meaning*, Dover Publications, p. 117.

20. Hancock, Graham and Faiia, Santha (1998), *Heaven's Mirror: Quest for the Lost Civilisation*, Michael Joseph, pp. 132, 152 etc.

21. Murphy and Moore, p. 178.

22. Allen (1963), p. 195.

23. For discussion, see Murphy and Moore, Chapter 7.

24. Ibid.

Chapter 5

1. Stout (2008), p. 96.

2. Ibid.

3. O'Kelly (1998) [1982], p. 24.

4. Ibid.

5. O'Kelly (1998), p. 33.

6. Stout (2008), p. 98.

7. Ibid.

8. Nevin, Mona, General Charles Vallancey 1725-1812, *Journal of the Royal Society of Antiquaries of Ireland*, Vol. 123 (1993), p. 34.

9. Ibid., p. 21.

10. Ibid., p. 28

11. http://www.iorarua.com/index.php?option=com_contentandview=articleandid=100:charles-vallanceyandcatid=67:gaelgeoritop25andItemid=136, extracted 11 April 2012.

12. Nevin (1993), p. 25.

13. General Charles Vallancey, from *A Compendium of Irish Biography*, 1878. http://www.libraryireland.com/biography/GeneralCharlesVallancey.php Extracted April 11th, 2012.

14. Ibid.

15. Nevin (1993), p. 23.

16. Vallancey, Charles, *Collectanea de Rebus Hibernicus*, Dublin, Vol. II, p. 210.

17. Nevin (1993), p. 25.

18. Vallancey, Charles (1804), *Collectanea de Rebus Hibernicus*, Vol. VI, Part II, Chapter IX, p. 314.

19. Ibid.

20. Ibid.

21. Shaw, Rev. William (1780), *A Gaelic and English Dictionary*, Volume I, London.

22. Vallancey, op. cit., p. 317.

23. Armstrong, R.A. (1825), *A Gaelic Dictionary in Two Parts*, London.

24. Vallancey, op. cit., p. 322.

25. Ibid., p. 323.

26. Ibid., p. 352.

27. Is it possible sodhac is just an anglicised form of zodiac?

28. Vallancey, op. cit., p. 354.

29. Shaw (1780) and McCionnaith, L. (1935), *Foclóir Béarla agus Gaedhilge, English-Irish Dictionary*, Dublin, p. 1217.

30. Vallancey, op. cit., p. 354.

31. Vallancey, op. cit., p. 369.

32. Ibid., p. 371

33. Shaw (1780). There are no page numbers in Shaw's dictionary.

34. Vallancey, op. cit., p. 376.

35. Vallancey, op. cit., p. 383.

36. Vallancey, Charles (1798), *Oriental Collections*, Vol. II, No. III, p. 213.

37. Higgins, Godfrey (1836), *Anacalypsis, An Attempt to Draw Aside the Veil of The Saitic Isis*, Vol. I., London, p. 181.

38. Vallancey (1804), p. 384.

39. Burl, Aubrey (1979), *Rings of Stone: The Prehistoric Stone Circles of Britain and Ireland*, Francis Lincoln, pp. 244-5.

40. Burl, Aubrey (2005) [1995], *A Guide to the Stone Circles of Britain, Ireland and Brittany*, Yale University, p. 31.

41. Vallancey (1804), p. 378.

42. Dinneen, Rev. Patrick S. (1927), *Foclóir Gaedhilge agus Béarla, An Irish-English Dictionary*, Educational Company of Ireland Ltd., p. 85.

43. Vallancey (1804), p. 382.

44. Vallancey (1798), p. 203.

45. Vallancey (1804), p. 388.

46. Ibid.

47. MacKillop, James (2000) [1998], *Dictionary of Celtic Mythology*, Oxford, p. 125.

48. Ibid., p. 126.

49. Vallancey (1804), p. 396.

50. Dinneen (1927), p. 1210.

51. McCionnaith (1935), p. 812.

52. Dinneen (1927), p. 17.

53. Vallancey (1804), p. 395.

54. Vallancey (1804), p. 397.

55. Vallancey (1804), p. 399.

56. MacKillop (2000), p. 10.

57. Vallancey (1804), pp. 404-8.

58. Brennan, Martin (1994), pp. 21-22.

59. Ibid., p. 23.

60. Ibid., p. 24.

61. Aveni, Anthony (2008), *People and the Sky: Our Ancestors and the Cosmos*, Thames and Hudson, p. 95.

Chapter 6

1. MacBain, Alexander (1998) [1896], *Etymological Dictionary of Scottish-Gaelic*, Hippocrene Books, p. 91. MacBain gives cnoc as 'a hillock, Ir, cnoc, O. Ir. cnocc, O. Br. cnoch, tumulus'.

2. Gwynn, Edward (1906), *The Metrical Dindshenchas*, Hodges and Figgis and Co. Ltd. (Royal Irish Academy Todd Lecture Series Volume IX),

3. O'Kelly, Michael J. (1997) [1989], *Early Ireland: An Introduction to Irish Prehistory*, Cambridge University Press, p. 97.

4. Ibid.

5. Cooney (2000), p. 92.

6. For more on Ireland's Stonehenge, see Murphy and Moore (2008), pp. 100-104.

7. O'Kelly (1998) [1982], p. 33.

8. Ibid.

9. Wilde, William (1847), Irish rivers, *Dublin University Magazine*, p. 741.

10. For an account of these excavations, see O'Kelly, Michael J. and O'Kelly, Claire (1983), 'The Tumulus of Dowth, County Meath', *Proceedings of the Royal Irish Academy* (PRIA), Vol. 83c., Appendix B., pp. 185-188.

11. Ibid., p. 143.

12. Graves, J. (1879), Letter in Proceedings, JRSAI 15, p. 13, quoted in O'Kelly and O'Kelly (1983), p. 144.

13. O'Kelly (1998), p. 24.

14. Stout (2002), p. 128.

15. See Eogan, George (1986), *Knowth and the Passage-Tombs of Ireland*, Thames and Hudson.

16. Prendergast, F.T., *Shadow Casting Phenomena at Newgrange*, Survey Ireland, November 1991, p. 11.

17. Ibid.

18. O'Kelly (1997), p. 72.

19. O'Kelly (1998), p. 72.

20. Ibid., p. 73.

21. Harbison, Peter (2003), *Treasures of the Boyne Valley*, Gill and Macmillan, p. 115.

22. From a letter by Edward Lhwyd in December 1699. See O'Kelly (1998), p. 24.

23. O'Kelly (1998), p. 33.

24. Stout and Stout (2008), p. 5.

25. Jones, Carleton (2007), *Temples of Stone: Exploring the Megalithic Tombs of Ireland*, The Collins Press, p. 111.

26. Ibid.

27. Nichols, Ross (1992) [1975], *The Book of Druidry: History, Sites and Wisdom*, Aquarian, p. 240.

28. Harbison (2003), p. 100.

29. Ibid.

30. MacKillop (1998), p. 200.

31. Ibid.

32. Ibid., p. 386.

33. Ibid., p. 202.

34. Ibid., pp. 201-2.

35. Ibid., p. 386.

36. Stout and Stout (2008), p. 95.

37. Ibid., p. 96.

38. Ibid.

39. Brennan, Martin (1994) [1983], *The Stones of Time: Calendars, Sundials, and Stone Chambers of Ancient Ireland*, Inner Traditions International, p. 18.

40. O'Kelly, Claire (1971) [1967], *Illustrated Guide to Newgrange*, John English and Co. Ltd., Wexford, p. 68.

41. O'Grady, S.H. (1892), *Silva Gadelica*, I–XXXI, London, and referenced in O'Kelly (1971), p. 68.

42. Murphy and Moore (2008), p. 159.

Chapter 7

1. Brennan (1994) [1983], p. 28.

2. Ibid.

3. O'Kelly, Claire, 'Stone Mad: A Review of *The Stars and the Stones*,' *Sunday Tribune*, 4 December 1983.

4. Ibid.

5. O'Callaghan, Chris (2004), *Newgrange: Temple to Life*, Mercier Press, p. 37.

6. Ibid.

7. Ibid., p. 36.

8. Ibid., p. 44.

9. Cooney (2000), p. 109.

10. Eogan, George (1986), *Knowth and the Passage-tombs of Ireland*, Thames and Hudson, p. 39.

11. Cooney (2000), p. 96.

12. Ibid., p. 98.

13. Lewis-Williams, David and Pearce, David (2005), *Inside the Neolithic Mind*, Thames & Hudson, p. 219.

14. Ibid., p. 90.

15. Ibid.

16. Twohig, Elizabeth (1990), Irish Megalithic Tombs, Shire Archaeology.

17. Ibid., p. 89.

18. Ibid.

19. Gimbutas, Marija (1999), *The Living Goddesses*, University of California Press, p. 55.

20. Battersby, William (1999), p. 1.

21. O'Callaghan (2004), p. 86.

22. Gimbutas (1999), p. 55.

23. Ibid.

24. Ibid.

25. Concannon, Maureen (2004), *The Sacred Whore: Sheela Goddess of the Celts*, The Collins Press, pp. 31-32.

26. Ibid., p. 32.

27. Knight and Lomas (1999), p. 287.

28. Gimbutas, Marija (1991), *The Language of the Goddess*, Harper p. 225.

29. This ancient trinity will be examined in greater detail in Chapter 10.

30. Murphy and Moore (2008), p. 172.

31. Hancock, Graham and Faiia, Santha (1998), *Heaven's Mirror: Quest for the Lost Civilisation*, Michael Joseph, p. 37.

32. O'Kelly (1998), p. 47.

33. Stout and Stout (2008), p. 103.

34. Reijs, Victor (2011), What feelings and/or experiences do visitors report having at heritage sites? A paper for the MA-CAA Research module at University of Wales.

35. Ham, Prof. Sam (2006), When a Place Means Something, It Matters: Adding Value Off the Main Road, a keynote address to Museums Australia. p. 4.

36. Otto, Rudolf (1958), *Idea of the Holy*, quoted in Ham (2006).

37. See chapter 13 for further exploration of this.

Chapter 8

1. Shirley, James, from his poem 'Death the Leveller'.

2. Moody, Raymond (2001) [1975], *Life After Life*, Rider, p. 49.

3. Kubler-Ross, Elisabeth, MD (2008) [1991], *On Life after Death*, Celestial Arts, p. 10.

4. Moody (2001), p. 20.

5. Ibid., p. 49.

6. Ibid.

7. Ibid., pp. 52-53.

8. Keane, Colm (2009), *Going Home: Irish Stories from the Edge of Death*, Capel Island, p. 26.

9. Ibid., p. 52

10. Ibid., pp. 63-64.

11. Ibid., p 67.

12. Keane, Colm (2010), *The Distant Shore: More Irish Stories from the Edge of Death*, Capel Island, pp. 29-30.

13. Ibid., p. 35.

14. Tales from the great unknown, *Limerick Leader*, 16 October 2010.

15. Ibid.

16. Kubler-Ross (2008), p. 84.

17. Keane (2009), p. 215.

18. Keane (2009), p. 211.

19. Colm Keane, personal communication, January 2012.

20. Ibid.

21. Ibid.

22. Colm Keane, personal communication, May 2012.

23. Jones, Carleton (2007), *Temples of Stone*, The Collins Press, p. 157.

24. Lewis-Williams, David and Pearce, David (2005), *Inside the Neolithic Mind*, Thames and Hudson, p. 52.

25. Jones (2007), p. 157.

26. Lewis-Willians and Pearce (2005), p. 195.

27. Knight, Christopher and Lomas, Robert (1999), *Uriel's Machine: The Prehistoric Technology that Survived the Flood*, Century, pp. 291, 294.

28. Murphy, Anthony and Moore, Richard (2006), *Island of the Setting Sun: In Search of Ireland's Ancient Astronomers*, The Liffey Press, p. 142.

29. O'Kelly (1998) [1982], p. 47.

30. Jones (2007), p. 162.

31. Ibid., p. 164.

32. Lewis-Williams and Pearce (2005), p. 225.

33. Ibid., p. 256.

34. Ibid., p. 195.

Chapter 9

1. From *The Annals of the Four Masters*, referenced in O'Kelly (1998), p. 46.

2. Mackillop (1998), p. 386.

3. Mackillop (1998), p. 200.

4. Mackillop (1998), p. 386.

5. Slavin, Michael (2005), *The Ancient Books of Ireland*, Wolfhound Press, p. 32.

6. Mackillop (1998), p. 414.

7. The battle between the Milesians and the Tuatha Dé Danann is described in some detail in Chapter 2 of *Island of the Setting Sun*.

8. Mackillop (1998), p. 415.

9. Mackillop (1998), p. 386.

10. Ó hÓgáin, Dáithí (2006), *The Lore of Ireland: An Encyclopaedia of Myth, Legend and Romance*, The Collins Press, p. 151.

11. Ó hÓgáin (2006), p. 151. Dagda's alternative name was *Eochaidh Ollathair*, meaning 'father of many'.

12. Ó Duinn, Seán (2011), *In Search of the Awesome Mystery: Lore of Megalithic, Celtic and Christian Ireland*, The Columba Press, p. 203.

13. Murphy and Moore (2006/2008). See in particular Chapters 11 and 12.

14. Carson, Ciaran (2007), *The Táin*, Penguin Classics, p. 104.

15. A theme explored in greater detail in *Island of the Setting Sun*.

16. Murphy and Moore (2008), p. 16.

17. Ó hÓgáin (2006), p. 38.

18. Ó hÓgáin (2006), p. 478.

19. Murphy and Moore (2006/2008). See Chapter 7, Newgrange: The Cygnus Enigma.

20. O'Kelly, Claire (1971) [1967], *Illustrated Guide to Newgrange*, John English & Co., Wexford, pp. 99-100.

21. Ibid., p. 100.

22. Stout and Stout (2008), p. 94.

23. O'Kelly (1998), p. 48.

24. O'Kelly (1998), p. 48.

25. Rolleston, Thomas (1998) [1911], *Myths and Legends of the Celts*, Senate, p. 90.

26. Whelan, Dolores (1999), 'Celtic Spirituality: A Holy Embrace of Spirit and Nature', from *Celtic Threads: Exploring the Wisdom of Our Heritage*, Veritas, p. 13.

27. Murphy and Moore (2006). See Chapter 6, Dowth: The Darkening of the Sky.

28. Rhys, John (1901), *Celtic Folklore: Welsh and Manx*, extracted from http://www.sacred-texts.com/neu/cfwm/cf202.htm Extracted: 3 June 2012.

29. Evans-Wentz, W.Y. (1911), *The Fairy-Faith in Celtic Countries*, Section II, Chapter IV.

30. Ibid.

31. Mackillop (1998), p. 405.

32. Ó hÓgáin (2006), p. 480.

33. MacIvor, Rev. Dermot (1958), 'The Legend of Gearóid Iarla of Hacklim', *County Louth Archaeological and Historical Journal* 9 CLAJ), Vol. XIV, No. 2, p. 78.

34. See Murphy and Moore (2006/2008), Chapter 12.

35. Dolan, Joseph (1929), *Louth Ordnance Survey Letters*, CLAJ, Vol. VII, No. 1, pp. 57-58.

36. Carey, John (1999), *A Single Ray of the Sun: Religious Speculation in Early Ireland*, Celtic Studies Publications Inc., p. 21

37. Carey (1999) says that the 'immortals outlasted even the Middle Ages, surviving down to our own day as the fairies or "good people" (daoine maithe).' He references Ó hEochaidh et al, Síscéalta ó Thír Chonaill where there is 'a list of twenty-two terms' for the fairy folk in Donegal alone, the most commonplace being bunadh na gcnoc, 'hill-folk'.

38. Mackillop (1998), p. 386.

39. Mackillop (1998), p. 202.

40. www.google.ie - extracted 4 June 2012.

41. Mackillop (1998), p. 145.

42. From a poem in the Lebor Gabála, quoted on http://en.wikipedia.org/wiki/Tuatha_D%C3%A9_Danann. Extracted 4 June 2012.

Chapter 10

1. Russell, George William (1921), 'A Dream of Angus Oge', from his book *Imaginations and Reveries*, Dublin, Maunsel and Roberts. The essay was written in 1897 but published in 1921.

2. Russell (1921).

3. Stout and Stout (2008), p. 47.

4. Brennan (1994) [1983] disputes this, suggesting that after the entrance to Newgrange was cleared in 1849, light would have been able to enter the passage, 'regardless of a certain amount of collapse closer to the opening'. See p. 30.

5. Russell, George (AE) (1919), *The Candle of Vision*, Macmillan and Co. Ltd., p. 168.

6. Brennan (1994), p. 22.

7. Brennan (1994), p.32.

8. Evans-Wentz, W.Y. (1911), *The Fairy-Faith in Celtic Countries*, p. 419.

9. Campbell, Joseph (1959), *The Masks of God: Primitive Mythology*, vol. I.

10. Murphy and Moore (2008), p. 165.

11. O'Kelly (1998), p. 123.

12. O'Kelly (1998), p. 123.

13. Murphy and Moore (2008), p. 175.

14. Mackillop (1998), p. 177.

15. Ó hÓgáin (2006), p. 21.

16. Ó Duinn (2011), p. 208.

17. Ibid.

18. Squire, Charles (1998) [1912], *Mythology of the Celtic People*, Senate, p. 139.

19. Ibid.

20. Ibid.

21. See Ó hÓgáin (2006), p. 37 and Squire (1998), p. 140.

22. Some versions of the story simply refer to Bodb as the king of Munster.

23. Squire (1998), pp. 141-142.

24. Ó hÓgáin (2006), p. 22.

25. Ó Duinn (2011), p. 234.

26. Collins (2006), p. 90.

27. Ó Duinn (2011), p. 232.

28. Carpenter, Edward (1920), *Pagan & Christian Creeds: Their Origin and Meaning*, Brace and Howe.

29. Each of these attributes is listed by Carpenter (1920), in Chapter II. 'Solar Myths and Christian Festivals'.

30, Mackillop (1998), p. 17.

31. Cross, Tom P., and Slover, Clark Harris (1996) [1936], *Ancient Irish Tales*, Barnes & Noble, p. 14.

32. Squire (1998), p. 125.

33. Most notably Mac Cuill, Ma Cecht and Mac Gréine. See Murphy and Moore (2006), p. 31.

34. Mackillop (1998), p. 416.

35. Mackillop (1998), p. 416.

36. Gregory (2004a, b). This quote is from *Gods and Fighting Men* (originally published in 1904 by John Murray, London), and is contained in Book IV, 'The Ever-Living Living Ones', Chapter III, 'Angus Og'.

37. In Kinsella's translation, Deichtine helps her brother Conchobar to drive away the birds from Emain Macha.

38. Kinsella, Thomas [1969] *The Táin*, Oxford University Press, p. 23.

39. Kinsella [1969], p. 22.

40. The Sétanta story, and *The Táin* in general, has long been considered an Iron Age myth, but some of its cosmology is Neolithic. Is Sétanta an 'Iron Age Celtic warrior in a Neolithic milieu'? See Murphy and Moore (2006), p. 225.

Chapter 11

1. http://www.knowth.eu/newgrange-solstice-lottery.htm Extracted June 17th, 2012.

2. Kavanagh, Peter, 'Trip Through Time', *Dundalk Democrat*, June 26, 2012.

3. Twohig, Elizabeth, personal communication, June 2012.

4. Stout (2002), p. 195.

5. Keane (2010), p. 10.

6. Whelan (2010), pp. 3-4.

7. Maggie McDonald, personal communication, June 2012.

8. Jeremiah Keogh, personal communication, June 2012.

9. Martin Dier, personal communication, July 2012.

10. The dawn of new beginnings despite the lack of sunshine, *Drogheda Independent*, 28 December 2005.

Chapter 12

1. Conor Brady, personal communication, May 2012.

2. Harbison (2003), p. 102.

3. Conor Brady, personal communication, May 2012.

4. Davies (2000), p. 19.

5. Ibid.
6. Smyth, Jessica (editor), (2009), *Brú na Bóinne World Heritage Site Research Framework*, The Heritage Council, p.37.
7. Stout (2002), p. 33.
8. O'Kelly (1998) [1982], p. 79.
9. Prendergast, Frank (1991), 'New Data on Newgrange', *Technology Ireland*, March 1991, pp. 22-25.
10. Conor Brady, personal communication, May 2012.
11. Ibid.
12. Murphy and Moore (2006), Chapter 5.
13. Ibid.
14. See Stout, Geraldine (1991), *Embanked Enclosures of the Boyne Region*, Proceedings of the Royal Irish Academy, Volume 91, C, No. 9.
15. Stout (2002), pp. 60-61.
16. Smyth (2009), p. 39.
17. Conor Brady, personal communication, July 2012.
18. Ibid.
19. Cooney (2000), p. 17.
20. Ibid., p. 18.
21. Ibid., pp. 18-19.
22. Smyth (2009), p. 70.
23. www.archaeology.co.uk/articles/features/bloody-stone-age-war-in-the-neolithic.htm Extracted July 17th 2012.
24. Conor Brady, personal communication, May 2012.
25. Stout (2002), p. 33.

Chapter 13

1. Ó Siocháin, P.A. (1983), *Ireland: A Journey Into Lost Time*, Fiolsiúcháin Eireann, p. 96.
2. http://cosmocentric.wordpress.com/ Extracted 18 July 2012.
3. Ó Duinn (2011), p. 236
4. Whelan, Dolores (2010) [2006], *Ever Ancient Ever New: Celtic Spirituality in the 21st Century*, Original Writing, p. 76.
5. Matthew 19:21.
6. Ó Duinn (2011), p. 188.
7. Ibid., p. 189.

8. Holden, John, 'Swanning off earlier than usual', *Irish Times*, 19 January 2012. www.irishtimes.com/newspaper/sciencetoday/2012/0119/1224310443944. html. Retrieved 2 August 2012.

9. Ibid.

Chapter 14

1. Some of this was discussed in Chapter 4.

2. Obviously you cannot actually see the constellations during daylight, but if you could eclipse the sun at that moment you would see its exact position among the stars. Ancient astronomers probably used observations of both the moon and heliacal star risings to determine the position of the sun among the stars. The full moon is always roughly opposite the sun, so a knowledge of the zodiac would allow early astronomers to determine which constellation the sun was located in. This was one of the rudimentary astronomy lessons discussed in Chapter 4. Heliacal risings of certain stars in the pre-dawn glow would help to further elucidate the exact position of the sun.

3. Nichols, Ross (1992) [1975], *The Book of Druidry: Historic Sites and Wisdom*, Aquarian, p. 239.

4. For further discussion about the many guises of Orion in Irish myth and folklore, see Murphy and Moore (2006), Chapter 11, 'Star Stories: Sky Myths of the Ancients'.

5. A video clip from Brennan's talk at The Boyne Valley Revision can be viewed at www.mythicalireland.com/theboynevalleyrevision/No-2012-doomsday-says-Maya-calendar-author.html (Extracted 4 August 2012).

6. Ibid.

7. www.mythicalireland.com/theboynevalleyrevision/No-2012-doomsday-says-Maya-calendar-author.html Extracted 4 August 2012.

8. Collins (2006), p. 171.

9. Ibid., p. 69.

10. Ibid.

11. Ibid., p. 71.

12. Ironically, if you live in Australia or in other southern parts of the world, Orion is now at his lowest ebb.

13. Whelan (2010), p. 76.

14. Ibid., p. 5.

15. Murphy and Moore (2006), p. 33.

16. Whelan (2010), p. 5.

17. Ibid.

INDEX